# Implementing Cisco UCS Solutions

*Second Edition*

A hands-on guide to deploy, manage, troubleshoot and automate Cisco UCS solutions in the data center

**Anuj Modi**
**Farhan Nadeem**
**Prasenjit Sarkar**

BIRMINGHAM - MUMBAI

# Implementing Cisco UCS Solutions

## *Second Edition*

First published: December 2013

Second edition: April 2017

Production reference: 1240417

Published by Packt Publishing Ltd.
Livery Place
35 Livery Street
Birmingham
B3 2PB, UK.
ISBN 978-1-78646-440-8

www.packtpub.com

# Credits

**Author**
Anuj Modi
Farhan Nadeem
Prasenjit Sarkar

**Reviewer**
Farhan Nadeem

**Acquisition Editor**
Namrata Patil

**Content Development Editor**
Amedh Pohad

**Technical Editors**
Prashant Chaudhari
Khushbu Sutar

**Production Coordinator**
Melwyn Dsa

**Copy Editors**
Safis Editing
Madhusudan Uchil

**Project Coordinator**
Judie Jose

**Proofreader**
Safis Editing

**Indexer**
Mariammal Chettiyar

**Graphics**
Kirk D'Penha

# About the Authors

**Anuj Modi** (@vConsultant) is a senior consulting engineer in the Advanced Service Group at Cisco Systems and has worked in architecting and implementing Cisco's cloud and data center solutions. He has more than 14 years' experience in the IT industry, including serving various roles as IT manager at IndSwift, senior system admin at Computer Science Corporation, and virtualization consultant at Hewlett Packard.

He holds a bachelor's and master's degree in computer applications and many industry-standard certifications, such as MCSE, VCP, ITIL, and CCA. He has co-authored a book on VMware NSX and Cisco Unified Computing System. His primary focus is orchestrating and automating infrastructures for private, public, and hybrid cloud solutions with Cisco and third-party products. He has extensive experience in data center assessment, and planning, designing, implementing, and optimizing infrastructure, and helping customers build and migrate to next-generation data centers.

- WordPress: https://anujmodi.wordpress.com/
- LinkedIn: https://www.linkedin.com/in/anuj-modi-2866481
- Other: https://communities.vmware.com/thread/528879?start=0&tstart=0

*Thanks to my family for having the patience with me in spite of all the time it took me away from them and couldn't spend quality time. I would like to dedicate this book to my family for all the encouragement and support while writing this book.*

**Farhan Nadeem** has been in the IT field for over 19 years. He has a master's degree in electrical engineering and holds several industry-recognized certifications, including VCAP-DCA, VCP, CCNP DC, CISSP, CCA, and MCIP-EA. Farhan has proven experience in successfully engineering, deploying, administering, and troubleshooting heterogeneous infrastructure solutions. Starting with the MCSE-NT Microsoft certification in 1997, he's always stayed abreast of the latest technologies and server hardware through proactive learning and successful real-world deployments. He has extensive work experience in complex heterogeneous environments comprising various hardware platforms, operating systems, and applications. This exposure has given him broad knowledge in investigating, designing, implementing, and managing infrastructure solutions. He progressively started focusing on virtualization technologies and the Cisco UCS platform and has completed several successful UCS deployments with multiple virtualization platforms. When not working with computers, he enjoys spending time with his family. He has also technically reviewed the second edition of this book.

*I would like to thank my family for providing their support during reviewing of this book.*

**Prasenjit Sarkar** is a product manager at Oracle for their public cloud, with a focus on cloud strategy, Oracle Ravello, cloud-native applications, and the API platform. His primary focus is driving Oracle's cloud computing business with commercial and public sector customers, helping to shape and deliver a strategy to build broad use of Oracle's Infrastructure as a Service offerings, such as Compute, Storage, and Database as a Service. He is also responsible for developing public/private cloud integration strategies, customers' cloud computing architecture visions, future state architectures, and implementable architecture roadmaps in the context of the public, private, and hybrid cloud computing solutions that Oracle can offer.

He is the author of a virtualization blog (`http://stretch-cloud.info`) and has also authored six industry-leading books on virtualization, SDN, and physical compute, among others.

He has six successful patents and six more patents pending at the US PTO. He has also authored numerous research articles.

# www.PacktPub.com

For support files and downloads related to your book, please visit www.PacktPub.com.

Did you know that Packt offers eBook versions of every book published, with PDF and ePub files available? You can upgrade to the eBook version at www.PacktPub.com and as a print book customer, you are entitled to a discount on the eBook copy. Get in touch with us at service@packtpub.com for more details.

At www.PacktPub.com, you can also read a collection of free technical articles, sign up for a range of free newsletters and receive exclusive discounts and offers on Packt books and eBooks.

https://www.packtpub.com/mapt

Get the most in-demand software skills with Mapt. Mapt gives you full access to all Packt books and video courses, as well as industry-leading tools to help you plan your personal development and advance your career.

## Why subscribe?

- Fully searchable across every book published by Packt
- Copy and paste, print, and bookmark content
- On demand and accessible via a web browser

# Customer Feedback

Thanks for purchasing this Packt book. At Packt, quality is at the heart of our editorial process. To help us improve, please leave us an honest review on this book's Amazon page at https://www.amazon.com/dp/1786464403.

If you'd like to join our team of regular reviewers, you can e-mail us at customerreviews@packtpub.com. We award our regular reviewers with free eBooks and videos in exchange for their valuable feedback. Help us be relentless in improving our products!

# Table of Contents

# Preface

Cisco **Unified Computer System** (**UCS**) is a powerful solution for modern data centers that is responsible for increasing efficiency and reducing costs. *Implementing Cisco UCS Solutions* is an update to the previous version and provides a similar hands-on approach. With actual examples of configuring and deploying Cisco UCS components, this book prepares readers for real-world deployments of Cisco UCS data center solutions.

This book starts with a description of Cisco UCS equipment options and introduces Cisco UCS Emulator, which is an excellent resource for practically learning Cisco UCS component deployment. Subsequent chapters introduce all areas of UCS solutions with practical configuration examples.

You will be introduced to the Cisco UCS Manager, which is the centralized management interface for Cisco UCS. Once the reader establishes elementary acquaintance with UCS Manager, we go deep into configuring LAN, SAN, identity pools, resource pools, and service profiles for the servers. We also present miscellaneous administration topics, including backup, restore, user roles, and high availability cluster configuration. The last few chapters introduce virtualized networking, third-party integration tools, testing failure scenarios, and automating your infrastructure with Cisco UCS Director.

If you want to learn and enhance your hands-on skills with Cisco UCS solutions, this book is certainly for you. You will learn everything you need for the rapidly growing Cisco UCS deployments.

# What this book covers

Chapter 1, *What's New with Cisco UCS*, will cover the third-generation of Cisco UCS products along with an introduction to Cisco UCS M-Series modular servers, UCS storage servers, and UCS Mini. This chapter can help you to understand various UCS products and select the best one for your data center and cloud computing solutions.

Chapter 2, *Installing Cisco UCS Hardware*, walks through UCS hardware component installation, such as Fabric Interconnect, chassis, blade, I/O module, and interface card, and discusses how to use Cisco Single Connect Technology to connect rack servers with Fabric Interconnect. It also covers power and cooling requirements.

Chapter 3, *Setting Up a Lab using Cisco UCS Emulator*, introduces the UCS Emulator, which is an excellent tool from Cisco that you can use to learn about UCS without a physical lab. Different UCS Emulator installation options are discussed, and configuring the UCS Emulator for lab usage is explained.

Chapter 4, *Configuring Cisco UCS using UCS Manager*, gives an overview of UCS Manager, which is the core management tool for the UCS platform. Readers will get acquainted with UCS Manager navigation and configuration options using both the graphical user interface and the command-line interface.

Chapter 5, *Configuring LAN Connectivity*, explains UCS network connectivity. UCS platform-unique features, including Fabric Interconnect operational modes, pin groups, port channels, virtual PortChannel, and Virtual Network Interface Card configuration, are explained along with both northbound and southbound network connectivities from Fabric Interconnects.

Chapter 6, *Configuring SAN Connectivity*, explains storage connectivity for different SAN protocols supported by the UCS platform. The configuration of protocols including FC, FCoE, and iSCSI is discussed, along with an introduction to unique UCS features, such as FC operational modes, VSANs, and uplink pinning.

Chapter 7, *Creating Identity Resource Pools, Policies, and Templates*, explains that pools are a very important topic in UCS, especially in relation to configuring service profiles. In this chapter, we'll discuss the different pools you create during UCS deployments. We'll start by looking at what pools are, and then we'll discuss the different types of pool and show how to configure each of them.

Chapter 8, *Creating and Managing Service Profiles*, introduces identity and resource pools, which include UUID, MAC addresses, WWN, and server pools. Identity and resource pools are used for abstracting unique identities and resources for devices such as vNICs; vHBAs and server pools can assign servers in groups based on similar server characteristics.

Chapter 9, *Managing UCS through Routine and Advanced Management*, introduces the most common and advanced management tasks performed with UCS, from startup and shutdown to logging, upgrading firmware, licensing, and role-based access. These routine management tasks are crucial to understand in order to effectively administer Cisco UCS.

Chapter 10, *Virtual Networking in Cisco UCS*, explains the integration of Cisco UCS and the virtualization of hypervisors with VMware vSphere and Cisco Nexus 1000V Distributed Virtual Switch.

Chapter 11, *Configuring Backup, Restore, and High Availability*, covers UCS backup and restore options. This chapter also provides details of high availability configuration for UCS Fabric Interconnects.

Chapter 12, *Cisco UCS Failure Scenarios Testing*, discusses various failure scenarios that provide solutions for UCS troubleshooting to identify and resolve issues.

Chapter 13, *Third-Party Application Integration,* covers third-party applications, including VMware vCenter extension, goUCS automation toolkit, and EMC UIM.

Chapter 14, *Automation and Orchestration of Cisco UCS*, introduces using Cisco UCS Central for domain management, Performance Manager for health monitoring, and Cisco UCS Director for automation, and orchestrating all the infrastructure components: compute, network, storage, and virtualization.

# What you need for this book

In order to create a lab without physical equipment and to practice the procedures provided in this book, you will need the following:

- A UCS Emulator virtual machine that provides UCS Manager and emulated hardware.
- A hypervisor that can run the UCS Emulator VM. Options include VM Player, VM Workstation, VM Fusion, vSphere, and Hyper-V.
- A client machine with an Internet Explorer- or Mozilla-compatible browser for accessing the UCS Manager application.

# Who this book is for

This book is intended for professionals responsible for Cisco UCS deployments, which include systems, network, and storage administrators. Readers should have basic knowledge of the server's architecture, network, and storage technologies. Although not necessary, familiarity with virtualization technologies is also recommended because a majority of real-world UCS deployments run virtualized loads. Even though UCS Fabric Interconnects running UCS Manager are based on the Nexus platform, knowledge of Nexus OS is not necessary, because the majority of the management tasks are handled in the graphical user interface, with very few exceptions using the CLI.

# Conventions

In this book, you will find a number of text styles that distinguish between different kinds of information. Here are some examples of these styles and an explanation of their meaning.

Code words in text, database table names, folder names, filenames, file extensions, pathnames, dummy URLs, user input, and Twitter handles are shown as follows: "None of the configurations get applied unless the `commit-buffer` command is used."

Any command-line input or output is written as follows:

```
switch(config)# feature vpc
switch(config)# feature lacp
```

**New terms** and **important words** are shown in bold. Words that you see on the screen, for example, in menus or dialog boxes, appear in the text like this: "Click on the **Equipment** tab in the navigation pane."

 Warnings or important notes appear in a box like this.

 Tips and tricks appear like this.

# Reader feedback

Feedback from our readers is always welcome. Let us know what you think about this book—what you liked or disliked. Reader feedback is important for us as it helps us develop titles that you will really get the most out of.

To send us general feedback, simply e-mail feedback@packtpub.com, and mention the book's title in the subject of your message.

If there is a topic that you have expertise in and you are interested in either writing or contributing to a book, see our author guide at www.packtpub.com/authors.

# Customer support

Now that you are the proud owner of a Packt book, we have a number of things to help you to get the most from your purchase.

# Downloading the color images of this book

We also provide you with a PDF file that has color images of the screenshots/diagrams used in this book. The color images will help you better understand the changes in the output. You can download this file from `https://www.packtpub.com/sites/default/files/down loads/ImplementingCISCOUCSSolutionsSecondEdition_ColorImages.pdf`.

# Errata

Although we have taken every care to ensure the accuracy of our content, mistakes do happen. If you find a mistake in one of our books—maybe a mistake in the text or the code—we would be grateful if you could report this to us. By doing so, you can save other readers from frustration and help us improve subsequent versions of this book. If you find any errata, please report them by visiting `http://www.packtpub.com/submit-errata`, selecting your book, clicking on the **Errata Submission Form** link, and entering the details of your errata. Once your errata are verified, your submission will be accepted and the errata will be uploaded to our website or added to any list of existing errata under the **Errata** section of that title.

To view the previously submitted errata, go to `https://www.packtpub.com/books/conten t/support` and enter the name of the book in the search field. The required information will appear under the Errata section.

# Piracy

Piracy of copyrighted material on the Internet is an ongoing problem across all media. At Packt, we take the protection of our copyright and licenses very seriously. If you come across any illegal copies of our works in any form on the Internet, please provide us with the location address or website name immediately so that we can pursue a remedy.

Please contact us at `copyright@packtpub.com` with a link to the suspected pirated material.

We appreciate your help in protecting our authors and our ability to bring you valuable content.

# Questions

If you have a problem with any aspect of this book, you can contact us at questions@packtpub.com, and we will do our best to address the problem.

# 1
# What's New with Cisco UCS

The data center computer industry has seen dramatic changes with the inception of Cisco's **Unified Computing System** (**UCS**). Within a few years, Cisco UCS has become the industry standard for converged compute infrastructures and is dominating the server market in the world. Unlike competitors who glued legacy rack server solutions into a chassis form factor, Cisco UCS is a truly unified platform that combines compute, network, and storage access in a single system. The current rate of increasing data and application traffic has made the network industry scale toward 40 Gig switches, whereas the server industry is way behind on this. To match with the network industry, Cisco brought out the third-generation hardware of UCS and breathed new life into it with 40 Gig Ethernet support. The Cisco third-generation UCS 6300 Fabric Interconnect series, and UCS 2300 Fabric Extender (I/O module) 2304 series integrated with B-Series and C-Series, enables an end-to-end 40 Gig Ethernet and FCoE solution, and extended 16 Gig native Fibre Channel support for high speed and performance.

In this chapter, we will acquaint ourselves with Cisco UCS products and the innovative UCS architecture, which abstracts underlying physical hardware and provides unified management to all devices. The chapter can help you understand various UCS products and new changes in the third-generation of UCS.

We'll explore the following topics:

- UCS architecture overview
- Fabric Interconnects
- Fabric Extenders
- Blade server chassis
- B-Series blade servers
- C-Series rack servers
- Mezzanine adapters

- Cisco storage servers
- Cisco UCS Mini

# UCS architecture overview

With ever-increasing demand on data centers, vendors started focusing on different aspects of server and networking hardware consolidation; however, most of the ad hoc solutions were based upon existing products that were not designed from the ground up for integration from the consolidation perspective and failed to address the requirements of a data center as a whole. Hence, the management of these amalgamated solutions was a nightmare for the IT administrator.

Cisco entered the blade server market with a holistic approach to blade server design. With a strong background in networking and storage products, Cisco developed a cohesive solution consolidating compute, network, and storage connectivity components along with centralized management of these resources. The purpose of Cisco UCS is to reduce the **total cost of ownership** (**TCO**) and improve manageability, scalability, and flexibility.

Cisco introduced the idea of stateless computing with its blade server design. Cisco blade servers do not need any initial configuration. Blade identity UUID, NICs, MAC addresses, storage WWN numbers, firmware, and BIOS settings are all abstracted from **Unified Computing System Manager** (**UCSM**), the management software running on the Fabric Interconnects.

Time for provisioning servers dramatically improves, as the servers can be provisioned using UCSM software even before they are physically available. Once the server is physically installed, it will abstract its identity from UCSM. Using server configuration templates, it is possible to create a server template once and apply it on hundreds of servers.

Replacing servers also becomes very easy. Since the servers are stateless, as soon as a replacement server is installed, it will abstract all the configuration of the old server from the associated service profile and will be available for use. Servers can also be easily migrated for different roles and workloads.

Virtualization in the form of modern bare-metal hypervisors is a major breakthrough for the optimal utilization of computational resources. The Cisco UCS solution supports all major hypervisor platforms, including VMware ESX/ESXi, Microsoft Hyper-V, and Citrix XenServer. Support and integration with VMware vSphere is very strong. UCSM can be integrated with vCenter to abstract and manage features at the individual **virtual machine** (**VM**) level. Leveraging the benefits of virtualization and increasing the density of physical servers, UCS can scale up to thousands of VMs.

Cisco UCS servers are available in two categories: B-Series blade servers and C-Series rack-mount servers. Both form factors are designed using the same industry-standard components and can address different computational requirements. Both B-series blade servers and C-Series rack-mount servers are designed using Intel® Xeon® CPUs. B-series servers are managed through UCSM, whereas C-Series servers can either be individually managed or can be integrated to UCSM.

Cisco also introduced patented extended memory technology for two CPU socket servers to increase the total amount of memory support, which could be more than double the amount of memory as compared to the industry standard for two-socket servers. Virtualized workloads can leverage this extra memory to support an even greater density of virtual machines in a reduced physical footprint, thus resulting in reduced **capital expenditure** (**CAPEX**) and **operational expenditure** (**OPEX**) costs. Extended memory technology is available in both B-Series blade servers and C-Series rack-mount servers.

# Changes in the third-generation UCS

Cisco has introduced native end-to-end 40 Gig support in the third-generation of UCS. With high-density 40 Gig ports in Fabric Interconnects and Fabric Extenders with 80 Gig Virtual Interface Cards. The following are the major changes:

- **Cisco UCS 6300 Series Fabric Interconnects**: These provide 40 Gig Ethernet/FCoE connectivity to upstream network switches and downstream to Cisco UCS B-Series servers and 4, 8, and 16 Gig native Fibre Channel connectivity to upstream storage switches with the 6332-16UP Fabric Interconnect Series
- **Cisco UCS 2304 Fabric Extenders**: These provide up to 160 Gig throughput to each Fabric Interconnect with 4x40 Gig uplink ports and 32x10 Gig backend ports to connect blade servers inside the chassis, totaling 320 Gig throughput to each chassis with two Fabric Extenders
- **Cisco UCS Virtual Interface Card (VIC) 1300**: This provides up to 80 Gig network throughput to a blade server with the correct combination of hardware
- **Cisco Nexus 2348UPQ 10GE Fabric Extenders**: These provide 6x40 Gig ports of upstream connectivity and downstream connectivity to C-Series rack servers

# Physical architecture of UCS

Cisco UCS consists of modular components that work together to provide a comprehensive solution that unifies compute, network, and storage technologies. Cisco UCS consists of the following components:

- Fabric Interconnects
- Blade server chassis
- Blade servers
- Rack-mount servers
- IOM modules and Fabric Extenders
- Mezzanine cards for network and storage connectivity
- Unified Computing System Manager

Here is a diagram of the Unified Computing System architecture:

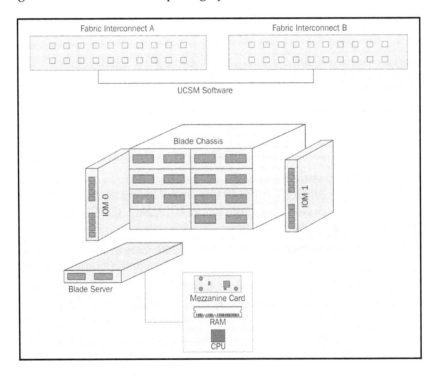

In this chapter, we will go into the details of various UCS components; we'll focus on their physical specifications and installation in the subsequent sections.

The Cisco interactive 3D model for Cisco 5100 series chassis and blades is an excellent resource for exploring Cisco UCS components physically. It is available for iPhone/iPad also (search for `UCS tech specs` in the market place): `http://www.cisco.com/en/US/prod/ps10265/ps10279/ucs_kaon _model_preso.html`.

# Fabric Interconnects

The **Fabric Interconnect (FI)** is the core component of a UCS solution, providing network, storage, and unified management capabilities to servers. Fabric Interconnects are typically configured as highly available clustered pairs in production environments and provide active-active data traffic. A single FI-based design is also possible for **proof of concept (POC)** but not recommended for a production environment. Fabric Interconnects provide the following two capabilities:

- Network connectivity to both LAN and SAN
- UCS infrastructure management through embedded management software UCSM for both hardware and software management

With Gen 3 UCS hardware, Cisco has introduced a new series of Fabric Interconnects, Cisco UCS Fabric Interconnect 6300. This generation has been upgraded from the earlier 10 GbE-port model to a high-density 40 GbE-port model with 2.56 Tbps throughput. At the time of writing this, the customer can still select the Cisco UCS Fabric Interconnect 6200 series from the second-generation to go with the 10 Gig unified port model. The first-generation Cisco UCS Fabric Interconnect 6100 series has reached end of life and will not be supported.

The core functionality is the same in all the generations, with a difference in the number of physical ports, and can be upgraded to the latest UCSM software.

Fabric Interconnects provide converged ports. **Converged** means that depending on physical SFP and Fabric Interconnect software configuration, each port can be configured as an Ethernet port, an FCoE, or an FC port.

In production, Fabric Interconnects are deployed in clustered pairs to provide high availability. A Cisco-supported implementation requires that clustered Fabric Interconnects be identical. The only scenario for having different Fabric Interconnects in a cluster is during a cluster upgrade.

Larger enterprises may consider deploying *Cisco UCS Central*, which can manage multiple UCS domains across globally distributed data centers.

The Gen 3 Fabric Interconnect comes in two models: UCS FI 6332, which is 32-port 40 Gig Ethernet/FCoE, and UCS FI 6332-16UP, which comes with 16 unified ports to support 1/10 Gig Ethernet/FCoE or 4, 8, and 16 Gig native Fibre Channel. The Fabric Interconnect is a **top-of-rack** (**ToR**) switch and provides 10 Gig/40 Gig LAN connectivity northbound, where 40 Gig I/O module connectivity southbound.

The Gen 2 Fabric Interconnect comes in two models: UCS FI 6248UP, which has 32 fixed ports and 16 ports with an expansion module, and UCS FI 6296UP, which has 48 fixed ports and 48 ports with three expansion modules (16 ports per expansion module). Both models provide unified ports that can be changed to any mode through a software configuration change.

## UCS third-generation 6332

Cisco 6332 is a 1U device with a maximum of 32 fixed ports with 2.56 Tbps throughput. The 32 ports support 10/40 Gig Ethernet/FCoE connectivity and don't support native Fibre Channel connectivity to a SAN switch. The fixed ports can be configured as 10 Gig with breakout cables to connect with a 10 Gig infrastructure but the last six 40 Gig at the Fabric Interconnect do not support breaking out and can be used only as 40 Gig network uplink ports:

"Courtesy of Cisco Systems, Inc. unauthorized use not permitted."

Its specifications are as follows:

- A maximum of 20 blade server chassis per UCS domain
- Fabric throughput of 2.56 Tbps

- 40 Gig ports providing at most 98x10 Gig ports with breakout cables
- Default 8-port license

# UCS third-generation 6332-16UP

Cisco 6332-16UP is a 1U device with a maximum of 40 fixed ports with 2.46 Tbps throughput. 24 ports support 40 Gig Ethernet/FCoE, and the remaining 16 support 1/10 Gig Ethernet/FCoE or 1/4/8/16 Gig Fibre Channel. The model can provide native Fibre Channel support to the FC infrastructure. Like the previous model, this model's fixed ports can be configured as 10 Gig with breakout cables to connect with a 10 Gig infrastructure, but the last six 40 Gig ports at the Fabric Interconnect do not support breaking out and can be used only as 40 Gig network uplink ports.

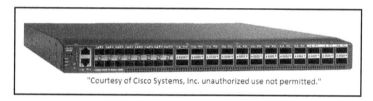

"Courtesy of Cisco Systems, Inc. unauthorized use not permitted."

Its specifications are as follows:

- A maximum of 20 blade-server chassis per UCS domain
- Fabric throughput of 2.46 Tbps
- 24-port base unit with one expansion slot, which can provide 16 extra ports
- 40 Gig ports providing a maximum of 72x10 Gig ports with breakout cables
- Default 12-port license (four from fixed ports and eight from an expansion module)

# UCS second-generation 6248UP

The Cisco 6248UP is a 1U device with a maximum of 48 converged ports. Ports can be configured as 1 Gig Ethernet, 10 Gig Ethernet, 10 Gig/FCoE, and 2/4/8 Gig Fibre Channel.

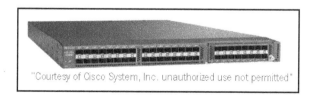

"Courtesy of Cisco System, Inc. unauthorized use not permitted"

The specifications of the 6248UP are as follows:

- A maximum of 20 blade-server chassis per UCS domain
- Fabric throughput of 960 Gbps
- 32-port base unit with one expansion slot, which can provide 16 extra ports

## UCS second-generation 6296UP

The Cisco 6296UP is a 2U device with a maximum of 96 converged ports. The ports can be configured as 1 Gig Ethernet, 10 Gig Ethernet, 10 Gig/FCoE, and 2/4/8 Gig Fibre Channel.

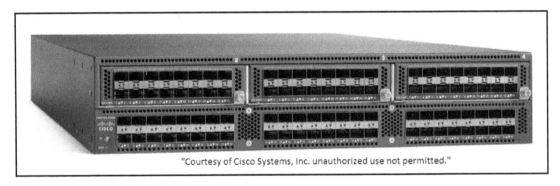

"Courtesy of Cisco Systems, Inc. unauthorized use not permitted."

The specifications of the 6296UP are as follows:

- A maximum of 20 blade-server chassis per UCS domain
- Fabric throughput of 1920 Gbps
- 48-port base unit with three expansion slots, which can provide 48 extra ports

## Fabric Extenders

**Fabric Extenders (FEX)** modules are also known as **IO Modules (IOMs)**. These modules serve as line cards to the Fabric Interconnects, in the same way as the Nexus series switches' remote line cards. IOMs also provide interface connections to blade servers. IOMs multiplex data from blade servers and provide this data to Fabric Interconnects and do the same in the reverse direction. In production environments, IOMs are always used in pairs to provide redundancy and failover.

Apart from data transfer between chassis and Fabric Interconnects, IOMs provide two other functions:

- **Chassis Management Controller** (**CMC**): This monitors chassis components, such as fan units, power supplies, and chassis temperature. It also reads chassis components' identification data and detects the insertion and removal of blade servers.
- **Chassis Management Switch** (**CMS**): This provides fast Ethernet links to embedded **Cisco Integrated Management Controller** (**CIMC**) instances on blade servers for KVM access, **serial over LAN** (**SoL**) access, and **Intelligent Platform Management Interface** (**IPMI**) data to travel from individual blades to FIs for monitoring and management purposes.

The following is a diagram of the Cisco UCS Fabric Extender (IO Module):

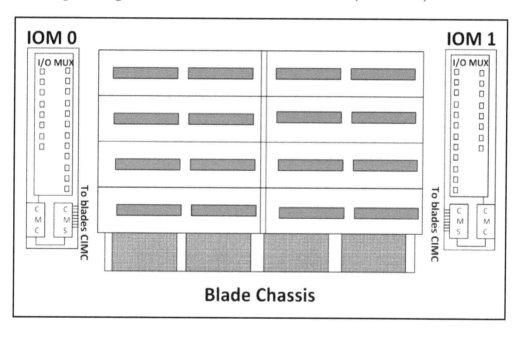

# UCS third-generation Cisco 2304 IOM

The Cisco UCS 2304 Fabric Extender is third-generation hardware and provides native 40 Gig Ethernet/FCoE uplinks to the Fabric Interconnect 6300 series. It includes 4x40 Gig **Network Interfaces** (**NIFs**) and 32x10 Gig backend ports to blade servers.

"Courtesy of Cisco Systems, Inc. unauthorized use not permitted."

The specifications of the 2304XP are as follows:

- 4x40 Gbps fabric ports for connecting to the Fabric Interconnect
- 32x10 Gbps server-facing ports with FCoE
- 160 Gbps throughput

# UCS second-generation Cisco 2208XP IOM

The Cisco UCS 2208XP Fabric Extender is second-generation hardware and provides 10 Gig Ethernet/FCoE uplinks to the Fabric Interconnect 6200/6300 series. It includes 8x10 Gig network interfaces and 32x10 Gig backend ports to blade servers.

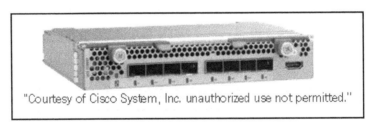

"Courtesy of Cisco System, Inc. unauthorized use not permitted."

Its specifications are as follows:

- 8x10 Gbps fabric ports for connecting to the Fabric Interconnect
- 32x10 Gbps server-facing ports with FCoE
- 80 Gbps throughput

# UCS second-generation Cisco 2204XP IOM

The Cisco UCS 2204 Fabric Extender is second-generation hardware and provides 10 Gig Ethernet/FCoE uplinks to the Fabric Interconnect 6200/6300 series. It includes 4x10 Gig network interfaces and 32x10 Gig backend ports to blade servers.

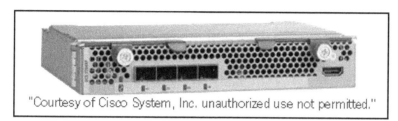

"Courtesy of Cisco System, Inc. unauthorized use not permitted."

The specifications of the 2204XP are as follows:

- 4x10 Gbps fabric ports for connecting to the Fabric Interconnect
- 16x10 Gbps server-facing ports with FCoE
- 40 Gbps throughput

# Cisco Nexus 2348UPQ 10GE Fabric Extender

The Cisco Nexus 2348UPQ 10GE Fabric Extender is third-generation hardware and provides native 40 Gig Ethernet upstream to the Fabric Interconnect 6200/6300 series and 1/10 Gig downstream connectivity to rack servers and other appliances.

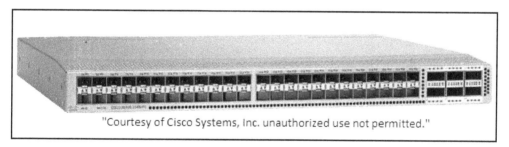

"Courtesy of Cisco Systems, Inc. unauthorized use not permitted."

The specifications of the N2248UPQ are as follows:

- 6x40 Gbps fabric ports for connecting to the Fabric Interconnect
- 48x10 Gbps server-facing ports
- 240 Gbps throughput

# Blade server chassis

The Cisco **5100 series blade server chassis** is a vital building block of the Cisco Unified Communication System solution. The chassis' form factor is 4U, and it can host:

- A maximum of eight half-width blade servers
- A maximum of four full-width servers

 Any other combination of half blade and full blade servers is also possible.

# Chassis front

Chassis front provides the access to manage the blades insertion and removal from it:

- Eight half-width empty slots for a maximum of eight half-width blade servers with a removable divider in the middle, which can be removed for installing full-width blades
- Four slots for single power supplies, which can be configured as non-redundant, N+1 redundant, and grid redundant

"Courtesy of Cisco System, Inc. unauthorized use not permitted."

# Chassis back

Chassis back provides access to manage IOM modules, fans and power supplies:

- Two slots for IOM modules, which act as remote line cards to the Fabric Interconnects
- Eight hot-pluggable fans for cooling
- Four power supply connectors

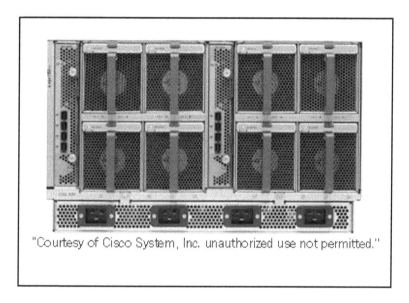

"Courtesy of Cisco System, Inc. unauthorized use not permitted."

# Environmental requirements

UCS System should meet all the environmental requirements before deploying in the data center:

- The chassis requires an industry-standard four-post 19-inch rack or cabinet. It cannot be mounted into a two-post relay rack because of weight and length.
- The chassis requires 6U rack space.
- Ensure proper cooling and ventilation for the rack. Chassis airflow is front to back and should not be obstructed.
- The chassis is floor loading.

Due to the weight and size of the chassis, at least two people are required to mount it to the rails. It is highly recommended to mount the chassis first and then insert power supplies, fan units, and blade servers.

# B-Series blade servers

While blade servers are the dominant deployment of UCS solutions, Cisco has strategically extended its offering to include the industry-standard rack-mount form factor as well to provide users a choice against competing rack-mount server vendors such as HP, IBM, and Dell. Blade servers are categorized as B-Series servers, and rack-mount servers are categorized as C-Series servers.

# Blade servers

Blade servers are at the heart of the UCS solution and come in various system resource configurations in terms of CPU, memory, and hard disk capacity. All blade servers are based on Intel® Xeon® processors, and there is no AMD option available. Businesses can choose from different blade configurations as required.

## B200 M3/M4

The B200 series is a half-width blade server and is in the third-generation of UCS hardware. The B200 M4 supports the latest Intel® Xeon® E5 v3 or v4 processor family, while B200 M3 supports the Intel® Xeon® E5-2500 or E5-2600 v1 or v2 processor family.

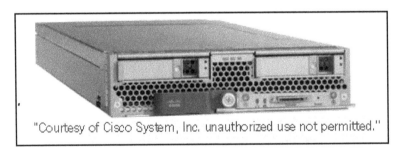
"Courtesy of Cisco System, Inc. unauthorized use not permitted."

The specifications of the latest B200 M3/M4 server are as follows:

- Two Intel® Xeon® E5-2600 v3 or v4 processor family CPUs for B200 M4 and Intel® Xeon® E5-2500 or E5-2600 v2 processor family CPUs for B200 M3.
- A maximum of 1.5 TB total memory capacity (using 64 GB DIMMs). Total memory slots are 24.
- Two drive bays for SAS/SATA/SSD internal hard drives for up to 2 TB maximum storage capacity with built-in RAID 0 and 1 controller
- Up to 80 GB I/O throughput with supported mezzanine card

A B200 series entry-level blade server is the most deployed blade server and is an excellent choice for virtualization, web server farms, distributed databases, and CRM applications.

# B260 M4

The B260 M4 series server is a full-width blade server with the power of Intel® Xeon® E7 series processor family CPUs.

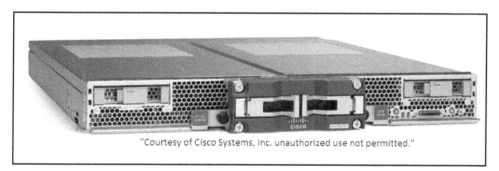

"Courtesy of Cisco Systems, Inc. unauthorized use not permitted."

These are its specifications:

- Two Intel® Xeon® E7 v2, v3, or v4 processor family CPUs
- A maximum of 3 TB total memory capacity with total 48 memory slots
- Two drives bays for SAS/SATA/SSD internal hard drives
- Up to 160 GB I/O throughput with supported mezzanine card

The B260 series server is an excellent choice for mission-critical and distributed workload with its latest addition of Intel® Xeon® E7 processors.

# B420 M3/M4

The B420 M3/M4 series server is a full-width blade server. The B420 M3/M4 series is based on an Intel® Xeon® E5 series processor.

"Courtesy of Cisco Systems, Inc. unauthorized use not permitted."

The following are the specifications of the B420 M3/M4 servers:

- Four Intel® Xeon® E5-4600 v3 or v4 for the B420 M4 and v2 for B420 M3
- A maximum of 3 TB total memory capacity with total 48 memory slots
- Two drive bays for SAS/SATA/SSD internal hard drives with an optional 2 GB flash-backed write cache
- Up to 160 GB I/O throughput with supported mezzanine card

B420 M3/M4 is full width blade server and can be best fit for enterprise performance and scalable architecture such as VDI, ERP and CRM applications.

# B460 M4

The B460 M4 series server is a dual full-width blade server and combine the power of two B260 M4 servers with four sockets.

"Courtesy of Cisco Systems, Inc. unauthorized use not permitted."

These are its specifications:

- Four Intel® Xeon® E7 v2, E7 v3, or E7 v4 processor family CPUs
- A maximum of 6 TB total memory capacity with total 96 memory slots
- Four drives bays for SAS/SATA/SSD internal hard drives
- Up to 320 GB I/O throughput with supported mezzanine card

The B460 M4 server is most in demand double full-width blade server for mission critical applications, in-memory analytics and large scale database applications so on. For a quick comparison of B-Series blade servers, visit `http://www.cisco.com/en/US/products/ps10280/prod_models_comparis on.html`. Select all servers and press the **Compare** button.
Cisco UCS B22 M3, B200 M1/M2, B230 M1/M2, B250 M1/M2, and B440 M1/M2 servers have reached end of sale and are no longer being sold.

# C-Series rack servers

UCS C-Series servers are available in industry-standard rack-mount form factor. Like B-Series blade servers, these servers are also based on Intel® Xeon® processors and there is no AMD option available.

C-Series servers can be managed independently through **out of band** (**OOB**) web management interface or can be integrated to UCSM software. The embedded controller known as CIMC provides the following services:

- Remote KVM to server console
- Remote power management
- Remote virtual media for operating system installation
- Industry standard IPMI support for monitoring
- Standard SNMP traps for monitoring

Connecting and managing C-Series rack servers through UCSM requires connection through Nexus 2300/2200 series Fabric Extenders which acts as line card to the Fabric Interconnects.

C-Series servers are available in various CPU, memory, I/Om, and storage configurations to address needs of different size of organizations. Following are the specifications of these servers as available at the Cisco website.

# C220 M3/M4

C220 M3/M4 is a 1U form factor rack-mounted server. C220 M4 supports the latest Intel® Xeon® E5 v3 or v4 processor family while C220 M3 supports Intel® Xeon® E5-2500 or E5-2600 v2 processor family.

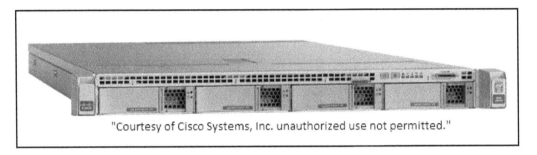

"Courtesy of Cisco Systems, Inc. unauthorized use not permitted."

Specifications of the C220 M3/M4 server:

- Two Intel® Xeon® processors E5-2600 v3 or v4 product family CPUs
- Maximum of 1.5 TB total memory capacity with total 24 memory slots in M4 while 512 GB total memory capacity with total 16 memory slots in M3
- Up to eight **small form factor** (**SFF**) or four **large form factor** (**LFF**) internal storage SAS/SATA/SSD hard disks with 12.8 TB (SFF) or 16 TB (LFF) storage capacity and optional RAID controller
- 2 x 1 GB I/O ports with optional 10 GB unified fabric
- Two PCIe generation three expansion slots

C220 M3/M4 series server has great performance and density for distributed database applications and web farms.

# C240 M3/M4

C240 M3/M4 is 2U formed factor rack-mounted server. C240 M4 supports latest Intel® Xeon® E5 v3 processor family while C240 M3 supports Intel® Xeon® E5-2600 v2 processor family.

Specifications of the C240 M3/M4 server:

- Two Intel® Xeon® processors E5-2600 v3 product family CPUs
- Maximum of 1.5 TB total memory capacity with total 24 memory slots in M4 while 768 GB total memory capacity with total 24 memory slots in M3

- Up to 26 SFF or 12 LFF internal storage SAS/SATA/SSD hard disks with 38.4 TB (SFF) or 48 TB (LFF) storage capacity and optional RAID controller
- 2 x 1 GB I/O ports with one modular LOM
- Up to six PCIe generation three expansion slots

"Courtesy of Cisco Systems, Inc. unauthorized use not permitted."

C240 M3/M4 series server provides great performance with storage extensibility for distributed database application and web farms.

## C460 M2/M4

C460 M2/M4 is 4U formed factor rack-mounted server. C460 M4 supports latest Intel® Xeon® E7-4800/8800 v2 or v3 processor family while B460 M2 supports Intel® Xeon® E7-4800/8800 v1 processor family.

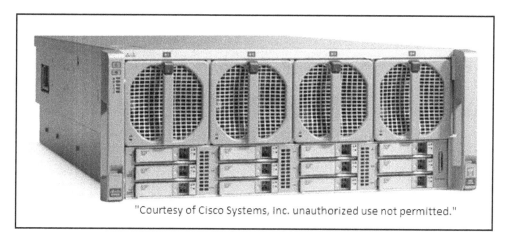

"Courtesy of Cisco Systems, Inc. unauthorized use not permitted."

Specifications of the C460 M2/M4 servers are as follows:

- Four Intel® Xeon® E7-4800/8800 v2 or v3 processor product family CPUs
- Maximum of 6 TB total memory capacity with total 96 memory slots
- Up to 12 LFF internal storage SAS/SATA/SSD hard disks with 21.6 TB (LFF) storage capacity and no RAID controller
- Two GE LAN on motherboard I/O ports with optional two 10 GB unified fabric ports
- 10 PCIe generation three expansion slots with optional LSI MegaRAID controller in the eleventh slot

The C460 M2/M4 series server provides exceptional computational resources for business critical applications, such as large databases both in bare metal and virtualized environments.

 For quick comparison of C-Series servers, please visit `http://www.cisco.com/en/US/products/ps10493/prod_models_comparis on.html`. Select all servers and press **Compare** button. Cisco UCS C22 M3, C24 M3, C200 M1/M2, C210 M1, C250 M1/M2, C260 M2, C420 M3, and B460 M1 servers have reached end of sale.

# Mezzanine adapters

A huge variety of **mezzanine adapters**, also known as **Virtual Interface Cards** (**VICs**), is available from Cisco for both B-Series blade servers and C-Series rack servers. Older adapters are fixed port and not optimized for contemporary virtualized server environments. There are some older third-party network cards also available as an option. Newer third-generation adapters are optimized for virtualization and can provide 256 dynamic virtual adapters. The number of virtual adapters is dependent on the VIC model. These virtual adapters can be configured as Ethernet (vNIC) or Fibre Channel (vHBA) devices. All virtualization-optimized VICs also support VM-FEX technology. Our focus will be on the mezzanine adapters, which are virtualization optimized.

# VICs for blade servers

VICs are available in the form factor of a mezzanine card. All new VICs provide dynamic virtual vNIC or vHBA interfaces for server-side connectivity. The latest Cisco 1300 VIC series can only support UCS 6200 and 6300 series Fabric Interconnects, whereas the Cisco 1200 VIC series can support UCS 6200 and 6100 series. In addition, 1300 series VICs support PCIe Gen 3.0 for greater bandwidth with the network offload support of NVGRE and VXLAN for enhanced performance and can create 256 NICs or HBAs without requiring SR-IOV support from hypervisors or operating systems.

## UCS third-generation VIC 1380

The specifications of VIC 1380 are as follows:

- 256 dynamic vNICs (Ethernet) or vHBAs (Fibre Channel) interfaces
- VM-FEX support for virtualized environments
- Hardware failover without OS driver
- 80 GB network throughput
- Mezzanine form factor
- Compatibility with UCS M3 and M4 blade servers

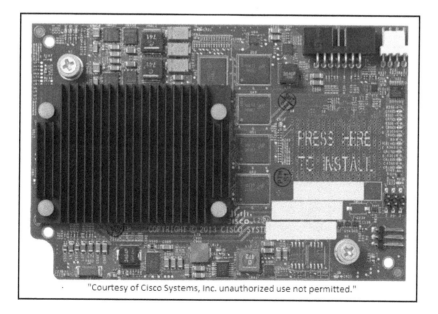

"Courtesy of Cisco Systems, Inc. unauthorized use not permitted."

# UCS third-generation VIC 1340

The specifications of the VIC 1340 are as follows:

- 256 dynamic vNIC (Ethernet) or vHBA (Fibre Channel) interfaces
- VM-FEX support for virtualized environments
- Hardware failover without OS driver
- 40-80 GB network throughput
- Modular LOM form factor
- Compatibility with UCS M3 and M4 blade servers.

"Courtesy of Cisco Systems, Inc. unauthorized use not permitted."

# UCS second-generation VIC 1280

The specifications of the VIC 1280 are:

- 256 dynamic vNIC (Ethernet) or vHBA (Fibre Channel) interfaces
- VM-FEX support for virtualized environments
- Hardware failover without OS driver
- 80 GB network throughput
- Mezzanine form factor
- Compatibility with UCS M2 (B230, B440) and all M3 blade servers

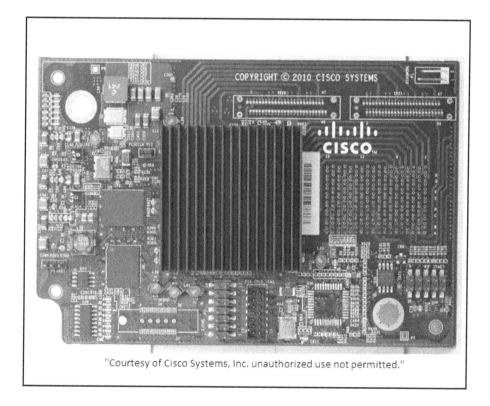

"Courtesy of Cisco Systems, Inc. unauthorized use not permitted."

# UCS second-generation VIC 1240

The specifications of the VIC 1240 are as follows:

- 256 dynamic vNIC (Ethernet) or vHBA (Fibre Channel) interfaces
- VM-FEX support for virtualized environments
- Hardware failover without OS driver
- 40 GB network throughput with optional 80 GB throughput using optional port expander in mezzanine slot
- LAN-on-motherboard form factor
- Compatibility with all M3 blade servers

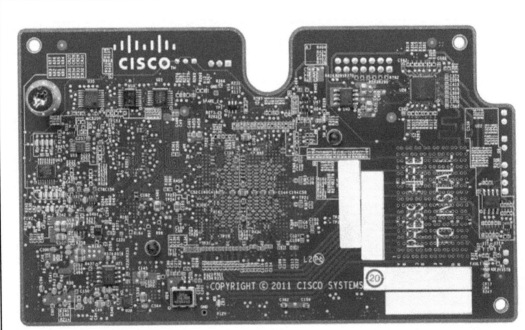

"Courtesy of Cisco Systems, Inc. unauthorized use not permitted."

# VICs for rack-mount servers

VICs are available as PCIe cards. All new VICs provide dynamic virtual vNIC or vHBA interfaces for server-side connectivity.

## UCS third-generation VIC 1387

The specifications of the VIC 1387 are as follows:

- 256 dynamic vNIC (Ethernet) or vHBA (Fibre Channel) interfaces
- VM-FEX support for virtualized environments
- Hardware failover without OS driver
- PCIe 3.0 x 8 form factor
- 80 GB network throughput
- Compatibility with UCS C220 M4, C240 M4, and 3160 rack-mount servers

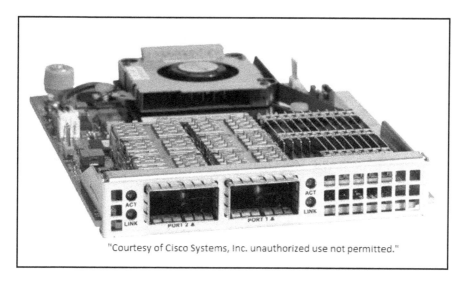

"Courtesy of Cisco Systems, Inc. unauthorized use not permitted."

# UCS third-generation VIC 1385

The specifications of the VIC 1385 are as follows:

- 256 dynamic vNIC (Ethernet) or vHBA (Fibre Channel) interfaces
- VM-FEX support for virtualized environments
- Hardware failover without OS driver
- PCIe 3.0 x 8 form factor
- 80 GB network throughput
- Compatibility with UCS C220 M4, C240 M4, and C460 M4 rack-mount servers

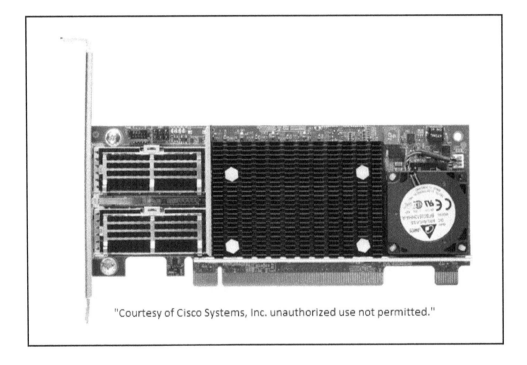

"Courtesy of Cisco Systems, Inc. unauthorized use not permitted."

# UCS second-generation VIC 1285

The specifications of the VIC 1285 are as follows:

- 256 dynamic vNIC (Ethernet) or vHBA (Fibre Channel) interfaces
- VM-FEX support for virtualized environments
- Hardware failover without OS driver
- 2 x 40 GB QSFP network throughput
- Compatibility with UCS C22 M3, C24 M3, C220 M3, C240 M3, and C460 M4 rack-mount servers

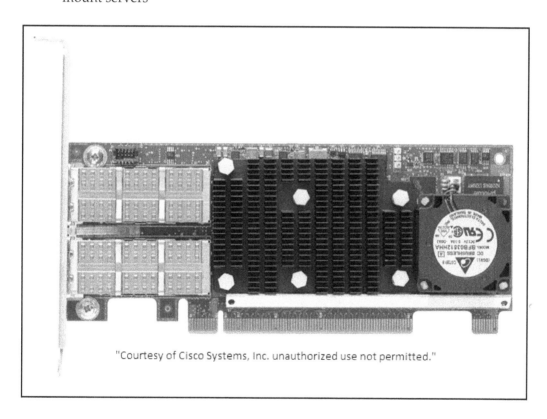

"Courtesy of Cisco Systems, Inc. unauthorized use not permitted."

# UCS second-generation VIC 1225

The specifications of the VIC 1225 are as follows:

- 256 dynamic vNIC (Ethernet) or vHBA (Fibre Channel) interfaces
- VM-FEX support for virtualized environments
- Hardware failover without OS driver
- 20 GB network throughput
- Compatibility with UCS M2 (C460, C260) and all M3 rack-mount servers

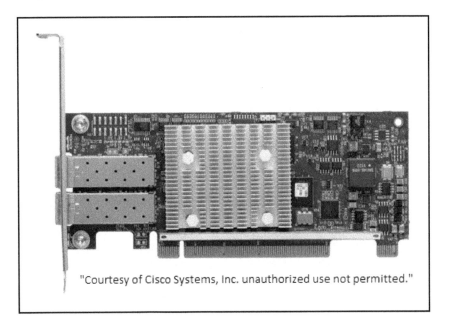

"Courtesy of Cisco Systems, Inc. unauthorized use not permitted."

For a quick comparison of mezzanine card specifications, visit `http://www.cisco.com/en/US/products/ps10277/prod_models_comparis on.html#~tab-a`.
Cisco VIC cards are also famous by their code name, **Palo**.

# UCS storage servers

To provide a solution to meet storage requirements, Cisco introduced the new C3000 family of storage-optimized UCS rack servers in 2014. A standalone server with a capacity of 360 TB can be used for any kind of data-intensive application, such as big data, Hadoop, object-oriented storage, OpenStack, and other such enterprise applications requiring higher throughput and more efficient transfer rates. This server family can be integrated with any existing B-Series, C-Series, and M-Series servers to provide them with all the required storage and backup requirements. This is an ideal solution for customers who don't want to invest in high-end storage arrays and still want to meet the business requirements. Cisco C3000 storage servers are an optimal solution for medium and large scale-out storage requirements.

Cisco UCS 3260 is the latest edition with better density, throughput, and dual-server support, whereas the earlier UCS 3160 provides the same density with a single server. These servers can be managed through CIMC like C-Series rack servers.

# UCS C3206

Cisco UCS **C3206** is 4U rack server with Intel® Xeon® E5-2600 v2 processor family CPUs and up to 320 TB local storage with dual-server nodes and 4x40 Gig I/O throughput using Cisco VIC 1300. This storage can be shared across two compute nodes and provide HA solution inside the box.

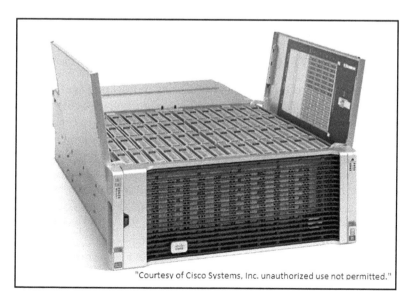

"Courtesy of Cisco Systems, Inc. unauthorized use not permitted."

# UCS C3106

Cisco UCS C3106 is a 4U rack server with Intel® Xeon® E5-2600 v2 processor family CPUs and up to 320 TB local storage with a single server node and 4x10 Gig I/O throughput.

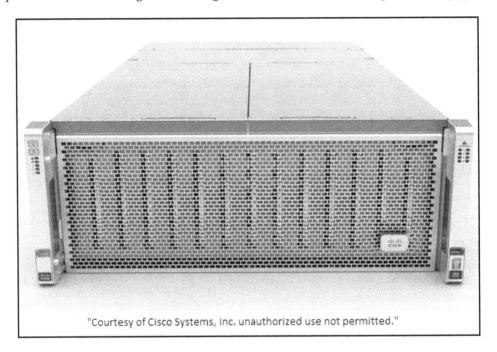

"Courtesy of Cisco Systems, Inc. unauthorized use not permitted."

# UCS M-Series modular servers

Earlier in 2014, Cisco unleashed a new line of M-Series modular servers to meet the high-density, low-power demands of massively parallelized and cloud-scale applications. These modular servers separate the infrastructure components, such as network, storage, power, and cooling, from the compute nodes and deliver compute and memory to provide scalable and resource demanding applications. These compute nodes provide processing and memory resources directly to applications without any virtualization with unified management capabilities through UCS Manager A modular chassis and compute cartridges are the building blocks of these M-Series servers. The M4308 chassis can hold up to eight compute cartridges. Each cartridge has a single or dual CPU with two memory channels and provides two nodes in a single cartridge to support up to 16 compute nodes in a single chassis. The cartridges are hot-pluggable and can be added or removed for the system. The Cisco VIC provides connectivity to UCS Fabric Interconnects from network and management.

The UCS M-Series modular server includes the following components:

- Modular chassis M4308
- Modular compute cartridges-M2814, M1414, and M142

# M4308

The M4308 modular chassis is a 2U chassis that can accommodate eight compute cartridges with two servers per cartridge, and this makes for 16 servers in a single chassis. The chassis can be connected to a pair of Cisco Fabric Interconnects, providing network, storage, and management capabilities.

"Courtesy of Cisco Systems, Inc. unauthorized use not permitted."

# M2814

The M2814 cartridge has dual-socket Intel® Xeon® E5-2600 v3 and v4 processor family CPUs with 512 GB memory. This cartridge can be used for web-scale and small, in-memory databases.

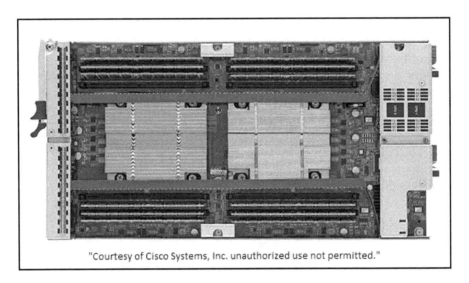

"Courtesy of Cisco Systems, Inc. unauthorized use not permitted."

# M1414

The M1414 cartridge has a single-socket Intel® Xeon® E3-1200 v3 and v4 processor family CPU with 64 GB memory. This cartridge can be used for electronic design automation and simulation.

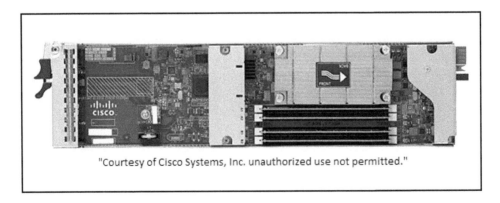

"Courtesy of Cisco Systems, Inc. unauthorized use not permitted."

# M142

The M142 cartridge has a single-socket Intel® Xeon® E3-1200 v3 and v4 processor family CPU with 128 GB memory. This cartridge can be used for content delivery, dedicated hosting, and financial modeling and business analytics.

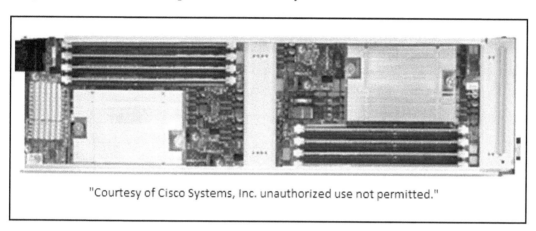

"Courtesy of Cisco Systems, Inc. unauthorized use not permitted."

# Cisco UCS Mini

Cisco brings the power of UCS in a smaller form factor for smaller business, remote, and branch offices with the UCS Mini solution, a combination of blade and rack servers with unified management provided by Cisco UCS Manager. UCS Mini is compact version with the specialized 6324 Fabric Interconnect model embedded into the Cisco UCS blade chassis for a smaller server footprint. It provides servers, storage, network, and management capabilities similar to classic UCS. The 6324 Fabric Interconnect combines the Fabric Extender and Fabric Interconnect functions into one plugin module to provide direct connections to upstream switches. A pair of 6324 Fabric Interconnects will be directly inserted into the chassis, called the primary chassis, and provide internal connectivity to UCS blades. A Fabric Extender is not required for the primary chassis. The primary chassis can be connected to another chassis, called the secondary chassis, through a pair of 2208XP or 2204XP Fabric Extenders.

Cisco UCS Mini supports a wide variety of UCS B-Series servers, such as B200 M3, 200 M4, B420 M3, and B420 M4. These blades can be inserted into mixed form factors. UCS Mini also supports connectivity to UCS C-Series servers C220 M3, C220 M4, C240 M3 and C240M4. A maximum of seven C-Series servers can be connected to a single chassis. It can support a maximum of 20 servers with a combination of two chassis with eight half-width blades per chassis and four C-Series servers.

Here is an overview of Cisco UCS Mini:

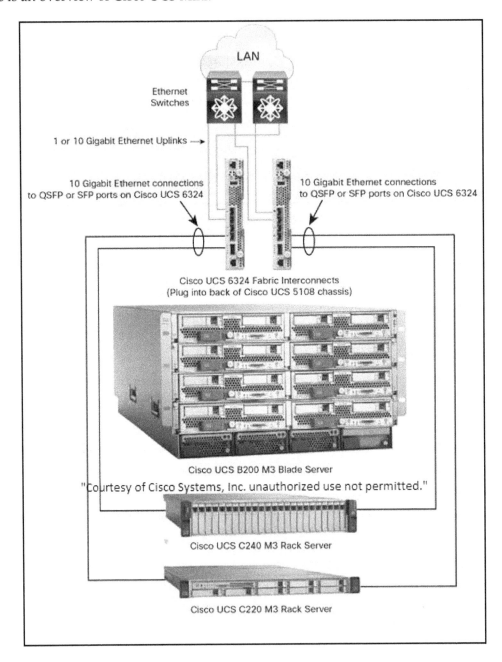

# 6324

Cisco 6324 is embedded into the Cisco UCS 5108 blade server chassis. The 6324 Fabric Interconnect integrates the functions of a Fabric Interconnect and Fabric Extender and provides LAN, SAN, and management connectivity to blade servers and rack servers with embedded UCS Manager. 1G/10G SFP+ ports will be used for external network and SAN connectivity, while 40 Gig QSPF can only be used for connecting another chassis, rack server, and storage. One or two Cisco UCS 6324 FIs can be installed in UCS Mini.

"Courtesy of Cisco Systems, Inc. unauthorized use not permitted."

The following are the features of the 6324:

- A maximum of 20 blade/rack servers per UCS domain
- Four 1 Gig/10 Gig SFP+ unified ports
- One 40 Gig QSFP
- Fabric throughput of 500 Gbps

# Summary

Cisco is the leader in integrated infrastructure, and over 50% of all integrated infrastructure deployments run on Cisco UCS servers and Nexus switches. The Gartner Magic Quadrant for integrated servers report published for the year 2015 placed Cisco as a market leader along with VCE, Oracle, and HP. Cisco's clustered Fabric Interconnect-based design provides a complete solution for converged data connectivity, blade server provisioning, and management whereas other vendors' offerings acquire the same functionality with added complexity.

Cisco UCS presented a paradigm shift for blade servers, data center design, and management to the industry. In this chapter, we acquired knowledge about the UCS solution's integral components and a broad portfolio of UCS servers to choose from various options based on application requirements.

We learned about the various available options for all UCS components, including Fabric Interconnects, blade chassis, blade servers, rack-mount servers, storage servers, modular servers, and UCS Mini.

In the next chapter, we will discuss installing UCS hardware components, including Fabric Interconnects, Fabric Extenders, chassis, blade servers, and rack servers. We'll also discuss the Cisco SingleConnect technology to connect blade and rack servers.

# 2
# Installing Cisco UCS Hardware

Before installing Cisco UCS hardware, the data center should meet the specific requirements for power, cooling, spacing, cabling, and environmental factors. These factors play a vital role in the performance and life span of Cisco UCS hardware and other devices in the data center. Proper planning of power, cooling, spacing, cabling, and environmental factors will not only save money but help improve the performance, operation cost, and life cycle of your data center infrastructure. Cisco UCS hardware has been designed in the most efficient way to consume less power by reducing the number of components. Converged fabric brings fewer cables, ports, connectors, and interfaces to further reduce power and cabling requirements. The simplified design of Unified Computing System with a 63% open center plane provides better cooling without compromising the performance of servers. Using the best practices of airflow management, such as strict hot aisle and cold aisle planning, can double the cooling capacity for servers and switches in the data center. However, poor airflow management can reduce both the efficiency and capacity of the data center.

In this chapter, we will walk through the installation of UCS hardware components such as Fabric Interconnects, chassis, I/O modules, blade servers, and rack servers with the configuration required to support these devices in the data center. Additionally, we will discuss the Cisco SingleConnect technology for connecting compute servers.

The topics that will be covered in this chapter are as follows:

- UCS hardware component installation
- Rack installation for UCS components
- UCS chassis installation
- UCS blade server installation
- Fabric Interconnect installation

- Cabling—Fabric Interconnect and Fabric Extender
- Cabling—Fabric Interconnect and Nexus
- Cisco SingleConnect technology

# Installing UCS hardware components

Now, as we have a better understanding of the various components of the Cisco UCS platform, we can dive into the physical installation of UCS Fabric Interconnects and chassis, including blade servers, IOM modules, fan units, power supplies, SFP+ modules, and physical cabling.

Before the physical installation of the UCS solution, it is also imperative to consider other data center design factors, including:

- Building floor load-bearing capacity
- Rack requirements for UCS chassis and Fabric Interconnects
- Rack **heating, ventilation, and air conditioning (HVAC)**

# Installing racks for UCS components

Any standard 19-inch rack with a minimum depth of 29 inches to a maximum of 35 inches from front to rear rails with 42U height can be an ideal rack solution for Cisco UCS equipment. However, rack size can vary based on different requirements and the data center's landscape. The rack should provide sufficient space for power, cooling, and cabling for all the devices. It should be designed according to data center best practices to optimize its resources. The front and rear doors should provide sufficient space to rack and stack the equipment and adequate space for all types of cabling. Suitable cable managers can be used to manage the cables coming from all the devices. It is always recommended that heavier devices be placed at the bottom and lighter devices at the top. For example, a Cisco UCS B-Series chassis can be placed at the bottom and Fabric Interconnect at the top of the rack. The number of UCS or Nexus devices in a rack can vary based on the total power available for it.

The Cisco R-Series R42610 rack is certified for Cisco UCS devices and Nexus switches, which provides better reliability, space, and structural integrity to data centers.

# Installing UCS chassis and components

Care must be taken during the installation of all components as failure to follow installation procedures may result in component malfunction and bodily injury.

**UCS chassis don'ts:**
Do not try to lift even the empty chassis alone. At least two people are required to handle a UCS chassis.
Do not handle internal components such as CPU, RAM, and mezzanine cards without an ESD field kit.

Physical installation is divided into three sections:

- Blade server component (CPU, memory, hard drives, and mezzanine card) installation
- Chassis and component (blade servers, IOMs, fan units, and power supplies) installation
- Fabric Interconnect installation and physical cabling

# Installing blade servers

Cisco UCS blade servers are designed with industry-standard components with some enhancements. Anyone with prior server installation experience should be comfortable installing internal components using guidelines provided in the blade server's manual and following standard safety procedures. Transient ESD charges may result in electricity, which can degrade or permanently damage electronic components.

The Cisco ESD training course can be found at
`http://www.cisco.com/web/learning/le31/esd/WelcomeP.html`.

All Cisco UCS blade servers have a similar cover design, with a button at the front top of the blade, which should be pushed down. Then, there are slight variations among models in the way that the cover slides off, which can be toward the rear and up or toward yourself and up.

# Installing and removing CPUs

The following is the procedure to mount a CPU into a UCS B-Series blade server:

1. Make sure you are wearing an ESD wrist wrap grounded to the blade server cover.
2. To release the CPU clasp, slide it down and to the side.
3. Move the lever up and remove the CPU's blank cover. Keep the blank in a safe place just in case you need to remove the CPU later.
4. Lift the CPU by its plastic edges and align it with the socket. The CPU can only fit one way.
5. Lower the mounting bracket with the side lever, and secure the CPU into the socket.
6. Align the heat sink with its fins in a position allowing unobstructed airflow from front to back.
7. Gently tighten the heat sink screws to the motherboard.

CPU removal is the reverse of the installation process. It is critical to place the blank socket cover back over the CPU socket. Damage could occur to the socket without the blank cover.

# Installing and removing RAM

The following is the procedure to install RAM modules into a UCS B-Series blade server:

1. Make sure you are wearing an ESD wrist wrap grounded to the blade server cover.
2. Undo the clips on the side of the memory slot.
3. Hold the memory module from both edges in an upright position and firmly push it straight down, matching the notch of the module to the socket.
4. Close the side clips to hold the memory module.

Memory removal is the reverse of the preceding process.

 Memory modules must be inserted in pairs and split equally between each CPU if all the memory slots are not populated. Refer to the server manual for identifying memory slots pairs, slot-CPU relation, and optimized memory performance.

# Installing and removing internal hard disks

UCS supports SFF, **serial attached SCSI (SAS)**, and SATA **solid-state disk (SSD)** hard drives. B200 M4 blade servers also support **non-volatile memory express (NVMe)** SFF 2.5-inch hard drives via PCI Express. The B200 M4 also provides the option of an SD card to deploy small footprint hypervisors such as ESXi.

To insert a hard disk into B200, B260, B420, and B460 blade servers, follow these steps:

1. Make sure you are wearing an ESD wrist wrap grounded to the blade server cover.
2. Remove the blank cover.
3. Press the button on the catch lever on the ejector arm.
4. Slide the hard disk completely into the slot.
5. Push the ejector lever until it clicks to lock the hard disk.
6. To remove a hard disk, press the button, release the catch lever, and slide the hard disk out.

 Do not leave a hard disk slot empty. If you do not intend to replace the hard disk, cover it with a blank plate to ensure proper airflow.

# Installing mezzanine cards

The UCS B200 supports a single mezzanine card, B260/B420 support two cards, and B460 supports four cards. The procedure for installing these cards is the same for all servers:

1. Make sure you are wearing an ESD wrist wrap grounded to the blade server cover.
2. Open the server's top cover.
3. Grab the card by the edges and align the male molex connector with the female connector on the motherboard.
4. Press the card gently into the slot.
5. Once card is properly seated, secure it by tightening the screw on the top.

Removing a mezzanine card is the reverse of the preceding process.

# Installing UCS chassis and rack rails

UCS chassis houses all the major components except Fabric Interconnect that can be connected as a standalone switch through copper and optical cables. It is extremely important to install the chassis with precautions as this is the heaviest device from all the components. UCS chassis comes with adjustable rack rails that can accommodate its whole weight including all other components. The following is the procedure for installing rails and chassis:

1. Insert the adjustable rails in one side in correct square holes. The holes should be the planned based on the number of devices that will be stacked in the rack.
2. Similarly insert the other rail on other side in the correct square hole, parallel to previous side.
3. Make sure the RU unit is same on both side and there should not be any angles between them.
4. Insert the empty chassis manually or through lift and place it on the mounting rail.
5. Slide the chassis on the rail till the depth of the rail.
6. Once chassis is properly seated, place all the components one by one in it.

# Installing blade servers into a chassis

The installation and removal of half-width and full-width blade servers is almost identical, with the only difference being that there's one ejector arm in a half-width blade server, whereas in a full-width blade server, there are two ejector arms. Only the B460 M4 blade server requires two full-width slots in the chassis with an additional Scalability Connector to connect two B260 M4 blade servers and allow them to function as a single server. The bottom blade in this pair serves as the *master* and top blade as *slave*. The process is as follows:

1. Make sure you are wearing an ESD wrist wrap grounded to the chassis.
2. Open the ejector arm for a half-width blade or both ejector arms for a full-width blade.
3. Push the blade into the slot. Once it's firmly in, close the ejector arm on the face of server and hand-tighten the screw.

The removal of a blade server is the reverse of the preceding process.

In order to install a full-width blade, it is necessary to remove the central divider. This can be done with a Philips-head screw driver to push two clips, one downward and the other upward, and sliding the divider out of the chassis.

# Installing rack servers

Cisco UCS rack servers are designed as standalone servers; however, these can be managed or unmanaged through UCS Managers. Unmanaged servers can be connected to any standard upstream switch or Nexus switch to provide network access. However, managed servers need to connect with Fabric Interconnects directly or indirectly through Fabric Extenders to provide LAN, SAN, and management network functionality. Based on the application requirement, the model of rack server can be selected from the various options discussed in the previous chapter. All the rack servers are designed in a similar way; however, they vary in capacity, size, weight, and dimensions. These rack servers can be fitted into any standard 19-inch rack with adequate air space for servicing the server. Servers should be installed on the slide rails provided with them. At least two people or a mechanical lift should be used to place the servers in the rack. Always place the heavy rack servers at the bottom of the rack, and lighter servers at the top.

Cisco UCS rack servers provide front-to-rear cooling, and the data center should maintain adequate air conditioning to dissipate the heat from these servers. A Cisco rack server's power requirement depends on the model and can be checked in the server data sheet.

# Installing Fabric Interconnects

The Cisco UCS Fabric Interconnect is a top-of-rack switch that connects the LAN, SAN, and management to underlying physical compute servers for Ethernet and Fibre Channel access. Normally, a pair of Fabric Interconnects can be installed either in a single rack or distributed across two racks to provide rack and power redundancy. Fabric Interconnects can be installed at the bottom in case the network cabling is planned under the floor. All the components in a Fabric Interconnect come installed by default from the factory; only external components such as Ethernet modules, power supplies, and fans need to be connected.

Interconnect includes two redundant hot-swappable power supply units. It is recommended that the power supply in the rack come from two different energy sources and installed with a redundant **power distribution unit** (PDU). It requires a maximum of 750 Watts of power.

Interconnect includes four redundant hot-swappable fans to provide the most efficient front-to-rear cooling design and is designed to work in hot aisle/cold aisle environments. It dissipates approximately 2500 BTU/hour, and adequate cooling should be available in the data center for getting better performance.

For detailed information on power, cooling, physical, and environmental specifications, check the data sheet.

UCS FI 6300 series data sheet:
http://www.cisco.com/c/dam/en/us/products/collateral/servers-u
nified-computing/ucs-b-series-blade-servers/6332-specsheet.pdf
UCS FI 6200 series data sheet:
http://www.cisco.com/c/en/us/products/collateral/servers-unifi
ed-computing/ucs-6200-series-fabric-interconnects/data_sheet_c
78-675245.pdf

Fabric Interconnects provide various options to connect with networks and servers. The 6300 Fabric Interconnect series can provide 10/40 Gig connectivity, while the FI 6200 series can provide 1/10 Gig to the upstream network.

The third-generation FI 6332 has 32x40 Gig fixed ports. Ports 1-12 and 15-26 can be configured as 40 Gig QSFP+ ports or as 4x10 Gig SFP+ breakout ports, while ports 13 and 14 can be configured as 40 Gig or 1/10 Gig with QSA adapters but can't be configured with 10 Gig SFP+ breakout cables. The last six ports, 27-32, are dedicated for 40 Gig upstream switch connectivity.

The third-generation FI 6332-16UP can be deployed where native Fibre Channel connectivity is essential. The first 16 unified ports, 1-16, can be configured as 1/10 Gig SFP+ Ethernet ports or 4/8/16 Gig Fibre Channel ports. Ports 17-34 can be configured as 40 Gig QSFP+ ports or 4x10 Gig SFP+ breakout ports. The last six ports, 35-40, are dedicated to 40 Gig upstream switch connectivity.

The second-generation FI 6248UP has 32x10 Gig fixed unified ports and one expansion module to provide an additional 16 unified ports. All unified ports can be configured as either 1/10 Gig Ethernet or 1/2/4/8 Gig Fibre Channel.

The second-generation FI 6296UP has 48x10 Gig fixed unified ports and three expansion modules to provide an additional 48 unified ports. All unified ports can be configured as either 1/10 Gig Ethernet or 1/2/4/8 Gig Fibre Channel.

# Cabling - Fabric Interconnects and Fabric Extenders

UCS is a network-and-computer integrated solution. All management and data movement intelligence for chassis components and blade servers is present in the Fabric Interconnects and Fabric Extenders (which are line cards for the FIs, also called **I/O modules**, or **IOMs**). Therefore, proper cabling between Fabric Interconnects and I/O modules is an important design consideration.

# Fabric Extenders - Fabric Interconnect cabling topology

Fabric Extenders are used to connect blade server chassis to Fabric Interconnects. The I/O modules act as line cards to the Fabric Interconnects. It is therefore necessary to maintain proper connectivity between IOMs and Fabric Interconnects. Since an IOM becomes part of the Fabric Interconnect, multiple links from a single IOM can only be connected to a single Fabric Interconnect and cannot be connected across to the other Fabric Interconnect. Depending on the IOM model, there can be 1, 2, 4, or 8 links from the IOM to a single Fabric Interconnect. These links can be configured in the port channel for bandwidth aggregation. The chassis discovery process starts as soon as the IOM is connected to the Fabric Interconnect.

In the following diagram on the left-hand side, all links from **IOM 0** are connected to a single Fabric Interconnect and can be combined into a single port channel. The diagram on the right shows a configuration in which links from a single IOM module are connected to different Fabric Interconnects. This is an invalid topology, and hence, chassis discovery will fail.

The chassis will also fail if a high-availability cluster is not established between Fabric Interconnects.

Fabric Interconnect and I/O module topologies:

# IOM - Fabric Interconnect physical cabling

IOMs provide connectivity to individual blade servers through backplane server ports and fabric uplink ports connectivity to the Fabric Interconnect. IOM interface connectivity to blade servers does not require user configuration.

IOM-to-Fabric Interconnect connectivity, however, requires physical cabling. Both IOM and Fabric Interconnects in the third-generation have **Quad Small Form-Factor Pluggable Plus (QSFP+)** slots, whereas the second-generation has **Small Form-Factor Plus (SFP+)** slots. The Fabric Interconnect 6300 series and I/O module 2300 series provide 40 Gig QSFP+ ports with a maximum of 320 Gig throughput from each chassis, while the Fabric Interconnect 6200 series and I/O module 2200 series provide 10 Gig SFP+ port with a maximum of 160 Gig throughput. There is a variety of possibilities in terms of physical interfaces. Some of the common configurations for the second-generation include the following:

- 10 GB FET SFP+ interface (special optical multimode fibre SFP+ module that can only be used with UCS and Nexus equipment)
- 10 GB CU SFP+ (copper Twinax cable)
- 10 GB SR SFP+ (short-range multimode optical fibre SFP+ module for up to 300 m)
- 10 GB LR SFP+ (long-range single-mode optical fibre SFP+ module for above 300 m)

The following diagram shows eight connections from **IOM 0** to **Fabric Interconnect A** and eight connections from **IOM 1** to **Fabric Interconnect B**. Depending on bandwidth requirements and model, it is possible to have only 1, 2, 4 or 8 connections from IOM to Fabric Interconnect.

Although a large number of links provide higher bandwidth for individual servers, as each link consumes a physical port on the Fabric Interconnect, they also decrease the total number of UCS chassis that can be connected to the Fabric Interconnects.

Fabric Interconnect and I/O module cabling:

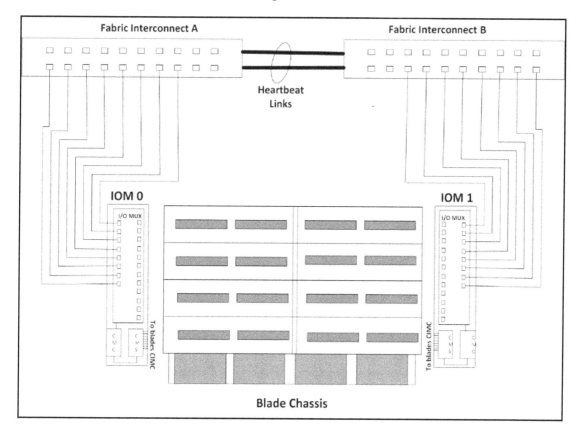

As shown in the preceding diagram, the IOM-to-Fabric Interconnect link only supports direct connection. However, Fabric Interconnect to northbound Nexus switches connectivity can either be direct and use the regular **port channel** (**PC**), or the connections from a single Fabric Interconnect may traverse two different Nexus switches and may use a **virtual PortChannel** (**vPC**).

The next diagram shows a direct connection between Fabric Interconnects and Nexus switches. All connections from **Fabric Interconnect A** are connected to **Nexus Switch 1**, and all connections from **Fabric Interconnect B** are connected to **Nexus Switch 2**. These links can be aggregated into a port channel.

There are two other connections that need to be configured:

- **Cluster heartbeat connectivity**: Each Fabric Interconnect has two fast Ethernet ports, L1 and L2. These ports should be connected using a Cat 6 UTP cable for cluster configuration. L1 and L2 ports needs to directly connect with Ethernet cables from L1 to L1 and L2 to L2 ports. These ports will be used to provide the cluster configuration between Fabric Interconnects and continuously monitor each other's status. The cluster configuration provides only management-plane redundancy, not data-plane redundancy. These ports don't forward any data traffic and can only be used for heartbeats between Fabric Interconnects.
- **Management connectivity**: Each Fabric Interconnect has one management port, mgmt0, which is also a fast Ethernet port and can be configured using a Cat 6 UTP cable for remote management of the Fabric Interconnect. The mgmt0 port will be connected to an out-of-band management switch from each Fabric Interconnect. An extra clustered (virtual) IP address along with two management IP addresses will be assigned to these management ports to provide management redundancy.

Fabric Interconnect and Nexus connectivity:

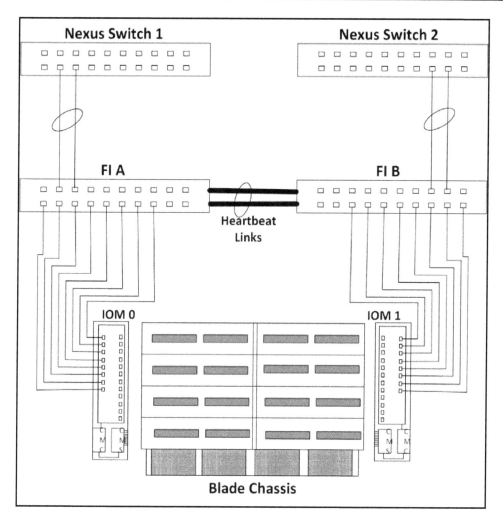

The next diagram shows Fabric Interconnect-to-Nexus switch connectivity where links traverse Nexus switches. One network connection from **Fabric Interconnect A** is connected to **Nexus Switch 1**, and the other connection is a connection from **Fabric Interconnect A** to **Nexus Switch 2**. Both these connections are configured in vPC configuration. Similarly, one connection from **Fabric Interconnect B** is connected to **Nexus Switch 2**, and the other is connected to **Nexus Switch 1**. Both these connections are also configured in vPC. It is also imperative to have vPC on the physical connections between both Nexus switches. This is shown as two physical links between **Nexus Switch 1** and **Next Switch 2**. Without this connectivity and configuration between Nexus switches, vPC will not work.

Physical slots in Nexus switches also support the same set of SFP+ modules for connectivity as Fabric Interconnects and IOM modules.

Fabric Interconnect and Nexus connectivity with vPC:

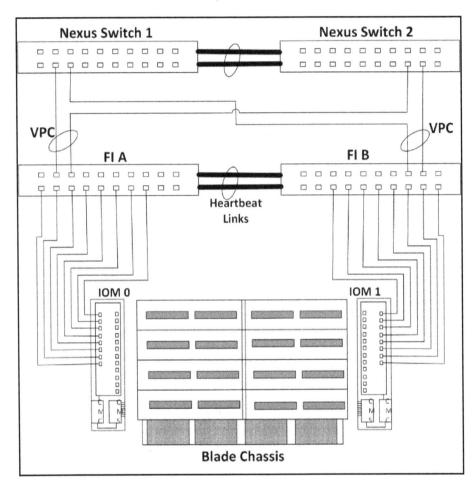

 For a complete list of SFP+ modules, visit this link and scroll down to table 3:

http://www.cisco.com/c/en/us/products/collateral/servers-unified
-computing/ucs-6300-series-fabric-interconnects/datasheet-
c78-732207.html

# Power capacity and power plug types

The UCS 5108 blade chassis comes with an option of up to four power supply units. Each power supply is a single-phase unit and provides 2500 Watts. Depending on the total number of power supplies in the chassis and input power sources, UCS 5108 can be configured in three modes.

## Non-redundant

In a non-redundant configuration, power supplies installed in the system provide adequate power. A power supply failure results in a chassis failure. Load is evenly distributed among power supplies; however, there is no power redundancy.

## N+1 redundant

In N+1 redundant mode, at least one extra power supply is available in the system in addition to the power supplies that are providing the required power for the chassis to be operational. The extra power supply is in standby mode, and load is evenly distributed among operational power supplies. In case of a single power-supply failure, standby power will replace the failed power supply on the fly.

## Grid-redundant

In grid-redundant mode, all four power supplies must be available in the system and power should be supplied from two different power sources. Power supplies must be configured in pairs. Power supplies 1 and 2 form one pair, and power supplies 3 and 4 form the second pair. Ideally, separate physical power cabling from two independent utility grids is recommended to feed each pair of power supplies. In case one source power fails, the remaining power supplies on the other circuit continue to provide power to the system.

# Cisco SingleConnect technology

Cisco SingleConnect is the most efficient and simplest way to connect and manage the compute servers in a data center. It unifies multiple types of traffic, such as LAN, SAN, and management, into a single channel with increased utilization and reduces the complex cabling structure in data centers. SingleConnect technology provides an end-to-end system I/O architecture with a single cable for Cisco blade servers, rack server, and virtual machines. Cisco SingleConnect can connect to:

- Physical servers and virtual machines
- LAN, SAN, and management networks
- Cisco B-Series and C-Series servers

Cisco VICs inside blade or rack servers connect through a Cisco **Fabric Extender (FEX/IOM)** to Fabric Interconnects with a single network link to provide data, storage, and management traffic. The single network layer uses the unified fabric to reduce the three-network layer into one, helping us save cables, ports, connectors, and so on. SingleConnect technology is an intelligent and virtualization-aware technology to automatically detect different types of traffic and isolate them at the Fabric Interconnect level to respective upstream switches and avoid any manual intervention to configure them. Virtual machines can be connected through Cisco VICs to provide them direct network access and offload CPU resources. The following diagram shows that any Cisco UCS blade server, rack server, or virtual machine can connect via a Cisco VIC to a Fabric Extender or I/O module in a chassis to a Fabric Interconnect through a single network layer to provide LAN, SAN, and management access. The VIC passes all traffic from blade servers, rack servers, and virtual machines to the Fabric Interconnect.

Cisco SingleConnect technology diagram:

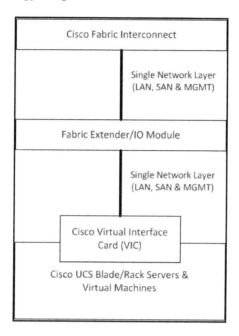

# Summary

Proper planning of data center power, cooling, spacing, and environmental factors will not only optimize the data center resources, it will also bring down the operational cost of manage devices. Cisco UCS hardware components have been designed with efficient power supplies, front-to-rear cooling, a unified fabric to reduce cabling requirements, and fewer network components for easy and simplified management of data centers. In this chapter, we learned rack installation and the installation of UCS hardware components such as chassis, blade, I/O module, Fabric Interconnect, and rack servers. We also discussed Cisco SingleConnect technology, an efficient way to connect blade servers, rack servers, and virtual machines in a data center.

In the next chapter, we will learn about Cisco UCS Emulator which is an excellent tool for exploring UCSM software.

# 3
# Setting Up a Lab Using Cisco UCS Emulator

Cisco UCS **Platform Emulator** (**PE**) is an excellent tool to demonstrate and practice the salient features provided by the UCS platform in order to get hands-on experience without setting up a UCS platform lab. UCS Emulator can be used to improve familiarity with the UCS platform and to provide demos to prospective clients. UCS Emulator mimics real UCS hardware with a configurable hardware inventory, including multiple chassis with multiple blade servers and multiple rack-mount servers. Working with UCS Emulator provides the feeling of real hardware and allows the user to set up UCS hardware virtually and become comfortable before configuring actual UCS hardware. It is an excellent resource for getting hands-on experience with the UCS platform. UCS Emulator's requirements are minimal, and it can be easily installed in a home-based lab on a standard laptop or desktop computer.

UCS Platform Emulator is freely downloadable from the Cisco website. In order to download it, a **Cisco Connection Online** (**CCO**) login is required, which can be created by anyone interested in learning and working with Cisco technologies. UCS Emulator is available on the Cisco Communities website (`https://communities.cisco.com`). You can download the latest Emulator package from the Communities website, and it can be installed under various virtualization platforms. Archives of previous UCS Platform Emulator versions are also available for download on the same page.

Using UCS Platform Emulator, it is possible to import configuration from a live UCS system. Also, configuration created on UCS Platform Emulator can be exported in XML, which can then be imported into a production system. This is extremely helpful for duplicating a production UCS system configuration for troubleshooting, testing, and development purposes.

 Cisco UCS Emulator can be downloaded from the following link: https://communities.cisco.com/docs/DOC-67121

In this chapter, we will use the term **UCSPE** for **Unified Computing System Platform Emulator** and **UCSM** for **Unified Computing System Manager**.

This chapter will cover the following topics:

- Configuring Cisco UCS Emulator
- Configuring Cisco UCS Emulator hardware settings
- Launching UCSM using UCS Emulator
- Limitations of UCSPE

# Configuring Cisco UCS Emulator

Cisco UCSPE is available in the OVA or ZIP file formats. It is packaged on CentOS Linux (a Red Hat Enterprise Linux clone open source operating system). This virtual machine can run Cisco UCS platform emulation on a standard laptop or desktop computer meeting the minimum system requirements. The UCS Emulator application OVA or ZIP file is approximately 800 MB in size.

# System requirements

The minimum system requirements for installing UCS Emulator are as follows:

- 8 GHz single core CPU
- 2 GB free RAM
- 20 GB free disk space
- Mozilla-compatible browser (Firefox or Chrome)
- Java Runtime Environment 1.6

# Hypervisor prerequisites

UCSPE can be installed on the following Type 1 and Type 2 hypervisor platforms:

- VMware Player 4.0 and higher (Windows and Linux versions)
- VMware Fusion 4.0 and higher for Apple macOS
- VMware Workstation 7 and higher (Windows and Linux versions)
- VMware vSphere ESXi 4.0 and higher
- Microsoft Hyper-V Server

VMware Workstation Player for Microsoft Windows is a free download from VMware. VMware has released a new version, VMware Workstation Player 12.0, and discontinued its previous version of VMware Player 7.0. For a home lab environment, VMware Workstation Player is an excellent choice. Users interested in advanced virtualization benefits such as snapshots may download VMware Workstation. Registration on the VMware website is required for downloading VMware Workstation, and it is not available as a free download. Users may also opt to run UCS Emulator on VMware ESXi or Microsoft Hyper-V environments if they do not want to install VMware Workstation Player, VMware Workstation, or VMware Fusion on their laptop or desktop.

In this chapter, we will be installing UCSPE on *VMware Workstation Player 12.0* installed on Microsoft Windows 7.

Make sure that the system on which VMware Workstation Player is installed has enough resources for running the guest UCSPE VM. VMware Workstation Player can be installed on a desktop or laptop even with lower specifications than the minimum system requirements for UCSPE. Newer laptops and desktops generally have more CPU speed than the minimum system requirements. Hard disk storage is very cheap, and usually, all new systems have an abundance of available hard disk space. System memory is usually a major consideration. As UCSPE VM's memory requirement is 2 GB, it is recommended you install VMware Workstation Player on a system with 4 GB of RAM.

The VMware Workstation Player installation is a typical Microsoft Windows click-next type of installation. It is recommended you close all running programs and save your data before installing VMware Workstation Player as the system may require a reboot.

VMware Player can be downloaded from the following link:
`https://my.vmware.com/web/vmware/free#desktop_end_user_computing`
`/vmware_player/5_0`

To download UCSPE, log on to the Cisco Communities website and download the file in the OVA or ZIP file formats. A simple Google search for `UCS emulator download` will take you to the right section of Cisco Communities website, where you will be required to enter your Cisco credentials to download the UCSPE.

UCSPE, Release 3.1(1ePE1) is the latest version while writing this book. VMware Workstation Player 12 and VMware Workstation 12.5 can be installed on Microsoft Windows 10.

# Installing UCSPE on VMware Workstation Player using the ZIP file

UCSPE can be installed through ZIP file on VMware Workstation Player with following steps:

1. Download the ZIP file.
2. Extract the downloaded file to an appropriate folder on the local system.

3.  In VMware Workstation Player, click on **Open a Virtual Machine**:

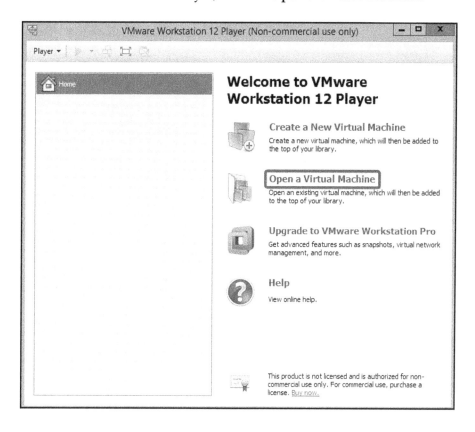

4. Browse to the folder where the extracted files are stored, select the VMX (VMware virtual machine configuration) file, and click on **Open**:

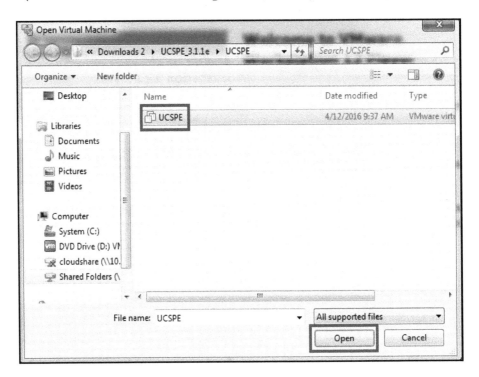

5. Once the VM is shown in the VMware Workstation Player inventory, click on **Play virtual machine**:

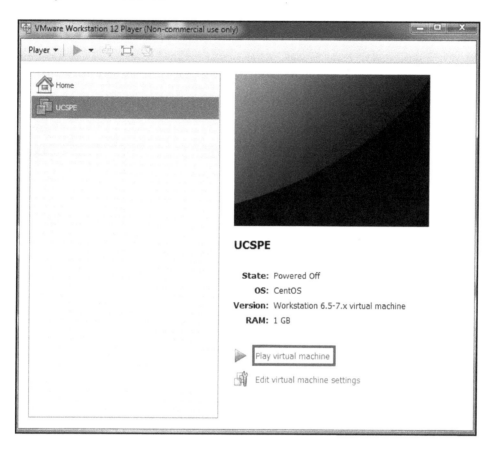

# Installing UCSPE on VMware Workstation Player using the OVA file

UCSPE can be installed through an OVA file on VMware Workstation Player with the following steps:

1. Download the OVA file.
2. In VMware Workstation Player, click on **Open a Virtual File**, and select the OVA file:

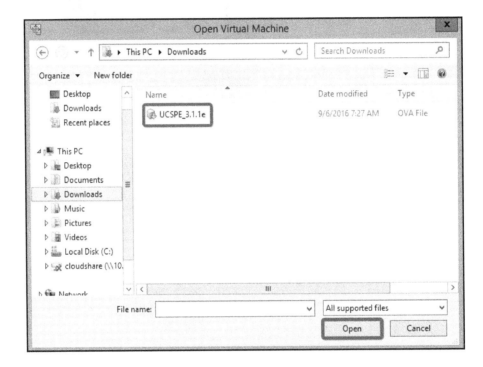

3. VMware Workstation Player will detect the OVA file and will ask where the UCSPE VM should be extracted to. Select an appropriate folder on the local system and click on **Import**:

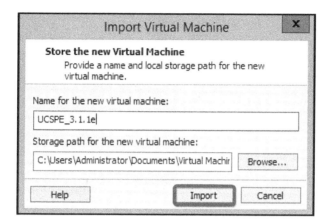

4. VMware Workstation Player will show the OVA import progress, which may take few minutes:

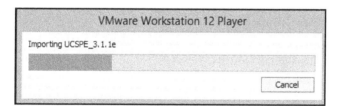

5. Once the import is complete, the VM can be played from VMware Player by clicking on **Play virtual machine**:

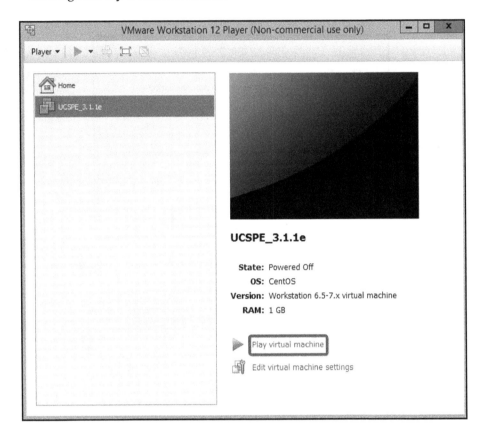

6. The console will display the automatic configuration of UCSPE and will assign an IP address. Use the default login credentials, username `ucspe` and password `ucspe`:

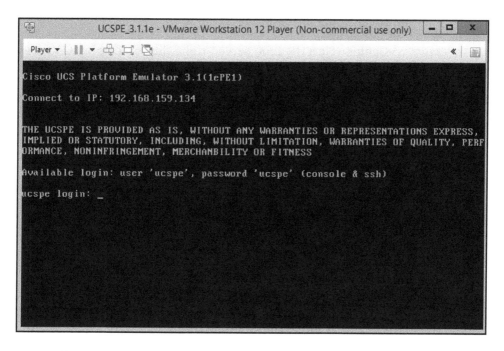

 For an older VMware Workstation Player or Workstation application, you need to convert the OVA format UCSPE VM using the VMware OVA conversion tool.

# Installing UCSPE on VMware Workstation

The procedure for installing UCSPE on VMware Workstation is identical to the VMware Player installation procedure for both the OVA and ZIP files. VMware Workstation provides some extra features, such as snapshots, not available in VMware Workstation Player. The latest version of VMware Workstation can also be installed on Microsoft Windows 10.

# Installing UCSPE on VMware vSphere ESXi

The UCSPE VM can be installed on vSphere ESXi using the OVA or ZIP files. The following are steps to install the OVA file:

1. Download the OVA file.
2. In VMware vCenter, select the ESXi server, right-click on **Deploy OVF Template**, and select the OVA file:

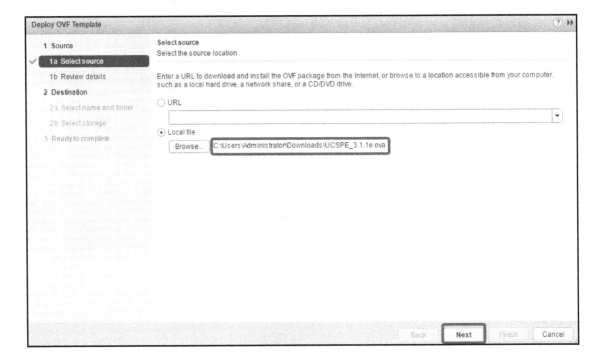

3. Review the details of the OVF template, its **Download size**, and **Size on disk**. Click on **Next**:

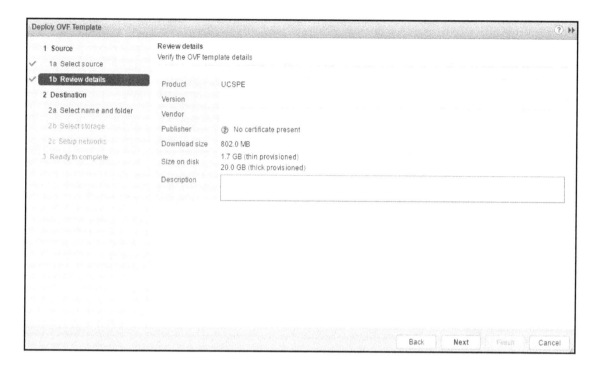

4. Modify the name of the UCSPE VM, select the folder or data center, and click on **Next**:

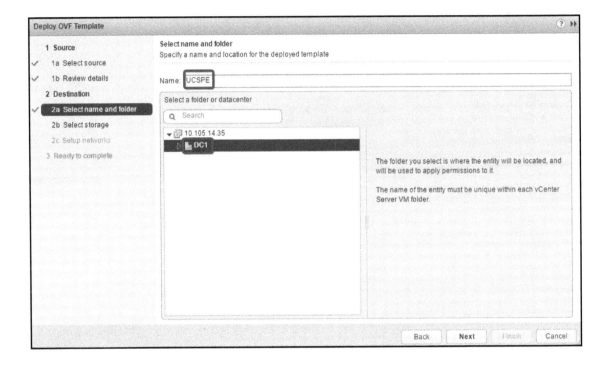

5. Select the virtual disk format and destination data store to store the UCSPE VM files, and click on **Next**:

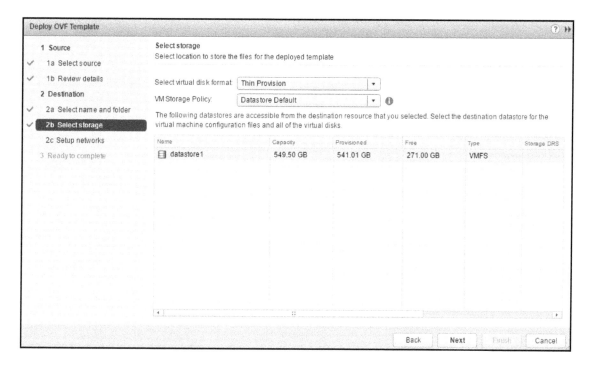

6. Select the destination network port group to communicate with the UCSPE VM management IP address and click on **Next**:

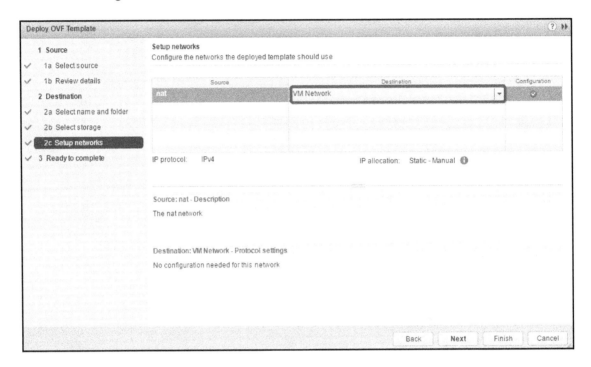

7. Review the summary of the UCSPE VM and click on **Finish** to start the deployment of the appliance:

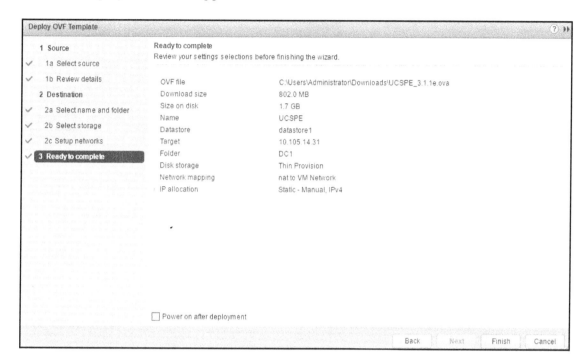

In order to run UCSPE using Microsoft Hyper-V, the VMDK file should be converted to the `.vhd` format using tools such as **System Center Virtual Machine Manager** (**SCVMM**) or any other supported third-party tools.

# Using Cisco UCSPE

UCSPE is packaged on a CentOS Linux-based VM. Keep in mind that the system boot time is long compared to regular Linux VMs as UCSPE and UCSM services are initialized before the VM can be used. Once the UCSPE VM is operational, it can be managed through a web browser or through a VM console CLI session. UCSM 3.1 added support for an HTML5 interface in addition to the previous Java-based interface. The HTML5 interface provides a similar look and functionality to the Java-based interface without requiring Java.

For web-based access, type the management IP as it appears in the VM console into the browser:

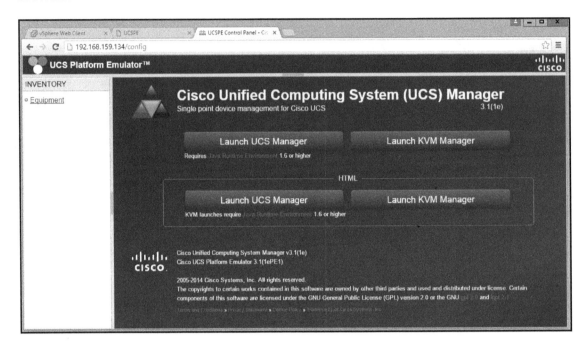

The web interface is divided into two main panes. On the left-hand side is the **navigation pane**, and on right-hand side is the main **work pane**. The navigation pane has the **Equipment** tab, as shown in the preceding screenshot, and is used to manage the UCSPE features, hardware inventory, and system reboots and launch UCS Manager. The work pane has two options: to launch UCS Manager or KVM Manager, using the Java-based interface or the HTML5 interface.

The other management option is CLI access, which is available from the VM console. CLI access provides a driven console interface for making the aforementioned changes.

For system hardware changes, the **Equipment** option needs to be selected under the **Inventory** tab in the navigation pane. The **Equipment** option is used to add, remove, and modify all chassis, blade servers, and rack-mount servers. For any hardware changes, a reboot of the UCSPE and UCSM services is required. For all system changes requiring a services reboot, for example, a **Factory Reset** option can be selected under the power menu for **Equipment**.

The next figure shows the **Factory Reset** configuration change, and these are the three steps required to complete this task:

1. Click on the **Equipment** tab in the navigation pane and select the power menu in the work pane:

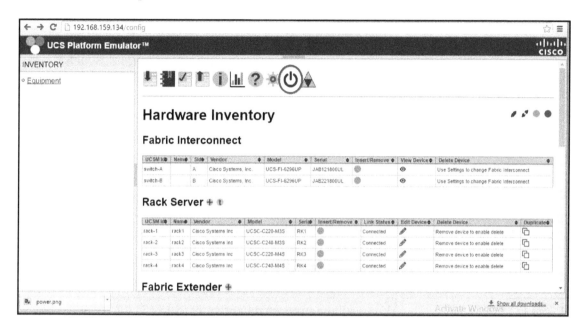

2. Select the **Factory Reset** option in the work pane:

3. Click on the **Yes** button to factory reset UCSPE:

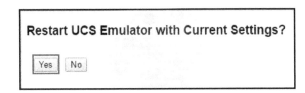

UCSPE provides the following icon options to manage the infrastructure and switch between inventory management and UCS Manager:

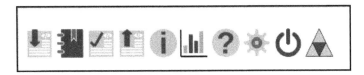

The following table describes the purpose of each of these icons:

| | |
|---|---|
| **Import configuration** | Import the UCSPE configuration using three options:<br>• **Import from a Saved XML**<br>• **Import from File**<br>• **Import from a Live UCS** |
| Hardware catalog | Verify all the supported hardware devices in the UCSPE |
| Validate present configuration | Validate the present configuration for any inconsistency in the configuration |
| Export configuration | Export the UCSPE configuration using two options:<br>• **Save the configuration**<br>• **Export XML** |
| Status summary | Display the status of various services running under UCSPE |

| | |
|---|---|
| Configure statistics | Customize the statistics of various devices under UCSPE |
| Help | Access the following information to manage UCSPE:<br>• **Managed Object Browser**<br>• **API Model Documentation**<br>• **XML Examples & XSD Schema**<br>• **UCS PowerTool Download**<br>• **UCS CDN**<br>• **Online Help** |
| Settings | Make the following changes to UCSPE:<br>• **Change Cluster State**<br>• **Change Fabric Interconnect**<br>• **UCSPE Restart settings** |
| Power | Perform the following power functions on UCSPE:<br>• **Restart UCSPE**<br>• **Factory Reset**<br>• **Reboot VM**<br>• **Shutdown VM** |
| UCSM Switch | Switch into UCS Manager from **Inventory** |

# Configuring network settings

The UCSPE VM supports DHCP and static IP address assignment. The default IP setting is **DHCP**, which can be changed to static using CLI access to the server interface after the first boot. DHCP is easier to configure for obtaining an IP address automatically. For VMware Workstation Player and Workstation, if you need to access UCSPE and UCSM only from the local system where it is installed, select the network type for the UCSPE VM NICs as **NAT** (the default option), and an IP will automatically be assigned that is accessible locally. If you need to access the UCSPE VM from a different computer on the network, you need to change the UCSPE VM network setting in VMware Workstation Player to **Bridged** and have a DHCP server running on the local office/home network, or the IP could be assigned manually.

Use the following method to assign an IP manually through the console:

1. Log in to the UCSPE VM console using username `ucspe` and password `ucspe`.
2. On the **Select** prompt, enter `n` to select **Modify Network Settings**.
3. For **Modify Connections**, enter `y` to change settings.
4. For **Custom Network Mode**, enter `c`.
5. Add the IP, subnet mask, and gateway in the following prompts.
6. The interface will reinitialize with the new IP settings:

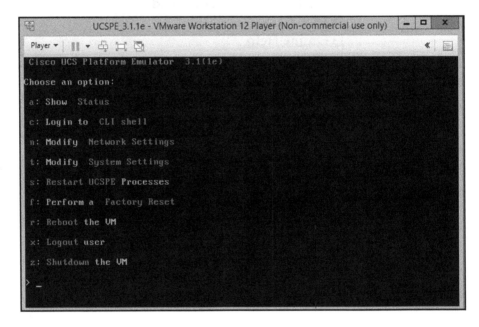

Changing the IP setting will stop and restart the UCSPE and UCSM services.

After initializing UCSPE, the management IP and the default username and password are shown on the VM console. This IP and username/password combination is used for accessing the VM:

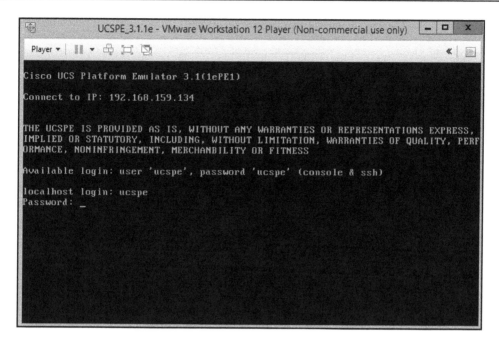

7. The Fabric Interconnect model and network uplinks from the blade server chassis to Fabric Interconnect is not managed under the **Hardware Inventory** tab. In order to change the Fabric Interconnect model and manage chassis uplinks, click on **Settings** in the work pane, as shown here:

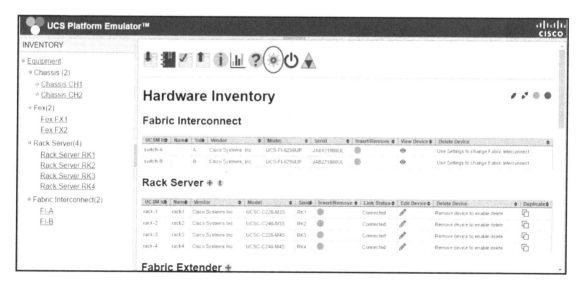

8. Select the **Change Fabric Interconnect** option:

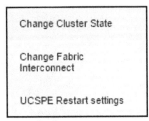

9. Select the desired model of Fabric Interconnect from the drop-down menu under **Fabric Interconnect**. Changing the Fabric Interconnect will reset the UCSPE VM:

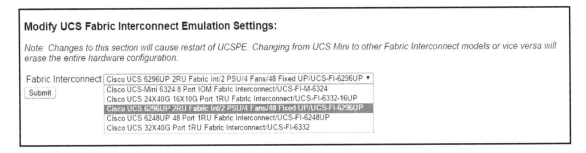

No network connectivity from Fabric Interconnects to any northbound switch is possible.

# Configuring hardware settings

UCSPE-supported hardware is available in the **Hardware Inventory**, which can be browsed by clicking on the hardware option, as shown here:

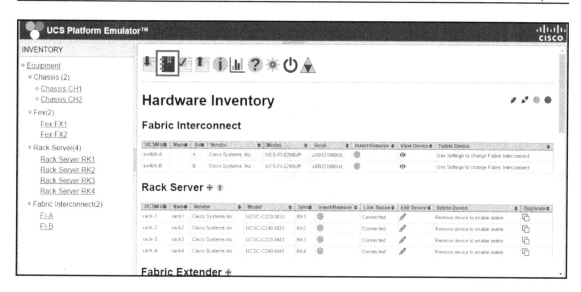

Always check the latest release notes for any hardware support on UCSPE.

This **Hardware Inventory** tab contains all supported hardware for Fabric Interconnects, chassis, and blade and rack-mount servers and is categorized as **Fabric Interconnect, Chassis, IOM, FEX, Blades, Rack Servers, Modular Servers, CPU, DIMM, Disks, Adaptors, Controllers, Fans**, and **PSU**:

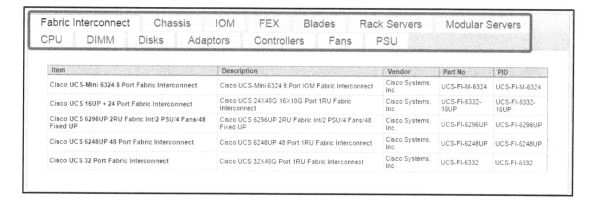

UCSPE is initially configured with two 6296UP Fabric Interconnects in clustered mode; two chassis, one C6508 B-Series blade chassis having seven assorted blades of B200 M3/M4 and B420M3 servers, and the second an M4308 M-Series modular chassis having seven assorted cartridges, two FEX C2232PP-10 GE, and four rack-mount servers, C220M3/M4 and C240M3/M4. Additional chassis, blades, FEX, and rack-mount servers can be added to UCSPE by configuring them in the hardware inventory.

New **Rack Server**, **Fabric Extender**, and **Chassis** can be added to existing hardware in the UCSPE as shown in the next figure. By clicking on the plus icon, any new device will be added to UCSPE as shown as follows:

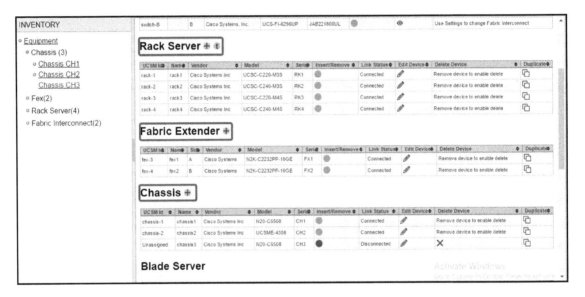

Changes to the blade servers, such as adding and removing components, can be done in the existing chassis. New blades servers can be added and removed from the hardware inventory. This can be accomplished by simply dragging and dropping the servers and other chassis components into the newly added chassis area, as shown in the following figure.

The chassis area is shown in the following highlighted area:

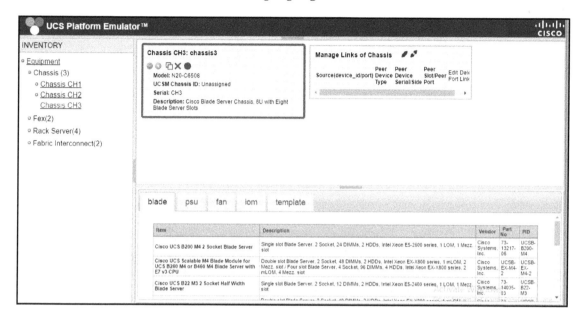

Components to the individual servers can also be dragged and dropped directly for addition and removal while the blade server is in the chassis. In order to modify an existing blade server's hardware configuration, it is recommended you eject the server and make the changes. The server removed from the chassis will preserve the slot identity.

Dragging and dropping from the hardware inventory to the blade server area is shown here:

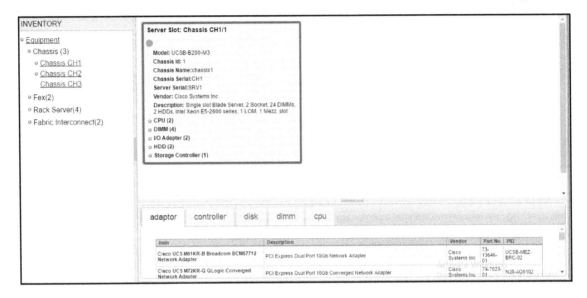

The following icons are used in the chassis in the working pane:

| | |
|---|---|
| 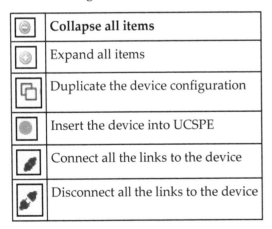 | **Collapse all items** |
| | Expand all items |
| | Duplicate the device configuration |
| | Insert the device into UCSPE |
| | Connect all the links to the device |
| | Disconnect all the links to the device |

# Adding a new chassis with blade servers

A new chassis with blades could be added in few different ways. The easiest is to duplicate the current chassis, which will create an exact replica including the blade servers. The blade servers can be added and removed to and from the chassis under the chassis section. The other method is to manually add the chassis and blade servers.

## Adding an empty chassis

The following steps can be used for adding an empty chassis:

1. Scroll down to the chassis section in the **Hardware Inventory** menu.
2. Click on the **Chassis +** icon, provide a chassis name, and select the chassis model from the drop-down:

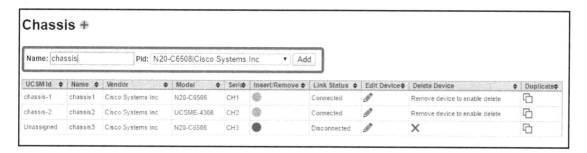

3. Click on the newly added chassis under the **Equipment** option in the navigation pane.
4. Add chassis fans by dragging them from the hardware inventory catalog area at the bottom of the page.
5. Add chassis PSUs by dragging the from the hardware inventory catalog area at the bottom of the page.
6. Add chassis IOMs by dragging the from the hardware inventory catalog area at the bottom of the page.

7. After adding all components, connect the links to the Fabric Interconnect under the **Manage Links of Chassis** area:

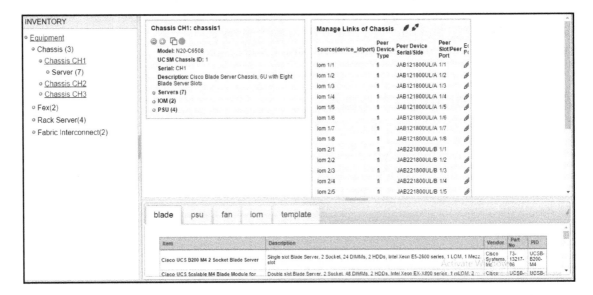

# Configuring and adding blade servers to the chassis

Blade servers can be directly added to the blade chassis. A key point to consider is that the new blade server does not have any components. It is therefore recommended to drag a new server to the **Stash** area, add server components such as CPU and RAM, and move the server to the chassis. Follow these steps:

1. Select **Chassis** from the **Equipment** tab.
2. Expand **Chassis**, and click on the **blade** tab at the bottom of the page.

3. Click and hold the left mouse button and drag the desired blade server to the chassis area. Enter the slot number of the blade server to successfully add it to the chassis:

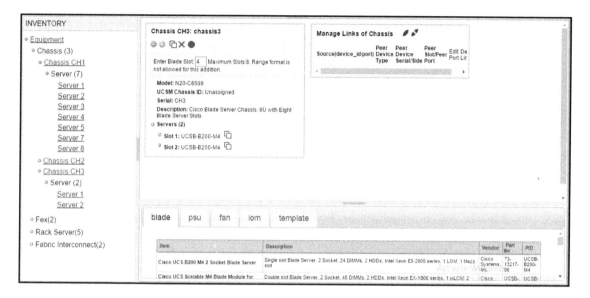

4. Select the blade server or edit it in the **Chassis** section.
5. Click on the **adaptor**, **controller**, **disk**, **dimm**, and **cpu** tabs to drag and drop required components onto the server.
6. Repeat step 4 for the required server components.
7. Once the server configuration is complete, insert the server into the chassis.
8. Repeat the same procedure for all new blade servers.

# Configuring and adding rack-mount servers

Rack-mount servers can be added directly to the appropriate rack-mount server area. It is recommended to configure the networking mode like direct attach, single mode or dual mode for rack-mount server. A Fabric Extender (2200 series) is automatically included in the rack-mount server area. Follow these steps:

1.  Scroll down to the **Rack Server** section in the **Hardware Inventory** menu. Click on the **Rack Server +** icon, provide the rack server **Name**, and select the rack server model from the drop-down:

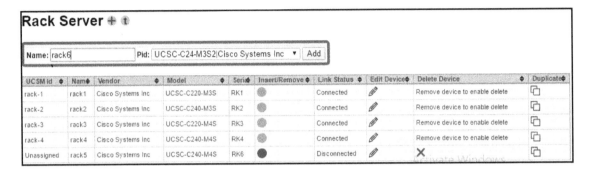

2.  Click on the newly added rack server under the **Equipment** option in the navigation pane.

3. Select the rack server connectivity **Mode** from the drop-down menu. Cisco rack servers provide the **Direct Attach Server**, **Single Wire Management**, and **Dual Wire Management** connectivity options. Click on **Manage Links of Rack** to choose from the various connectivity options:

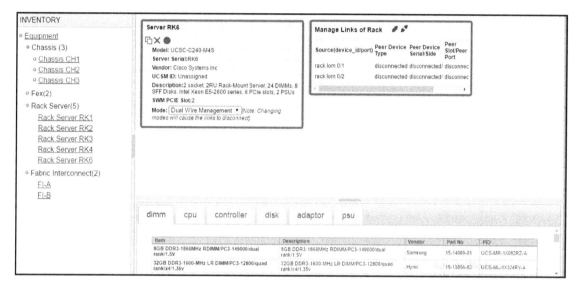

4. Click on the **adaptor**, **controller**, **disk**, **dimm**, **cpu**, and **psu** tabs to drag and drop the required components to the server.
5. Repeat step 4 for all the required server components.
6. Repeat the same procedure for all new rack-mount servers.

# Modifying server components

In order to remove blade servers from a chassis, click on the ⊜ icon with slot number under the **Servers** option in the chassis to remove the server. The server will be removed from the chassis:

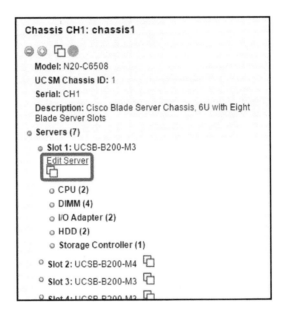

Individual components from servers can be removed by clicking on the ⊜ icon to delete the component under the **Edit Server** option:

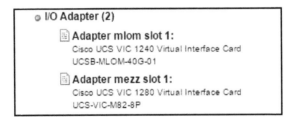

Server components can be added by dragging and dropping components directly on the server.

# Launching UCS Manager using Platform Emulator

Launching UCS Manager from UCSPE is done using a web browser. It is recommended you use a Mozilla-compliant browser such as Firefox or Chrome. Java is required for the Java-based interface, while the HTML5-based interface doesn't require Java. In Microsoft Windows, you can check your version of Java in the **Control Panel** Java icon.

1. Click on **Launch UCS Manager** in the right-hand pane under the **HTML** section:

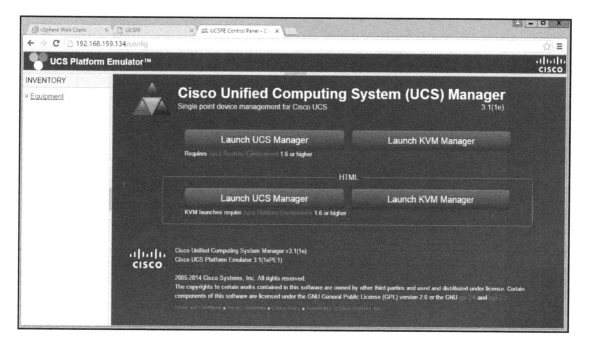

2. UCSM will display the login page; type `ucspe` as the **Username** and **Password**, and click on **Log In**:

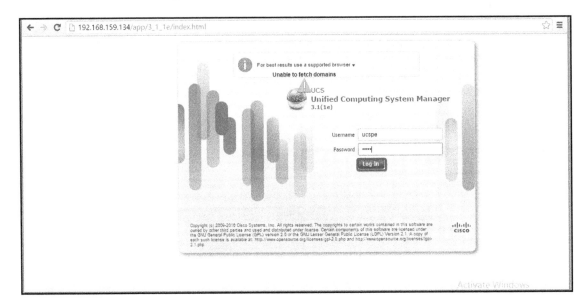

3. After you log in, the UCSM interface will display the currently configured hardware available from the hardware inventory. The following screenshot shows a system with the default hardware inventory configured in UCSPE:

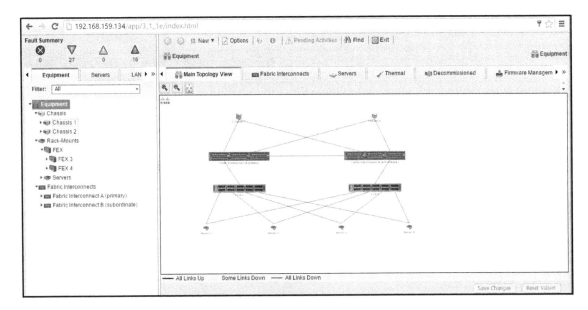

# UCSPE limitations

UCSPE is an excellent platform for those looking to gain hands-on experience with Cisco Unified Communication System Platform and UCSM software without setting up a costly lab. UCSPE provides a profound awareness of all the hardware available for the UCS platform, and it also provides hands-on configuration experience with UCSM software.

But UCSPE has some limitations compared to the real UCSM software:

- The system cannot be integrated with a directory server (such as AD) for user authentication
- Server profiles configured can be assigned to the server, but an operating system cannot be installed on the UCSPE servers
- No KVM interface to the servers is available
- Remote monitoring data (syslog, SNMP, call home, smart call home, and so on) cannot be sent out
- High availability of the Fabric Interconnect cluster cannot be simulated

# Summary

In this chapter, we learned about the various options of installing UCSPE and learned about the methods to add, remove, and modify different hardware components. We also launched the UCS Manager software from UCSPE using a web browser and looked at the user interface. In subsequent chapters, we will use UCSM running on UCSPE to configure various settings, such as server profiles, resource pools, organizations, networking, and storage.

In the next chapter, we will get introduced to UCSM and learn about the GUI and the options that are available in the tabs and nodes under the two main screen panes, which are used for the configuration and management of UCS hardware and software components.

# 4
# Configuring Cisco UCS Using UCS Manager

In this chapter, we will provide an introduction to the **Unified Computing System Manager** (**UCSM**) and updates on the latest HTML5 support for UCSM. We will discuss the changes in the latest version of the **graphical user interface** (**GUI**), as well as the options that are available in tabs and nodes under the two main screen panes that are used for the configuration and management of UCS hardware and software components. We will look at some global configuration policies that provide information on DNS, **Simple Network Management Protocol** (**SNMP**), and power redundancy during initial configuration. We will then look at the basic steps to set up the initial configuration. In subsequent chapters, we will delve deep into individual configuration topics such as policies, identity or resource pools, templates, and service profiles for configuring servers.

We will then discuss the **command-line interface** (**CLI**), which provides the same UCS component configuration as that of the GUI. All UCS configurations are possible from both the GUI and CLI.

Throughout this book, we will extensively use the UCSM GUI for the configuration of various UCS components and policies.

The topics that will be covered in this chapter are as follows:

- Introduction to Cisco UCSM
- What's new with HTML5
- Walking through the UCSM interface
- Starting with the initial configuration

- Initial configuration step-by-step
- Global configuration policies
- UCS Manager—command-line interface

# Introducing Cisco UCSM

Cisco UCSM provides unified management of all hardware and software components for the Cisco UCS solution. UCSM also provides both GUI and CLI user interfaces. UCSM is embedded into Fabric Interconnects.

UCSM controls multiple UCS chassis. The maximum number of chassis that can be controlled by UCSM is 20, but the actual number of manageable chassis is dependent upon the model and the number of physical uplinks from each chassis' IOM or Fabric Extender module to FIs. UCSM provides unified visibility and management for servers, network, and storage resources. The core functions that UCSM provides are as follows:

- **Identity and resource pools**: UCSM provides identity and resource pools to abstract the compute-node identities for stateless servers, whereas traditional servers use the hardware's burned-in identities. These identities and resources include **universally unique identifiers (UUIDs)**, **media access controls (MACs)**, **world-wide node (WWN)** numbers, and IP pools for remote KVM.
- **Policies**: UCSM provides multiple policies that govern the behavior of system devices like service policy provides different configurations for UCS servers, including BIOS settings, firmware versions, **Virtual Network Interface Cards (vNICs)**, **virtual host bus adapters (vHBAs)** policies, scrub policies, **Quality of Service (QoS)**, and **Intelligent Platform Management Interface (IPMI)** policies, whereas global policy can be assigned to change the number of active links between FI and IO Module and so on. A service profile policy, once configured, can be assigned to any number of blade servers in order to provide the configuration baseline
- **Templates**: A template is an excellent feature of UCSM that assists in provisioning multiple physical servers, vNICs, and vHBAs, with similar hardware configuration through a single source. A template can be configured for each type of server in the environment, different vNICs, and vHBAs, as per the business requirement. Templates can be used to quickly create services profiles, vNICs, and vHBAs for the servers.

- **Service profiles**: A service profile is the principal feature of the UCS platform that enables stateless computing. It combines information and features abstracted from identity and resource pools, templates, and server policies. It is a software entity residing in UCSM, which has the specifications of a complete server when associated with a stateless physical hardware server. Service profiles radically improve server provisioning and troubleshooting.

UCSM provides the following benefits:

- **Agility**: With an appropriate initial configuration, UCSM facilitates the system administrator with rapid provisioning of any number of new chassis and blade servers using resource pools, policies, and templates to create service profiles.
- **Flexibility**: UCSM abstracts hardware resources using software configurations. A system administrator can quickly modify vNICs, vHBAs, and other resources using software configurations.
- **Troubleshooting**: Since UCS hardware is stateless, in case of catastrophic failures, servers can be replaced with all the existing identities and configurations without having to deal with lengthy configuration steps.

With Cisco UCS central software, UCS management can be extended centrally to thousands of servers in multiple UCS domains.

# What's new with UCSM

With the 3.1 version release of UCSM, Cisco added support for the HTML5 interface in addition to the existing Java-based interface. The HTML5 interface provides a similar look and feel to the Java-based GUI and removes the unnecessary pain of installing a supported Java version. To launch the KVM console of a blade server, Java is still required. The HTML5 GUI provides full functionality to manage all support UCS hardware components; however, Gen 1 UCS hardware components will be supported with the earlier UCSM 2.2 version. Don't upgrade the UCS firmware version to 3.1 if you have a mix of Gen 1 and Gen 2 UCS hardware components.

Some of the features included in UCSM are as follows:

- It supports Cisco UCS B-Series blade servers, C-Series rack servers, M-Series modular servers and Cisco storage servers infrastructure
- It is embedded in Fabric Interconnect and provides unified and policy-driven capabilities to manage server, network, and storage infrastructure without the need to install any separate software

- UCSM auto-discovery detects discover, inventory, manage, and provision system components that are added or changed
- It facilitates an open XML API architecture to integrate with third-party system-management tools
- It provides multitenant architecture to share the infrastructure among different clients for service providers
- **Role Based Access Control (RBAC)** provides controlled access to authorized users

# UCSM firmware version

The most recent UCSM firmware version available at the time of writing this book is UCSM 3.1. Always check the Cisco website to acquire the most recent firmware. It is necessary to have a CCO account and authorization in order to download the UCSM firmware. Older firmware versions are also available in the archive area of the same web page.

The following are the major firmware releases:

- UCSM version 1.4
- UCSM version 2.2
- UCSM version 3.0 (UCS Mini only)
- UCSM version 3.1

For each major release, there are some minor revisions as well. When performing a firmware upgrade, always read the firmware release notes carefully in order to avoid breaking a production environment. For example, if you have configured default SAN zoning (not recommended, but configurable in version 2.0) for production systems running on firmware version 2.0, upgrading to firmware version 2.1 will break the SAN access unless proper zoning is configured, as default zoning is not an option in version 2.1.

It is always recommended to refer to the latest release notes before making any changes to the system.
http://www.cisco.com/c/en/us/td/docs/unified_computing/ucs/rel
ease/notes/CiscoUCSManager-RN-3-1.html

# Walking through the UCSM interface

The UCSM GUI is accessed through a web URL pointing to the cluster IP or DNS name of the cluster. UCSM requires an HTML5-supported browser such as Internet Explorer, Mozilla Firefox, or Chrome, or **Java Runtime Environment** (**JRE**) 1.6 for a Java-based interface.

The UCSM GUI is an HTML5 or Java-based application. Java **Web Start** (**WS**) is used to display the UCSM GUI. The UCSM GUI is divided into the following parts:

- **Navigation pane**: On the left-hand side of the screen is the navigation pane. It provides navigation to all equipment and components, such as resource pools, policies, and so on. When a component is selected in the navigation pane, its details appear on the right-hand side, that is, on the work pane.
- **Work pane**: On the right-hand side of the screen is the work pane, which is larger in width than the navigation pane. Tabs in the work pane can be used to display information about the components, modify the configuration, create new components, launch the KVM console, and observe the status of a finite-state machine. The work pane also includes a navigation bar at the top to indicate current position in the equipment hierarchy.
- **Fault summary area**: The fault summary area is on the upper-left corner of the navigation pane. It provides a summary of all the faults, in different colors.
- **Status bar**: The status bar is at the bottom of the screen, under both navigation and work panes. It displays the system time and provides information on the logged-in user and the status of the applications.

The following screenshot shows the different sections of the UCS Manager graphical user interface:

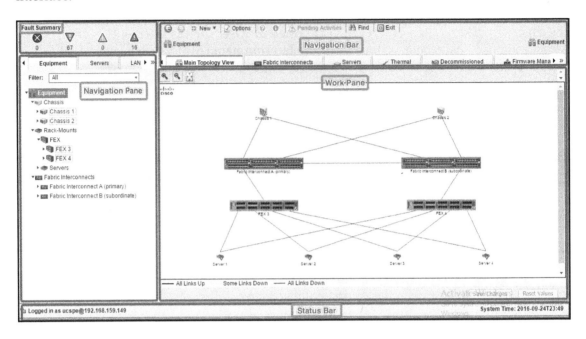

# Navigation pane

As discussed previously, the navigation pane provides navigation to all equipment and components, such as resource pools, policies, and so on. The navigation pane has seven main tabs that categorize UCS hardware and software components into physical equipment, servers' software configuration, LAN settings, SAN settings, UCSM administration configuration, and integration with the virtualization platform (usually VMware). These tabs are shown in the following screenshot. When a tab is selected, it expands to give further information, configuration, and action options in the navigation pane:

We will now walk through the main configuration options under each tab in the navigation pane.

# The Equipment tab

The **Equipment** tab provides a view of the physical hardware of the UCS equipment, including chassis, FEXs, blade servers, rack-mount servers, FIs, and other hardware, along with connectivity. Any type of failure can be easily detected as it is indicated with a red, orange, yellow, or blue rectangle on that particular piece of equipment, as shown in the following screenshot:

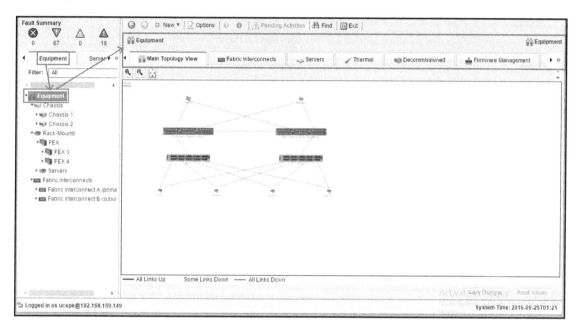

Details about the chassis, FEXs, servers, and FIs can also be gathered by clicking on the specific equipment. As an example, the following screenshot shows details of the UCS chassis in the work pane when **Chassis 1** is selected from the **Equipment** tab. Also note the number of options available in the work pane that provide further details and configuration options.

The main nodes under this tab are listed as follows:

- **Chassis**
- **Rack-Mounts**
- **Fabric Interconnects**

The **Equipment** tab is shown in the following screenshot:

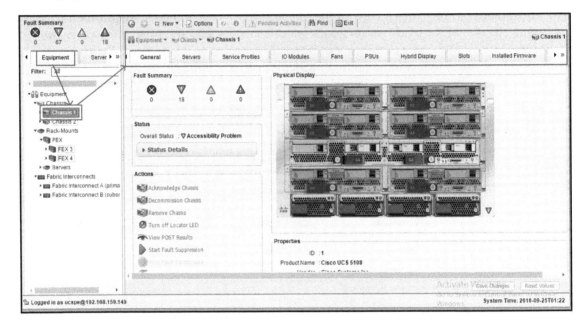

The Fabric Interconnect shows the details under The **Equipment** tab in the following screenshot:

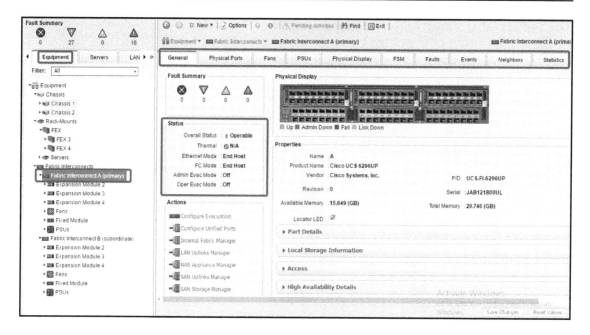

# The Servers tab

The **Servers** tab provides server-related software configuration and components, such as service profiles, service profile templates, policies, and pools. All server software configurations are done under this tab by configuring service profiles for physical servers.

The main nodes under this tab are listed as follows:

- **Service Profiles**
- **Service Profile Templates**
- **Policies**
- **Pools**
- **Schedules**

The **Servers** tab is shown in the following screenshot:

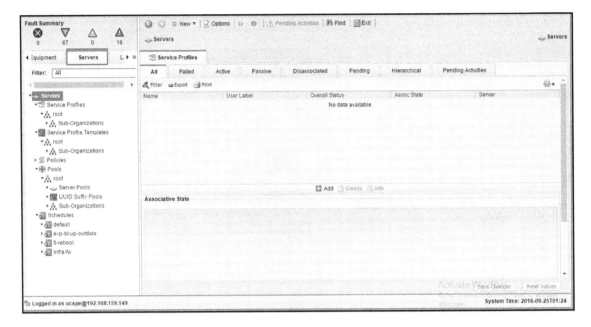

# The LAN tab

The **LAN** tab contains components related to network configuration, such as VLANs, vNIC templates, LAN policies, pin groups, QoS policies, and MAC pools. vNICs created as templates can be assigned to configure virtual server vNICs for service profiles under the **Servers** tab. Network-related policies configured under the **LAN** tab are also assigned to service profiles.

The main nodes under this tab are listed as follows:

- **LAN Cloud**
- **Appliances**
- **Internal LAN**
- **Policies**
- **Pools**
- **Traffic Monitoring Sessions**
- **Netflow Monitoring**

The **LAN** tab is shown in the following screenshot:

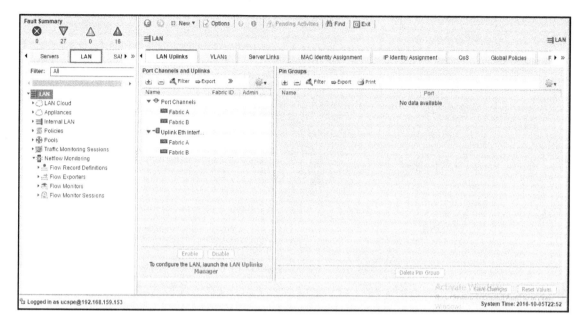

## The SAN tab

The **SAN** tab provides SAN-related information and configuration such as VSANs, policies, zoning configuration, and WWN pools.

The main nodes under this tab are listed as follows:

- **SAN Cloud**
- **Storage Cloud**
- **Policies**
- **Pools**
- **Traffic Monitoring Sessions**

The **SAN** tab is shown in the following screenshot:

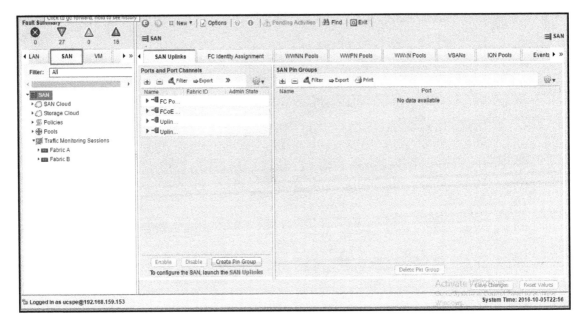

## The VM tab

The **VM** tab provides information on the configuration of the connection between Cisco UCSM and VMware vCenter to configure distributed virtual switches and port profiles, and to view the virtual machines hosted on servers in the Cisco UCS domain. Have a look at the following screenshot for more details:

# The Storage tab

The **Storage** tab provides storage profiles and storage policies to meet the entire local storage requirements for service profiles. The storage profile provides access to single LUN or multiples LUNs to the servers, and can be served as either boot LUN or data LUN, whereas storage policies are used to create disk group policies such as RAID 0 or RAID 1.

The main nodes under this tab are listed as follows:

- **Storage Profiles**
- **Storage Policies**

The **Storage** tab is shown in the following screenshot:

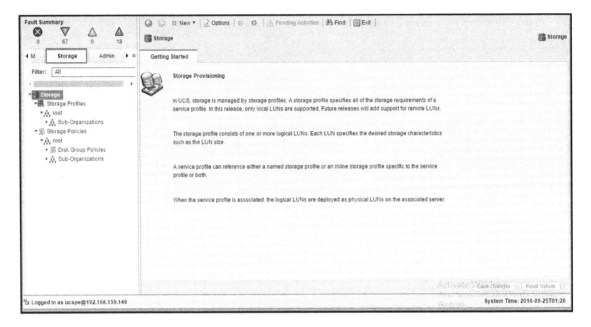

# The Admin tab

The **Admin** tab provides global system administration settings such as faults, events, users, **Role Based Access Control** (**RBAC**), external directory services, backup, restore, communication services, and licensing.

The main nodes under this tab are listed as follows:

- **Faults, Events and Audit Log**
- **User Management**
- **Key Management**
- **Communication Management**
- **Stats Management**
- **Time Zone Management**
- **Capability Catalog**
- **Management Extension**
- **License Management**

The **Admin** tab is shown in the following screenshot:

In the navigation pane, there is a **Filter** drop-down box that can be used to filter the navigation tree to view all the sub-components, or only one, as per our need.

# The Fault Summary area

The **Fault Summary** area is in the upper-left corner of the UCSM GUI, at the top of the navigation pane. This area displays a summary of all the faults that have occurred in the Cisco UCS infrastructure.

Faults are represented by different-colored icons. The total number of specific faults is indicated by a small number below each fault icon. If you click on a fault icon in the **Fault Summary** area, Cisco UCSM GUI changes the view to the **Faults, Events and Audit Log** tab, under the **Admin** tab, and displays all such similar faults.

The following is a list of the alarms displayed in the **Fault Summary** area:

- **Critical alarm**: This is displayed by the red-colored icon; this alarm indicates that there is a critical fault with a very high probability of services getting disrupted. This requires immediate user intervention for the fix.

- **Major alarm**: This is displayed by the orange-colored icon; this alarm indicates that there is a fault issue that may affect some services. It also requires immediate user action.
- **Minor alarm**: This is displayed by the yellow-colored icon; this alarm indicates that there is a minor fault that may partially affect some services. Immediate user action is recommended, before the services get adversely affected.
- **Warning message**: This is displayed by the blue-colored icon; this alarm that indicates there is a minor fault that may affect any of the services. It should be corrected as soon as possible.

# Starting with the initial configuration

Before using the UCSM software for configuration, it is necessary to make sure that the following prerequisites are met:

- Physical cabling of the FIs, specially the L1 and L2 dedicated ports for control pane connectivity is working fine
- FI cluster configuration is complete and the cluster status is up

Details on physical cabling and cluster configuration of FIs are provided in Chapter 11, *Configuring Backup, Restore, and High Availability*.

Although it is possible to use a single FI for data connection as a proof of concept implementation, it is, however, not recommended in the production environment.

# Step-by-step initial configuration

The following are the rudimentary steps for the initial configuration of UCSM:

1. First ensure the presence of proper physical cabling between FIs, IOMs, and north-bound switches, as explained in Chapter 2, *Installing Cisco UCS Hardware*.
2. Access FIs using a serial console as there is no IP assigned initially (most modern PCs and laptops do not have serial port, and a USB-to-serial converter might be required).
3. UCSM 3.1 provides the option for initial configuration through GUI and CLI. FI will run an initial configuration wizard that will assign IP and other necessary configurations (detailed steps are provided in Chapter 11, *Configuring Backup, Restore, and High Availability*)

**TIP**

Please refer the link for more information: `http://www.cisco.com/c/en/u`
`s/td/docs/unified_computing/ucs/ucs-manager/GUI-User-Guides/Ge`
`tting-Started/3-1/b_UCSM_Getting_Started_Guide_3_1/b_UCSM_Init`
`ial_Configuration_Guide_3_0_chapter_011.html`

4. Make sure that the L1 port is connected to L1 and the L2 port is connected to L2
   between FIs so that, when the second FI is powered up, it automatically detects
   the first FI and configures the cluster settings as part of the initial configuration
   (detailed steps are provided in `Chapter 11`, *Configuring Backup, Restore, and High
   Availability*).

5. Assign a cluster IP to get centralized management access to the cluster, also
   known as **Virtual IP** (**VIP**).

6. Once the IPs have been assigned, it is also possible to access FIs through **Secure
   Shell** (**SSH**).

7. Log in to FI and use the following commands to get the status of the cluster, as
   shown in the following screenshot:

   ```
   show cluster state
   show cluster extended-state
   ```

```
Lesser General Public License (LGPL) Version 2.1. A copy of each
such license is available at
http://www.opensource.org/licenses/gpl-2.0.php and
http://www.opensource.org/licenses/lgpl-2.1.php

ucspe# show cluster state
Cluster Id: 0x80d1192c0ac511e7-0xa0ce000c2925886a

A: UP, PRIMARY
B: UP, SUBORDINATE

HA READY
ucspe# show cluster extended-state
Cluster Id: 0x80d1192c0ac511e7-0xa0ce000c2925886a

Start time: Fri Mar 17 03:55:18 2017
Last election time: Fri Mar 17 03:55:33 2017

A: UP, PRIMARY
B: UP, SUBORDINATE

A: memb state UP, lead state PRIMARY, mgmt services state: UP
B: memb state UP, lead state SUBORDINATE, mgmt services state: UP
   heartbeat state PRIMARY_OK

INTERNAL NETWORK INTERFACES:
eth0, UP

HA READY
Detailed state of the device selected for HA storage:
Chassis 1, serial: CH1, state: active
Chassis 2, serial: CH2, state: active
Server 1, serial: RK1, state: active
ucspe#
```

8. After confirming the status of the cluster, log in to the UCSM GUI using the cluster VIP IP or DNS name using a compatible browser, as shown in the following screenshot:

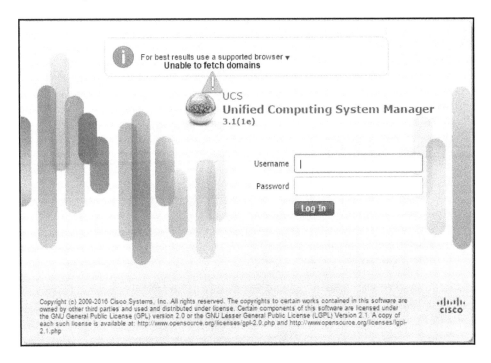

9. Configure the UCS global policies, which will be explained in the next section.

In case it is necessary to reinitialize FI to default factory settings, use the following commands:

```
connect local-mgmt
erase-config
```

 On a primary FI, A is automatically added to the name, and on a secondary FI, B is automatically added to the name, so pay attention to the naming convention.

In this chapter, we will only discuss the configuration of UCS policies that have global impact on chassis discovery, connectivity, and power management.

In subsequent chapters, we will be exploring different blade-server-specific policies and other configurations using the UCSM.

# Global configuration policies

Most of the policies and configurations are assigned to servers by assigning those policies and configurations to service profiles associated with physical servers. There are a few global policies and configurations for UCS infrastructure that are not assigned to servers but are necessary for proper functioning of all the components.

These policies and configurations include the following:

- **Chassis/FEX Discovery Policy**
- **Rack Server Discovery Policy**
- **Rack Management Connection Policy**
- **Power Policy**
- **MAC Address Table Aging Policy**
- **DNS Server**
- **Time Zone Management**
- **SNMP configuration**

These policies and settings are configured under various navigation pane tabs. We will now look into the configuration of each of these.

# Chassis/FEX Discovery Policy

This is the first policy we need to configure so that the UCS chassis is detected by the UCSM software. The Following are the steps to configure this policy:

1. Log in to the UCSM screen.
2. Click on the **Equipment** tab in the navigation pane.
3. Select **Policies** from the work pane and click on **Global Policies**.
4. In the **Chassis/FEX Discovery Policy** area of the work pane, from the **Action** drop-down menu, select the option with the number of connections that is equal to or less than the actual number of physical connections from IOM/FEX of chassis to the FIs.
5. In the **Link Grouping Preference**, select the **port-channel** for bundling the links between Fabric Interconnect and chassis.
6. Click on **OK**.

# Rack Server Discovery Policy

The following are the steps to configure this policy:

1. Follow the same steps as you did for **Chassis/FEX Discovery Policy** and select **Global Policies**.
2. Select the appropriate **Action** option from the available radio buttons to discover the rack servers.
3. Select the **Scrub Policy** for the rack server to scrub the disk drives.
4. Click on **OK**.

# Rack Management Connection Policy

The following are the steps to configure this policy:

1. Follow the same steps as you did for **Chassis/FEX Discovery Policy** and select **Global Policies**.
2. Select the appropriate **Action** option from the available radio buttons to connect the rack servers.
3. Click on **OK**.

# Power Policy

The following are the steps to configure this policy:

1. Follow the same steps as you did for **Chassis/FEX Discovery Policy** and select **Global Policies**.
2. Select the appropriate **Redundancy** option, which is dependent on the total number of power supplies and power feeds to the data center.
3. Click on **OK**.

The following screenshot highlight the above settings.

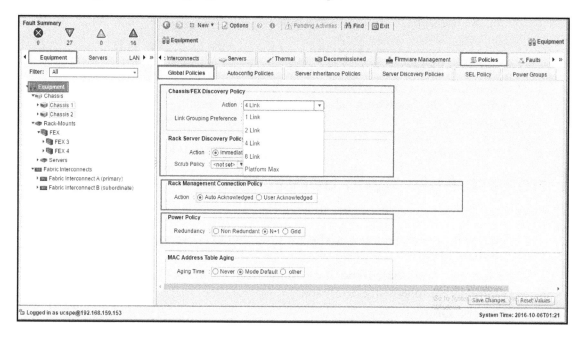

# MAC Address Table Aging

The following are the steps to configure this policy:

1. Follow the same steps as you did for **Chassis/FEX Discovery Policy** and select **Global Policies**.
2. Select the appropriate **Aging Time** option from the available radio buttons.
3. Click on **OK**.

# Global Power Allocation Policy

The following are the steps to configure this policy:

1. Follow the same steps as you did for **Chassis/FEX Discovery Policy** and select **Global Policies**.
2. Select the appropriate **Allocation Method** option from the available radio buttons for power allocation to the chassis and blade servers.
3. Click on **OK**.

# Firmware Auto Sync Server Policy

The following are the steps to configure this policy:

1. Follow the same steps as you did for **Chassis/FEX Discovery Policy** and select **Global Policies**.
2. Select the appropriate **Sync State** option from the available radio buttons for manual or auto-syncing firmware.
3. Click on **OK**.

# Global Power Profiling Policy

The following are the steps to configure this policy:

1. Follow the same steps as you did for **Chassis/FEX Discovery Policy** and select **Global Policies**.
2. Select the **Profile Power** option to use the power profile.
3. Click on **OK**.

# Info Policy

The following are the steps to configure this policy:

1. Follow the same steps as you did for **Chassis/FEX Discovery Policy** and select **Global Policies**.
2. Select the appropriate **Action** option from the available radio buttons to enable the info policy.
3. Click on **OK**.

Following screenshot highlight the preceding settings.

The other global configurations are under the **Admin** tab in the navigation pane. Go through the following sections to get an idea of the steps required to configure these settings.

# DNS server

The following are the steps to configure the DNS server:

1. Log in to the UCSM screen.
2. Click on the **Admin** tab in the navigation pane.
3. Expand **Communication Management**.
4. Select **DNS Management** from the work pane.

5. Click on **Specify DNS Server**, which will pop up another window for providing the IP address of the DNS server.

6. Click on **OK**.

7. Click on **Save Changes**, as shown in the following screenshot:

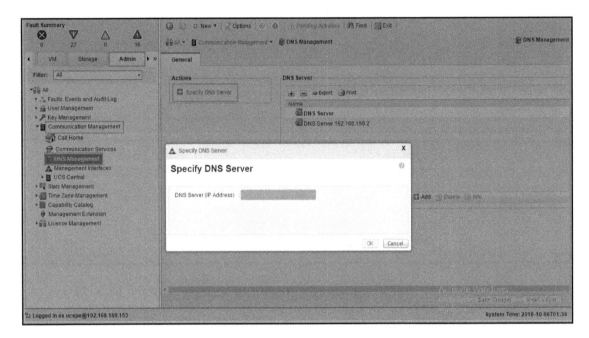

# Time-zone management

The following are the steps to configure time zone and NTP servers:

1. Log in to the UCSM screen.

2. Click on the **Admin** tab on the navigation pane.

3. Select **Time Zone Management** from the work pane.

4. Click on **Add NTP Server**, which will pop up another window for providing the IP address of the NTP server.

5. Click on **OK**.

6. Click on **Save Changes**, as shown in the following screenshot.

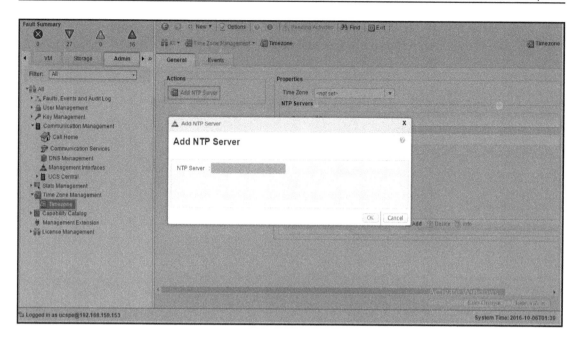

# SNMP

The following are the steps to configure SNMP for sending alerts to a remote SNMP server:

1. Log in to the UCSM screen.
2. Click on the **Admin** tab on the navigation pane.
3. Expand **Communication Management**.
4. Select **Communication Services** from the work pane.

5. In the **SNMP** section, select the **Enabled** radio button for the **Admin State** option, as shown in the following screenshot:

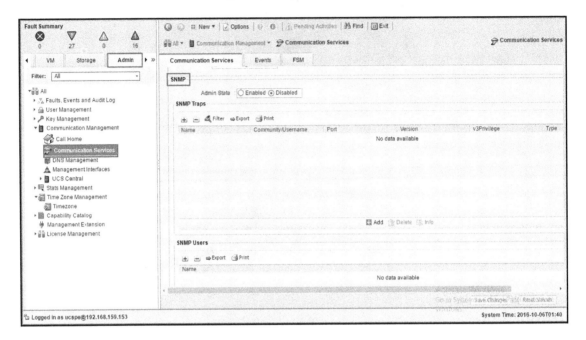

6. Click on the green **Add** sign under the **SNMP Traps** heading; a new pop-up window will appear for configuring SNMP.

7. Provide the **IP Address** value of the remote collection server, SNMP string in the **Community/Username** field, server **Port** value, SNMP **Version** type, and **Type** of data collection. The last option, the **v3Privilege** field, is only applicable for SNMP v3.

8. Click on **OK**.

9. Click on **Save Changes** as shown in the following screenshot.

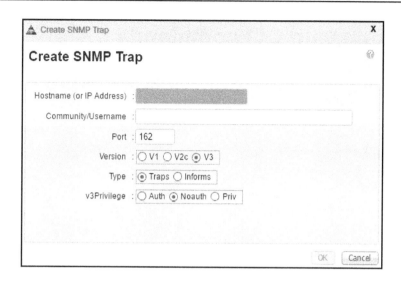

# UCS Manager - command-line interface

UCSM's command line is different from Cisco's regular IOS and even NX-OS (Nexus is the base platform of FIs that runs UCSM). The UCSM CLI provides the same tab completion options as IOS and NX-OS. You can either SSH to log in remotely, or log in locally through the console access to the FI to get access to the UCS CLI.

Each UCS component can be configured using the GUI or CLI commands. Each GUI tab, and each component present in the infrastructure and represented in the GUI, has an equivalent CLI configuration command. You can navigate through various UCS components using the `scope` command.

Once connected to the CLI, it is also possible to connect the other advanced CLIs to individual components introduced later in the chapter.

# Getting help with CLI commands

On the blank command prompt, typing ? lists all the available commands for the mode you are in. It lists all the available keywords and arguments for the command at the current position in the command syntax, as shown in the following screenshot:

```
ucspe#
   acknowledge      Acknowledge
   backup           Backup
   clear            Clear managed objects
   commit-buffer    Commit transaction buffer
   connect          Connect to Another CLI
   decommission     Decommission managed objects
   delete           Delete managed objects
   discard-buffer   Discard transaction buffer
   end              Go to exec mode
   exit             Exit from command interpreter
   recommission     Recommission Server Resources
   remove           Remove
   restore-check    Check if in restore mode
   scope            Changes the current mode
   set              Set property values
   show             Show system information
   terminal         Terminal
   top              Go to the top mode
   up               Go up one mode
   where            Show information about the current mode

ucspe# 
```

Typing ? with a partially completed command provides the syntax completion option. In this case, ? should be typed without any space, as shown in the following screenshot:

```
ucspe# scope fc
   fc-storage       FC Storage
   fc-traffic-mon   FC Traffic Monitoring Domain
   fc-uplink        FC Uplink

ucspe# 
```

# Accessing the history of CLI commands

UCS automatically saves all the typed commands during a session. You can use the up and down arrow keys in order to step through the commands, and the right and left arrow keys to make any modifications before executing:

```
ucspe# scope fc-
fc-storage        fc-traffic-mon  fc-uplink
ucspe# scope fc-uplink
ucspe /fc-uplink #
  acknowledge  Acknowledge
  create       Create managed objects
  delete       Delete managed objects
  enter        Enters a managed object
  scope        Changes the current mode
  set          Set property values
  show         Show system information

ucspe /fc-uplink #
```

# Accessing component-level CLIs

It is also possible to connect to other CLI interfaces of individual components, for example, mezzanine adapters, server **Cisco Integrated Management Controllers** (**CIMCs**), IOMs, and the underlying Nexus OS. It is usually not required to connect to these CLIs for a normal operation. However, during troubleshooting scenarios, Cisco technicians may ask you to connect to other CLIs to collect logs and other advanced troubleshooting. This is done using the `connect` command with the desired CLI option. The options include the following as shown in the screenshot:

- `connect adapter`
- `connect cimc`
- `connect clp`
- `connect iom`
- `connect local-mgmt`
- `connect nxos`

```
ucspe# connect
  adapter          Mezzanine Adapter
  chassis-adapter  Adapter
  cimc             Cisco Integrated Management Controller
  clp              Connect to DMTF CLP
  iom              IO Module
  local-mgmt       Connect to Local Management CLI
  nxos             Connect to NXOS CLI

ucspe# connect
```

# Scope commands

The UCS scope commands provide hierarchical access to UCS components. The following table lists some of the main categories of the scope command. Scope command categories are mostly self-explanatory and provide access to a major area or component. Under each major category, there are subcategories for specific components. This is equivalent to the hierarchy of different tabs in the GUI:

| Component | CLI command to access |
|---|---|
| **Chassis** | `FI# scope chassis`<br>`FI/chassis#` |
| Fabric Interconnect | `FI# scope fabric-interconnect`<br>`FI/ fabric-interconnect#` |
| Service profile | `FI# scope service-profile`<br>`FI/ service-profile#` |
| Firmware | `FI# scope firmware`<br>`FI/firmware#` |
| Host Ethernet interface | `FI# scope host-eth-if`<br>`FI/host-eth-if#` |
| Host Fibre Channel interface | `FI# scope host-fc-if`<br>`FI/host-fc-if#` |
| Virtual NIC | `FI# scope vnic`<br>`FI/vnic#` |
| Virtual HBA | `FI# scope vhba`<br>`FI/vhba#` |
| Organization | `FI# scope org`<br>`FI/org#` |
| Security Mode | `FI# scope security`<br>`FI/security#` |
| Ethernet uplink | `FI# scope eth-uplink`<br>`FI/eth-uplink#` |
| System | `FI# scope system`<br>`FI/system#` |
| Mezzanine Adapter | `FI# scope adapter`<br>`FI/adapter#` |

| Component | CLI command to access |
|---|---|
| Cabling | `FI# scope cabling`<br>`FI/cabling#` |
| Cartridge | `FI# scope cartridge`<br>`FI/cartridge#` |
| Ethernet Flow Monitoring Domain | `FI# scope eth-flow-mon`<br>`FI/ eth-flow-mon#` |
| Ethernet Server Domain | `FI# scope eth-server`<br>`FI/ eth-server #` |
| Ethernet Storage | `FI# scope eth-storage`<br>`FI/ eth-storage#` |
| Ethernet Traffic Monitoring Domain | `FI# scope eth-traffic-mon`<br>`FI/ eth-traffic-mon#` |
| FC Storage | `FI# scope fc-storage`<br>`FI/ fc-storage#` |
| FC Traffic Monitoring Domain Storage | `FI# scope fc-traffic-mon`<br>`FI/ fc-traffic-mon#` |
| FEX Module | `FI# scope fex`<br>`FI/ fex#` |
| License | `FI# scope license`<br>`FI/ license#` |
| Monitoring the System | `FI# scope monitoring`<br>`FI/ monitoring#` |
| Power Cap Mgmt | `FI# scope power-cap-mgmt`<br>`FI/ power-cap-mgmt#` |

The following screenshot shows the list of scope option:

```
ucspe# scope
  adapter              Mezzanine Adapter
  cabling              Cabling
  cartridge            Cartridge
  chassis              Chassis
  eth-flow-mon         Ethernet Flow Monitoring Domain
  eth-server           Ethernet Server Domain
  eth-storage          Ethernet Storage
  eth-traffic-mon      Ethernet Traffic Monitoring Domain
  eth-uplink           Ethernet Uplink
  fabric-interconnect  Fabric Interconnect
  fc-storage           FC Storage
  fc-traffic-mon       FC Traffic Monitoring Domain
  fc-uplink            FC Uplink
  fex                  FEX (fabric-extender) Module
  firmware             Firmware
  host-eth-if          Host Ethernet Interface
  host-fc-if           Host FC Interface
  license              License
  monitoring           Monitor the system
  org                  Organizations
  power-cap-mgmt       Power Cap Mgmt
  security             security mode
  server               Server
  service-profile      Service Profile
  system               Systems
  vhba                 vHBA
  vnic                 vNIC

ucspe# scope
```

Once inside a specific configuration, you can use the following commands to show, create, or delete configurations:

- show
- create
- delete

Use the exit command to go one level higher in the hierarchy.

# Applying changes

None of the configurations get applied unless the commit-buffer command is used. You can make configuration changes, but you do need this final command in order to apply those changes. The commit-buffer command is analogous to the **OK**, **Apply**, and **Save Changes** buttons to apply changes in the GUI.

If you have not executed the `commit-buffer` command, it is possible to discard the changes by using the `discard-buffer` command. It is also possible to accumulate multiple configurations and use a single `commit-buffer` command to apply all the changes. You can view the pending commands by entering the `show configuration pending` command in any command mode.

# An example configuration using CLI commands

As an example, we will configure the DNS and NTP servers with the IP address `8.8.8.8` for UCSM.

The following command changes the CLI focus to system scope, as DNS is a system-wide setting:

```
FI-A# scope system
```

The following command changes the CLI focus to services scope:

```
FI-A /system # scope services
```

The following command creates a DNS server entry:

```
FI-A /system/services # create dns 8.8.8.8
```

The `commit-buffer` command applies the changes and saves the configuration:

```
FI-A /system/services* # commit-buffer
```

The following command changes the CLI focus to system scope, as NTP is also a system-wide setting:

```
FI-A# scope system
```

The following command changes the CLI focus to services scope:

```
FI-A /system # scope services
```

The following command creates a DNS server entry:

```
FI-A /system/services # create ntp-server 8.8.8.8
```

The `commit-buffer` command saves the configuration:

```
FI-A /system/services* # commit-buffer
```

# Summary

In this chapter, we learned about the UCSM GUI. We looked at how the GUI is divided into different panes and sections, and the various methods to find the required information or set up the necessary configuration. We briefly described the main tabs in the navigation pane and some tabs in the work pane in subsequent chapters, we will go into the details of navigation and work-pane tabs. We then went through the initial configuration of UCSM. We walked through the minimum configuration steps. We also learned about the CLI UI and how its syntax is a bit different than regular IOS or NX-OS syntax. We also configured some global policies and other settings, which are necessary for UCS components, using the GUI. In subsequent chapters, we will be using the UCSM GUI extensively for the configuration of various UCS physical and software objects.

In the next chapter, we will learn about the UCS LAN configuration. We will start using UCSM extensively, and will explore different configurations, pools, templates, policies, and so on, related to the LAN configuration.

# 5
# Configuring LAN Connectivity

UCS Fabric Interconnect provides connectivity for Ethernet and storage data traffic. UCS Fabric Interconnect also runs the **Unified Computing System Management** (**UCSM**) software. UCS Fabric Interconnect hardware is based on the Nexus series of switches and runs NX-OS; however, Fabric Interconnect has some features that are different from a standard Nexus Ethernet switch. In this chapter, we'll focus on Fabric Interconnect Ethernet connectivity to the servers and upstream switches.

In this chapter, we'll discuss the following topics:

- Understanding Fabric Interconnect switching modes
- Introduction to Fabric Interconnect port types
- Configuring northbound connectivity to upstream switches
- Configuring southbound connectivity to IOMs/FEXs
- Configuring the last piece of the puzzle-vNICs

We'll configure Fabric Interconnect's downstream (southbound) connectivity to IOMs/**Fabric Extenders** (**FEXs**) in the blade chassis and upstream (northbound) connectivity to the physical switches. Network configuration is done under the **LAN** and **Equipment** tabs in the navigation pane of the UCS Manager software. In this chapter we, will thoroughly explore the **LAN** and **Equipment** tabs in the navigation pane.

# Understanding Fabric Interconnect switching modes

UCS Fabric Interconnect supports two types of switching modes: **end-host mode (EHM)** and the standard Ethernet switching mode. The default switching mode is the EHM, which eliminates the use of the **Spanning Tree Protocol (STP)** on Fabric Interconnect. The standard Ethernet switching is rarely used and it is recommended that you do not implement this option unless there is a use case.

 Switching mode conversion is a disruptive change requiring a Fabric Interconnect reboot and hence should be planned during a scheduled maintenance window.

## Ethernet end-host mode

The end-host mode is the default mode of operation for UCS Fabric Interconnect Ethernet connectivity. In this mode, UCS Fabric Interconnect is presented to the northbound LAN switch as an end host with many adapters. STP is not configured on the uplink switch ports. Since there is no STP, all FI ports are in the forwarding state irrespective of the northbound topology. This means that data traffic can use any of the FI uplink ports/port channels. In this mode, Fabric Interconnect is in the active/active usage state.

The data traffic flow is accomplished through the pinning of host interfaces to the Fabric Interconnect uplink ports. Host interface pinning can be configured dynamically or statically. All Fabric Interconnect uplink ports are configured as 802.1q trunks. No control protocol is used on the uplinks. **MAC Address learning** only happens for southbound server ports and not on uplink ports:

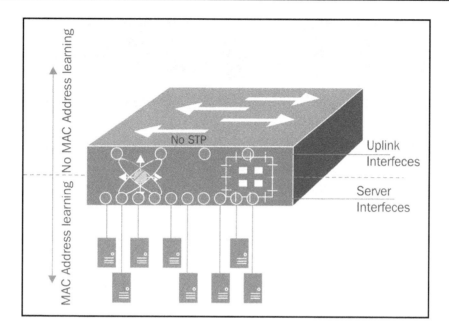

In order to configure or verify EHM for Fabric Interconnects, follow these steps:

1. Log into UCS Manager.
2. Click on the **Equipment** tab in the navigation pane.
3. On the **Equipment** tab, click on **Fabric Interconnect A** (as shown in the following screenshot).
4. The **Status** area in the work pane shows the current **Ethernet Mode** configuration which is **End Host**.

5. In the **Actions** area of the work pane, the currently configured **Ethernet Mode**, which in this case is **End Host**, will be shown grayed:

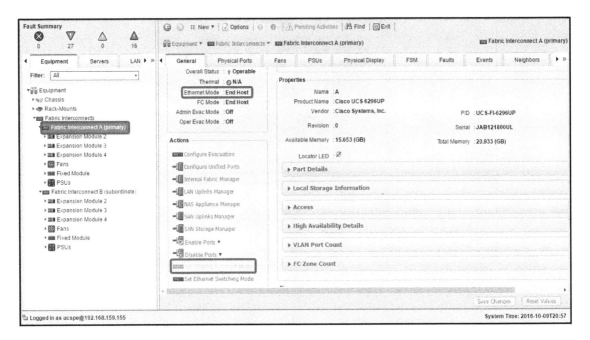

A Fabric Interconnect reboot is required in order to change the **Ethernet Mode** from **End Host** to **Switch** and vice versa.

In order to change the **Ethernet Mode** from **End Host** to **Switch**, perform the following steps:

1. Log into UCS Manager.
2. Click on the **Equipment** tab in the navigation pane.
3. In the **Equipment** tab, click on **Fabric Interconnect A** (as shown in the following screenshot).
4. In the **Actions** area of the work pane, the currently configured **Ethernet Mode**, which in this case is **End Host**, will be shown grayed and cannot be selected.
5. Click on **Set Ethernet Switching Mode** in the **Actions** area of the work pane.
6. Click on **Yes** on the pop-up warning message to restart Fabric Interconnect:

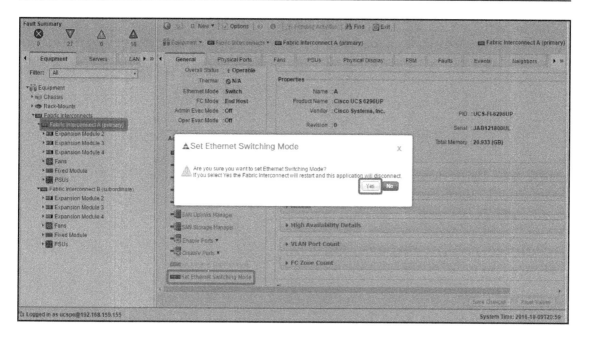

7. After Fabric Interconnect restarts, the **Ethernet Mode** is changed to **Switch**.

 You can also right-click on a Fabric Interconnect in the **Equipment** tab in the navigation pane in order to change the switching mode.

# Ethernet switching mode

In this mode, UCS Fabric Interconnect is configured as a standard Ethernet switch with STP configured for loop avoidance. The up-link's ports are configured as forwarding or blocking as per the STP algorithm.

In order to verify or configure the switching mode for Fabric Interconnect, perform the following steps:

1. Log into UCS Manager.
2. Click on the **Equipment** tab in the navigation pane.
3. In the **Equipment** tab, click on **Fabric Interconnect A** (as shown in the following screenshot).

4. The **Status** area in the work pane shows the current **Ethernet Mode** configuration which is the switching mode.

5. In the **Actions** area of the work pane, the currently configured **Ethernet Mode**, which in this case is **Switch**, will be shown grayed:

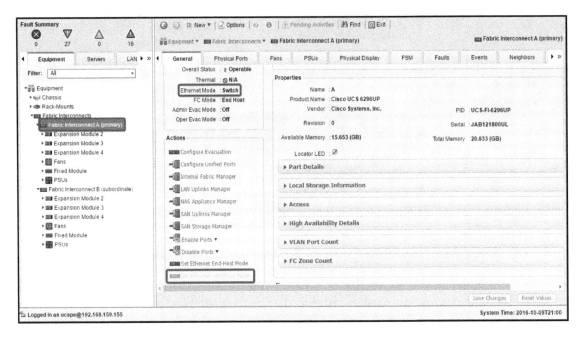

A Fabric Interconnect reboot is required in order to change the **Ethernet Mode** from the **Switch** mode to the **End Host** mode and vice versa.

In order to change the **Ethernet Mode** from **Switch** to **End Host**, follow these steps:

1. Log into UCS Manager.
2. Click on the **Equipment** tab in the navigation pane.
3. In the **Equipment** tab, click on **Fabric Interconnect A** (as shown in the following screenshot).
4. In the **Actions** area of the work pane, the currently configured **Ethernet Mode**, which in this case is **Switch**, will be shown grayed and cannot be selected.
5. Click on **Set Ethernet End-Host Mode** in the **Actions** area of the work pane.
6. Click **Yes** on the pop-up warning message to restart Fabric Interconnect.

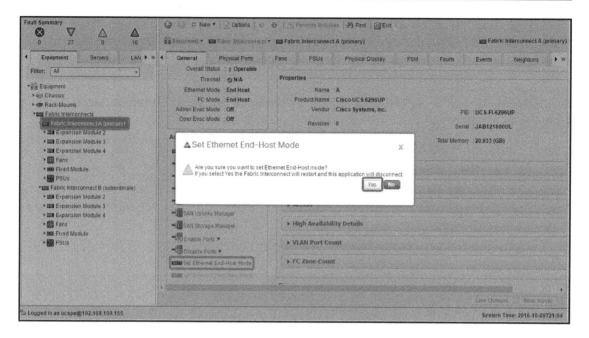

7. After Fabric Interconnect restarts, the **Ethernet Mode** is changed to the **End Host** mode.

# Introduction to Fabric Interconnect port types

By default, all Fabric Interconnect ports are unconfigured. Fabric Interconnect ports can be in the following states:

- **Unconfigured**: Port is not configured and cannot be used.
- **Server port**: Port is configured for southbound connection to an IOM **Fabric Extender** (**FEX**) module in a blade chassis.
- **Uplink port**: Port is configured for northbound connection to the upstream Ethernet switch. Uplink ports are always configured as trunk ports.
- **Disabled**: Port is configured either as an uplink or server port and is currently disabled by the administrator.

For the 6200 series FI, all ports are unified ports; hence all the ports can also be configured as 1/10 Gig Ethernet, FC, FC uplink, appliance port, or FCoE port. For the 6300 series, FC configurations are only available with expansion module ports with 6332-16UP model.

To define, change, or check the state of a port, expanding the **Fabric Interconnect** inventory from the **Equipment** tab in the navigation pane, follow these steps:

1. Log into UCS Manager.
2. Click on the **Equipment** tab in the navigation pane.
3. In the **Equipment** tab click on **Fabric Interconnect A** and expand the ports.
4. Click a port, and its current configuration will be displayed in the right-hand side working pane.
5. Right-click on a port and select a new configuration for the port from the pop-up menu.
6. Ports can be enabled or disabled from the menu as well:

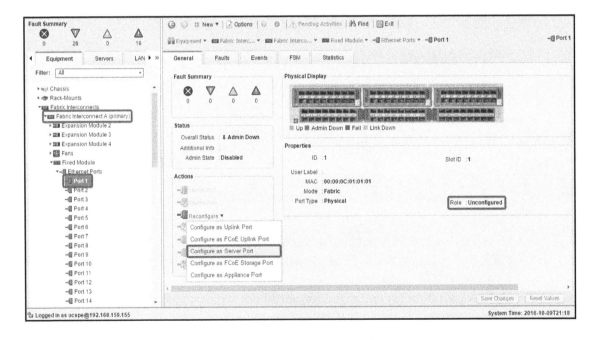

The other option to configure the ports is the **LAN Uplinks Manger** tool, which can be accessed using the following steps:

1. Log into UCS Manager.
2. Click on the **Equipment** tab in the navigation pane.
3. In the **Equipment** tab, click on **Fabric Interconnect A**.
4. In the work area pane, select **LAN Uplinks Manager**.

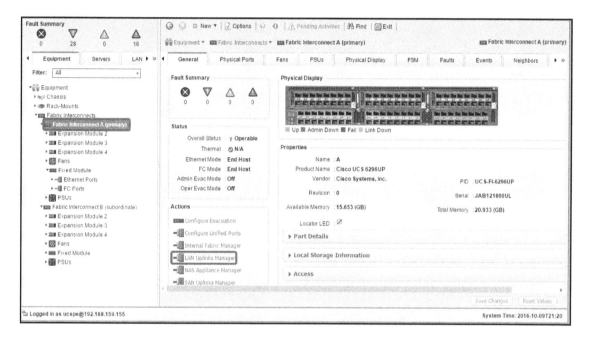

 **LAN Uplinks Manager** is a pop-up pane that can be used to configure LAN configurations from a single view, which are otherwise configured from different tabs in the navigation and work panes. **LAN Uplinks Manager** shows all the ports in various categories. Ports can be configured, enabled, and disabled. Ethernet **Port Channels**, **VLANs**, **Pin Groups**, and **QoS** policies can be created and assigned. Ethernet related **Events**, **Faults**, and **FSM** status can also be viewed using the tab available at the top in **LAN Uplinks Manager**.

5. The **LAN Uplinks Manager** user interface is as shown in the following screenshot:

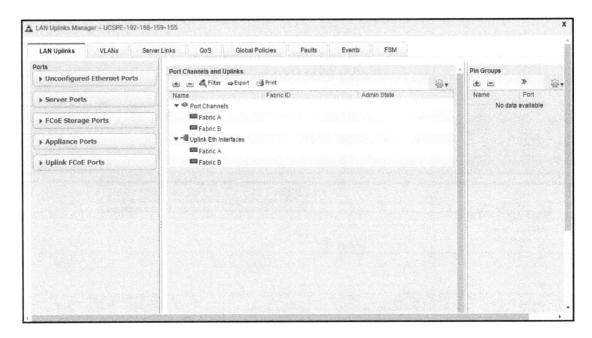

# Configuring northbound connectivity to upstream switches

Cisco recommends using Nexus 5k/7k/9k switches for Fabric Interconnect northbound network connectivity because of the features such as **virtual PortChannel** (**vPC**). It is, however, possible to connect Fabric Interconnect to other Ethernet switches as well, including Cisco Catalyst series switches and even switches from Cisco competitors, as long as those switches use the industry standard protocols.

The majority of UCS field deployments are designed using Nexus 5k/7k switches. Therefore, we will explain the upstream configuration using Cisco Nexus 5k switches. However, with the introduction of the **Application Centric Infrastructure** (**ACI**), Cisco supports UCS connectivity with the latest spin/leaf architecture with Nexus 9k and provides tight integration with the **Application Programming Interface Controller** (**APIC**).

# Configuring upstream switches

Northbound connectivity from Fabric Interconnect can be achieved through a standard uplink, a port channel, or vPC configuration. The recommended configuration for the northbound connectivity is through Nexus switches and configuring a vPC.

The vPC configuration aggregates bandwidth and provides redundancy across two physical northbound Nexus switches to each Fabric Interconnect. In the vPC configuration, northbound Nexus switches logically appear as a single entity to Fabric Interconnect. A MAC address learned by an individual Nexus switch is shared between both switches.

vPC consists of the following components:

- **Two peer Nexus switches**: One is configured as primary and the other is configured as secondary
- **vPC domain ID**: This is a logical ID assigned to vPC and should be unique for **Link Aggregation Control Protocol (LACP)** negotiations
- **vPC peer link**: This is a high throughput link configured between the two Nexus switches for synchronizing the forwarding of information and data movement, if needed
- **vPC keep alive link**: This is configured between two Nexus switches for sharing heartbeat information
- **vPC member links**: These are southbound links to Fabric Interconnects:

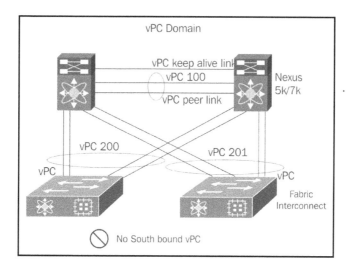

To enable the vPC feature on Nexus switches, use the following steps:

1. The vPC feature needs to be enabled on Nexus switches. Also enable the LACP feature for port trunking:

```
switch(config)# feature vpc
switch(config)# feature lacp
```

These features should be enabled on both switches.

2. Configure the vPC domain ID:

```
switch(config)# vpc domain 1
```

The domain ID should be configured on both switches.

3. Configure `peer-keepalive`:

```
switch(config-vpc-domain)# peer-keepalive destination x.x.x.x
```

`peer-keepalive` is also configured on both switches where the destination IP is usually the management port IP of the peer switch, which is used as a heartbeat link for vPC.

4. Configure the peer link between directly connected ports of both switches:

```
switch(config)# interface ethernet 1/10-11
switch(config-if-range)# channel-group 100 mode active
switch(config-if-range)# interface port-channel100
switch(config-if)# switchport mode trunk
switch(config-if)# switchport trunk allowed vlan x
```

5. Create a port channel on both switches, enable the trunk mode, and allow the required VLANs:

```
switch(config-if)# vpc peer-link
```

Enable the port channel as the vPC peer link.

6. Configure Nexus member ports connecting to Fabric Interconnects:

```
switch(config)#interface ethernet1/1-2
switch(config-if-range)#channel-group 200
switch(config-if-range)#interface port-channel200
switch(config-if)#switchport mode trunk
switch(config-if)#switchport trunk allowed vlan x
switch(config-if)#vpc 200
```

Similar configuration is required for vPC 200 on the second Nexus switch connectivity to the same FI.

7. Now configure the second vPC on both switches for connecting to both Fabric Interconnects:

```
switch(config)#interface ethernet1/3-4
switch(config-if-range)#channel-group 201
switch(config-if-range)#interface port-channel201
switch(config-if)#switchport mode trunk
switch(config-if)#switchport trunk allowed vlan x
switch(config-if)#vpc 201
```

A similar configuration is required for vPC 201 on the second Nexus switch connectivity to the same FI.

# Learning how to configure Fabric Interconnect uplink ports

Fabric Interconnect ports configured as uplink ports are used to connect to northbound upstream network switches. These uplink ports can be connected to upstream switch ports as individual links or links configured as **port channels** (**PC**), which provides bandwidth aggregation as well as link redundancy.

The Fabric Interconnect port channel configuration is based on LACP. It is also possible to configure a port channel as a vPC where port channel uplink ports from a Fabric Interconnect are connected to different upstream switches.

It is recommended to configure Fabric Interconnect uplink ports in vPC configuration, as shown in the following diagram:

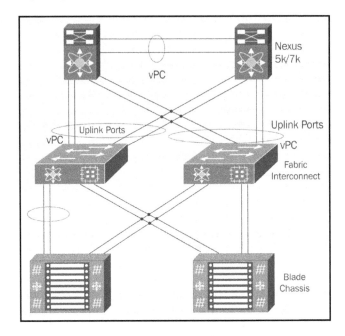

The following are the steps to configure the ports and the port channels for the preceding network topology:

1. Log into UCS Manager.
2. Click on the **Equipment** tab in the navigation pane.
3. In the **Equipment** tab, click on a Fabric Interconnect.
4. In the work area pane, select **LAN Uplinks Manager**.
5. Expand **Ports** in the **Fixed Module** or **Expansion Module** (if present).
6. Right-click on a single port or hold the *Ctrl* key and select multiple ports.
7. Select **Configure as Uplink Port**.
8. A pop-up menu will allow us to configure a new status for the port(s).
9. Select the new port status and click on **Yes**.

Repeat these steps to configure all the uplink ports for both Fabric Interconnects.

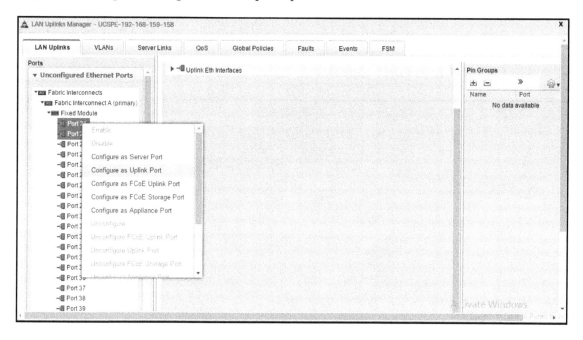

After all the uplink ports are configured, a port channel can be created for these ports by performing the following steps:

1. Right-click on a Fabric Interconnect in the middle pane labeled **Port Channel and Uplinks** of LAN Uplinks Manager.

2. Click on **Create Port Channel**.

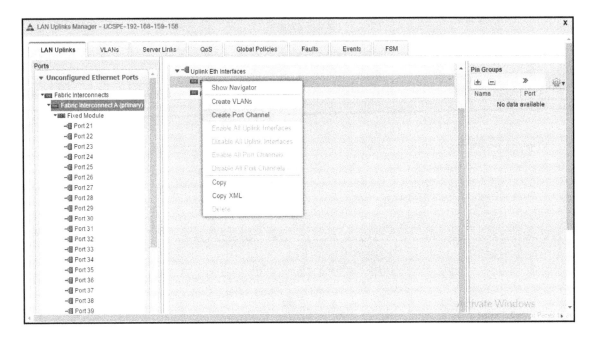

3. In the pop-up window, assign an ID and a name for the port channel and click on **Next**.

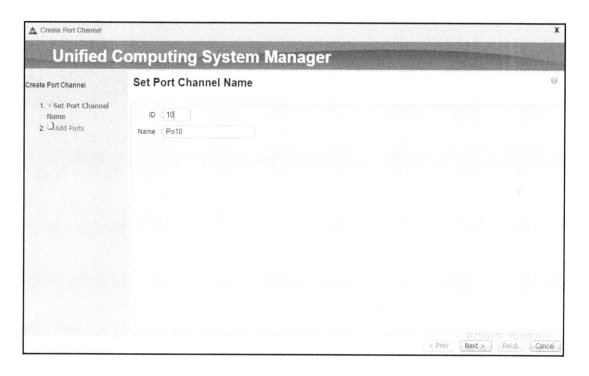

4. In the next window, click the uplink ports which should be added to the port channel and click on the arrow sign to add ports to the port channel.

5. After adding ports, click **Finish** to complete the port channel configuration:

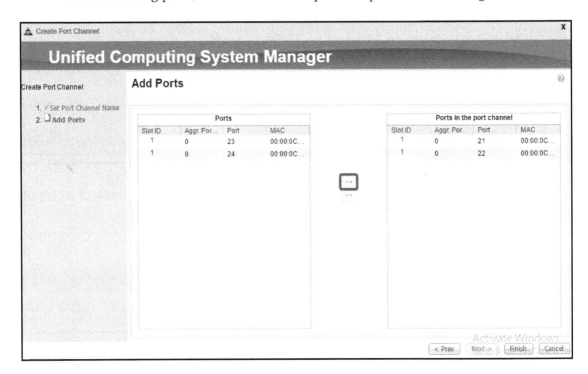

 The port channel name and ID configured on Fabric Interconnect should match the name and ID configuration on the upstream Ethernet switch for easy troubleshooting.

# Configuring VLANs

VLAN configuration on Fabric Interconnects can be done either through **LAN Uplink Manager** or through the **LAN** tab in the navigation pane. Typically, both Fabric Interconnects have the same VLAN configuration, which is called **global VLAN configuration**. It is possible to configure VLANs that are available on only one of the two Fabric Interconnects which is called **FI-specific VLAN configuration**. It is also possible to configure a same VLAN differently on both Fabric Interconnects. Fabric Interconnects also support the creation of private VLANs.

The default VLAN is `VLAN 1`, which cannot be deleted and is available on both FIs. `VLAN 1` is also the native VLAN. VLANs can be configured in the range of 1-3967 and 4049-4093. The 3968-4048 and 4094 VLAN IDs are reserved for system use on FIs and cannot be configured.

As the uplink ports on Fabric Interconnects are always trunk ports, UCS Manager automatically manages the allowed VLANs on FI uplink ports whenever a VLAN is created, deleted, or changed. Using the USC Manager VLAN wizard, it is possible to create a single VLAN or multiple VLANs, as shown in the following steps:

1. Log into UCS Manager.
2. Click on the **LAN** tab in the navigation pane.
3. In the **LAN** tab, right-click on any Fabric Interconnect or the **VLAN** tab and click on **Create VLANs**:

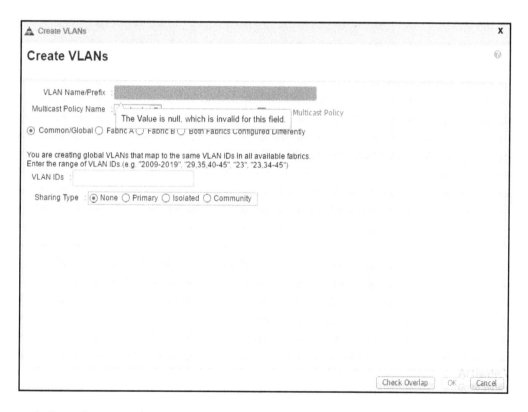

4. In order to configure a single VLAN, assign a VLAN name and ID.
5. Select the VLAN configuration type as **Common/Global** if the same VLAN configuration is required on both Fabric Interconnects.

6. Leave **Sharing Type** as **None**, which is the default selection. This selection can be changed if a private VLAN configuration is required.
7. Click on the **Check Overlap** button in order to verify uniqueness of the VLAN ID.
8. Click on **OK** to create the VLAN.

In order to create a VLAN range, perform the following steps:

1. Open the LAN tab in UCS Manager.
2. In the **LAN** tab, right-click on any Fabric Interconnect or the **VLAN** tab and click on **Create VLANs**.
3. In order to configure a VLAN range, assign a **VLAN Name/Prefix** and enter the range of **VLAN IDs** and click on **OK**.

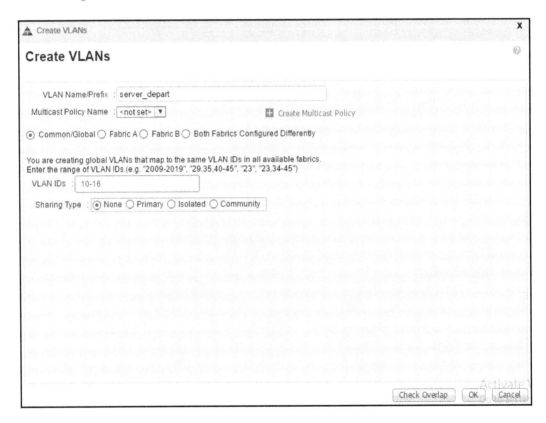

4. VLANs will be created with a combination of prefix and VLAN numbers.

5. On the next window, click on **OK** again after verifying the new VLAN names.

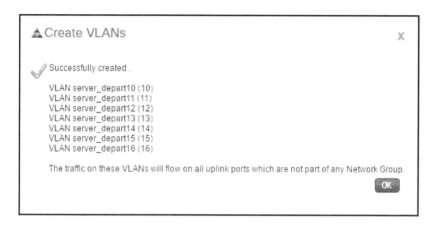

Fabric Interconnect does not participate in **VLAN Trunking Protocol** (**VTP**)

# Using pin groups

In the end-host mode, Fabric Interconnect does not work as a traditional layer 2 switch. In this mode, UCS Fabric Interconnect is presented to the northbound LAN switch as an end host with many adapters. Traffic from individual servers' vNICs is mapped to a specific Fabric Interconnect uplink port or port channel. This mapping of Ethernet traffic is known as **LAN pin groups**.

Pin groups can be configured as a static or dynamic pin group. The default configuration is dynamic pin groups.

# Dynamic pin groups

This is the default pin group setting. In dynamic pinning, Fabric Interconnect automatically binds server vNICs to uplink FI ports. The mapping of server vNICs to uplink FI ports depends upon the total number of active uplinks configured, which could be either 1, 2, 4, or 8 (for older 6100 series FIs, uplinks could only be 1, 2, and 4).

# Failure response

Both Fabric Interconnects are in active/active mode with respect to Ethernet data traffic movement. Each server is pinned to a single Fabric Interconnect uplink port or port channel. This means that the data traffic from some servers will move using Fabric Interconnect A and for other servers using Fabric Interconnect B.

In case of a northbound uplink or port channel failure where a server is currently pinned to, the server connection will be automatically pinned to another port or port channel on the same Fabric Interconnect. In case of a complete Fabric Interconnect failure, the server will be automatically pinned to any uplink port or port channel on the second Fabric Interconnect provided that the Fabric failover is configured for the vNIC. The Fabric Interconnect will update the northbound switch about this change using the **Gratuitous Address Resolution Protocol** (**GARP**).

The dynamically pinned server vNIC uplinks are automatically rebalanced after 300 seconds to distribute the data traffic load on both Fabric Interconnects.

No user configuration is required for dynamic pinning. If no static pin groups are configured, dynamic pinning will be automatically used. Dynamic pinning is the recommended configuration and static pinning should only be used for business use cases.

# Static pin groups

In static pinning, LAN pin groups are defined by the administrator on Fabric Interconnects using UCSM, which can be assigned to vNICs or vNIC templates. Static pin groups are defined under the **LAN** tab of the UCSM navigation pane.

The steps for creating a static pin group and assigning them to a vNIC are as follows:

1. Log into UCS Manager.
2. Click on the **LAN** tab in the navigation pane.
3. In the **LAN** tab, right-click on **LAN Pin Groups** or click on the + sign on the right-hand side to create a new global LAN pin group:

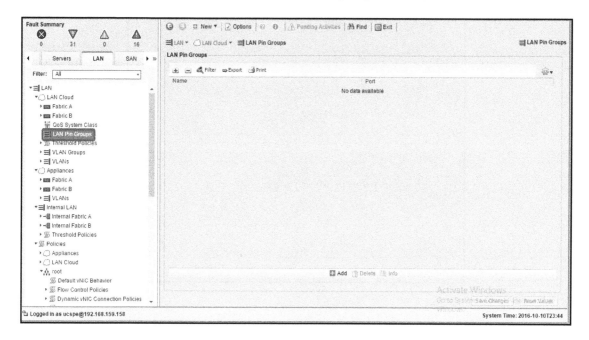

4. In the pop-up window, provide a name for the LAN pin group and bind interfaces (uplink ports or port channels).

5. Click on **OK** to complete the configuration. A pop-up message will remind you to make sure that the selected uplinks are in the same layer 2 network:

# Failure response re-pinning

Each server is statically pinned to a single Fabric Interconnect uplink port or port channel using manual configuration. The administrator will have to make sure the data traffic from the servers is equally distributed among Fabric Interconnects.

In case of a northbound uplink, port channel, or Fabric Interconnect failure where a server is statically pinned to, the server connection will be transferred to other Fabric Interconnects where the server will be dynamically pinned to available uplink ports or port channels, provided the fabric failover is configured for the vNIC.

# Configuring southbound connectivity to IOMs

Each Fabric Interconnect is connected to IOMs in the UCS chassis, which provides connectivity to each blade server. Internal connectivity from blade servers to IOMs is transparently provided by UCS Manager using the **10BASE-KR** Ethernet standard for backplane implementations and there is no configuration required.

Connectivity between Fabric Interconnect server ports and IOMs is required to be configured. Each IOM module, when connected with the Fabric Interconnect server port, behaves as a line card to Fabric Interconnect, hence IOMs should never be cross-connected to the Fabric Interconnect. Each IOM is connected directly to a single Fabric Interconnect using the following cabling configuration:

- **Cisco UCS 2200 IOM**: Possible connections are 1, 2, 4, or 8 depending on the model, because 2204 provides four ports and 2208 provides eight ports

- **Cisco UCS 2300 IOM**: Possible connections are 1, 2, or 4 as there are only four ports

With UCSM 2.0 and UCS 2200 series IOMs, it is possible to create port channels for IOM to FI, connectivity as shown in the following diagram:

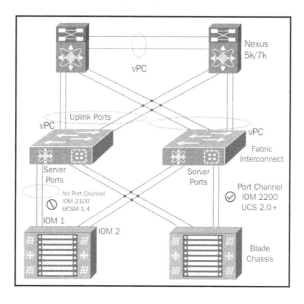

# Learning how to configure Fabric Interconnect server ports

Fabric Interconnect ports that should be connected to southbound IOM cards should be configured as server ports.

The following are the steps to configure the server ports:

1. Log into UCS Manager.
2. Click on the **Equipment** tab in the navigation pane.
3. In the **Equipment** tab, click on a Fabric Interconnect.
4. In the work area pane, select **LAN Uplinks Manager**.
5. Expand **Ports** in the **Fixed Module** or **Expansion Module** (if present).
6. Right-click on a single port or hold the *Ctrl* key and select multiple ports.
7. Select **Configure as Server Port**.
8. A pop-up menu will appear which allows configuring new statuses for the port(s).
9. Select the new port status and click on **Yes**.

Repeat these steps to configure all the server ports for both Fabric Interconnects:

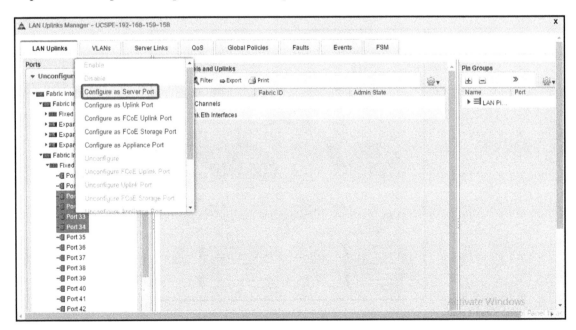

# Configuring IOM ports

First, make sure there is physical connectivity between the Fabric Interconnect and IOM. For the IOM ports configuration, the global chassis discovery policy, discussed in `Chapter 4`, *Configuring Cisco UCS Using UCS Manager*, needs to be configured using the following steps:

1. Log into UCS Manager.
2. Click on the **Equipment** tab in the navigation pane.
3. In the **Equipment** tab, click on **Equipment**.
4. In the work area pane, select **Policies** and select **Global Policies**.
5. Under the **Chassis/FEX Discovery** section, click on the down arrow and select the desired number of IOM links in the **Action** field:

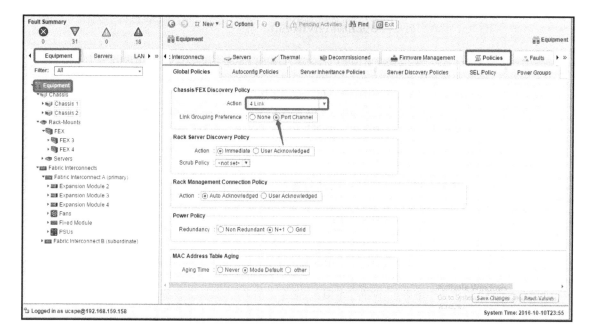

6. For UCS 2200/2300 IOMs, select the **Port Channel** option and all IOM connected server ports will be automatically added to a port channel.
7. Click on **Save Changes**.

# Configuring the last piece of the puzzle - vNICs

Once the connectivity between northbound uplink switches and southbound IOMs is established, we can connect vNICs from blade servers configuring vNICs. It is recommended to create a vNIC template that provides ease of management in the future. A vNIC template can be configured as either of the following:

- **Initiating template**: This vNIC template will provide one-time configuration for the vNICs created using this template. Any subsequent changes to the template are not propagated to abstracted vNICs.
- **Updating template**: This vNIC template will provide initial configuration for the vNICs created using this template. Any subsequent changes to the template will also be propagated to abstracted vNICs. It is recommended to create an updating vNIC template for production environments.

 While updating a template, some changes to the vNIC template setting may trigger an immediate reboot of the associated server depending on the **Maintenance Policies** setting in the **Servers** tab. It is recommended to make **Maintenance Policies** as **User Acknowledge** in order to avoid an immediate reboot of the associated servers.

# What is MAC address abstraction?

vNIC MAC addresses can be assigned manually or by configuring a MAC address pool. It is possible to either use the burned-in MAC addresses or abstract MAC addresses from an identity pool with system-defined prefixes. Stateless computing is the salient feature of the Cisco UCS platform; it is therefore recommended to abstract vNIC MAC addresses for server profiles and hence server vNIC MAC addresses from MAC address identity pools instead of using burned-in NIC MAC addresses.

The main benefit of abstracting the MAC addresses from an identity pool is that in the event of physical server failure, the server profile can be easily associated with the replacement server and the new server will acquire all the identities associated with the old server including the vNIC MAC addresses. From the operating system perspective, there is no change at all.

It is recommended to create vNIC templates with required configurations and create individual vNICs from vNIC templates as per the requirement. Also, define MAC address pools and assign MAC addresses to individual vNICs using MAC address pools.

The following screenshot shows a vNIC template with the MAC address pool server configuration for providing vNIC MAC addresses to server profiles created using a vNIC template:

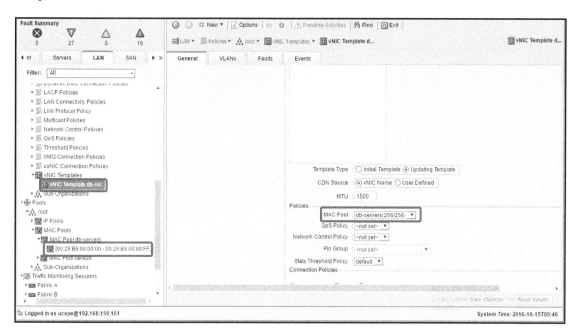

# Learning to create vNICs

A vNIC is abstracted from the physical mezzanine card. Older Emulex, QLogic, and Intel NIC cards have fixed ports. The Cisco mezzanine NIC card, also known as the **Virtual Interface Card** (**VIC**), provides dynamic server interfaces. Cisco VICs provide up to 256 dynamic interfaces.

vNICs can be created directly into server profiles or by using a vNIC template. Using a vNIC template is the recommended method for configuring the NIC settings once for each template and quickly creating vNICs with the desired configuration. The vNIC configuration settings can be optimized for various operating systems, storage devices, and hypervisors.

The vNIC template can be created by performing the following steps:

1. Log into UCS Manager.
2. Click on the **LAN** tab in the navigation pane.
3. In the **LAN** tab, click on **Policies** and expand **vNIC Templates** on the root organization or the sub-organization (if created).
4. Right-click on **vNIC Templates** and select **Create vNIC Template,** as shown in the following screenshot:

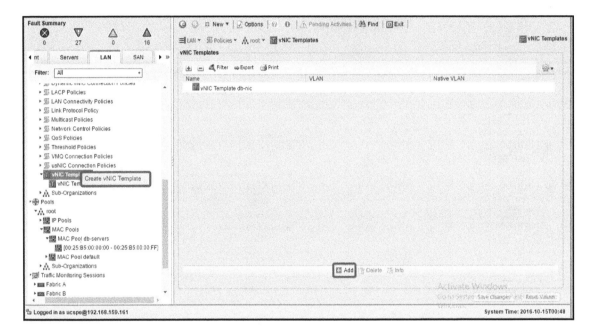

5. A new pop-up window will appear which allows configuring various settings for the vNIC template. These settings are summarized in the following screenshots:

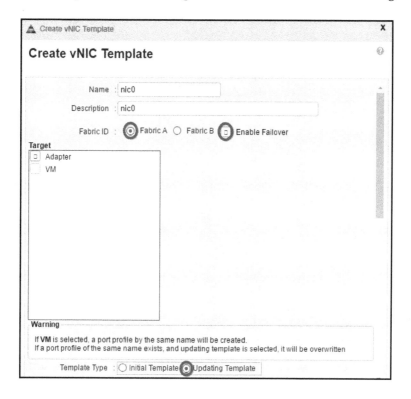

The following screenshot shows the VLANs setting:

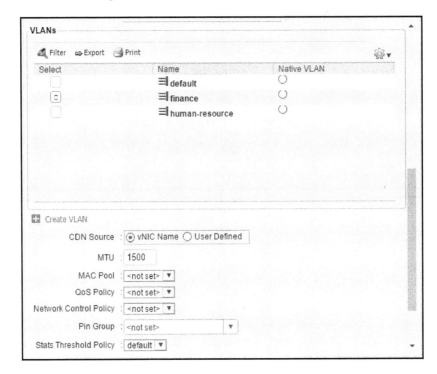

The following screenshot shows the **Connection Policies** settings:

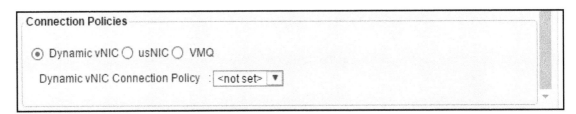

The vNIC configuration options shown in the preceding screenshot are summarized in the following table:

| Option | Description |
|---|---|
| Name | Name for the vNIC template |
| Description | General description about the purpose of the vNIC |
| Fabric ID | Select the Fabric A or B for NIC traffic and choose fabric hardware lever failover |
| Target | Can be a VM template for VN-Link implementation or an adapter template for creating a vNIC for a server profile |
| Template type | Initiating or updating template |
| VLANs | Select a VLAN or initiate creation of a new VLAN |
| CDN Source | Can be a vNIC Name or User Defined CDN Name |
| MTU | Set the Message Transfer Unit size |
| MAC Pool | Select a MAC identity pool |
| QoS Policy | Select a QoS policy |
| Network Control Policy | Select a network control policy |
| Pin Group | Select a static pin group |
| Stats Threshold Policy | Select a statistics threshold policy |
| Dynamic vNIC Connection Policy | Select a dynamic vNIC connection policy |

The vNIC creation for servers is part of the server profile or server profile template creation. Once **Create Service Profile Template** or **Service Profile (Expert)** is started to create a service profile for the blade servers, the vNIC creation is the second step in the configuration wizard. The steps involved in creating a vNIC in the **Service Profile Template** using a vNIC template are as follows:

1. Log into UCS Manager.
2. Click on the **Servers** tab in the navigation pane.
3. In the **Servers** tab, click on **Server Profile Templates** and expand the root organization or the sub-organization (if created).
4. Right-click on **root** and select **Create Service Profile Template**, as shown in the following screenshot:

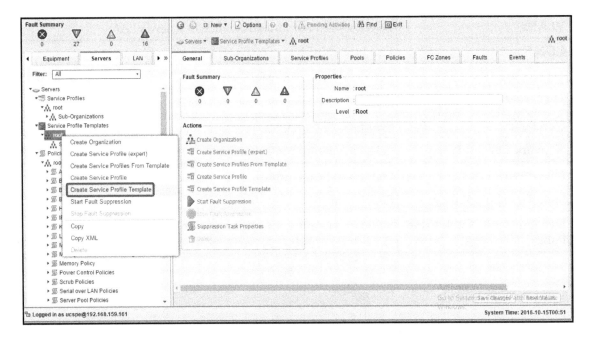

5. In the pop-up window, name the service profile template and click on **Next**.

6. For networking, select the **Expert** option for creation of vNICs and the window display will change:

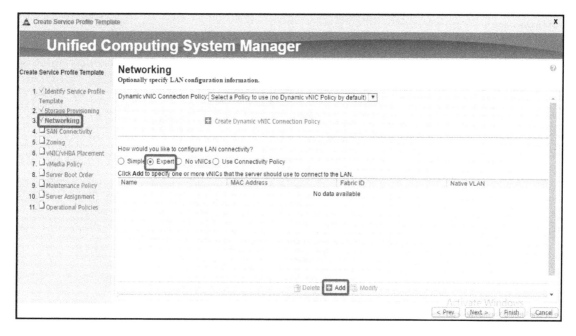

7. Click on **Add** for a new vNIC from the template.

8. In the next window, provide a vNIC name and select the **Use vNIC Template** checkbox. The display will change to select an existing vNIC template.

9.  It is also possible to create a new vNIC template on the same window in which the template configuration window appears.

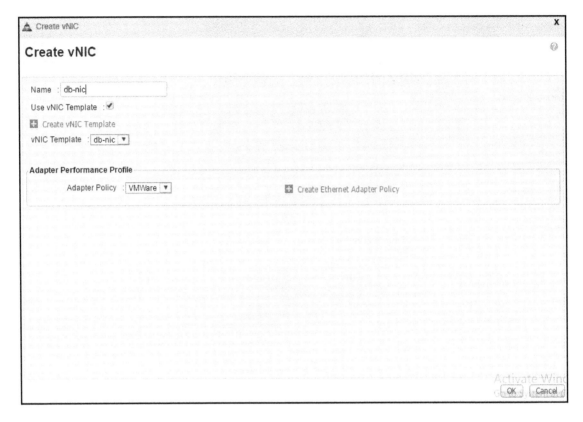

10.  Select **OK** to create the new **vNIC** from the existing template.

# Summary

In this chapter, we learned about the Fabric Interconnect Ethernet features and how to configure those features. We learned about the Fabric Interconnect switching modes, port types, and port states. We looked into the FI uplink ports and upstream Ethernet switch ports configuration including port channels. We looked into VLANs, pin groups, vNIC MAC address abstraction, and configuration of vNICs for the server profile. We also learned that UCS Fabric Interconnects provide some unique features such as EHM switching and pin groups which are not available in the standard Ethernet switches. We looked into the Fabric Interconnect to IOM connectivity and also learned how to configure vNIC templates for the server's vNICs.

Now that we understand the network connectivity, we will learn about the SAN connectivity in the next chapter, in addition to learning about various options including standard Fibre Channel, FCoE, iSCSI, and NAS appliances connectivity.

# 6
# Configuring SAN Connectivity

In this chapter, we'll start looking at the different types of storage supported by UCS and the benefits of each. We'll provide an overview of **Fibre Channel** (**FC**), **Fibre Channel over Ethernet** (**FCoE**), and iSCSI. We will look into how UCS integrates with the FC fabric and configuring zoning on the Fabric Interconnects We'll walk through connecting SAN ports and configuring service profiles for single initiator and single target zoning for the SAN. We will also look into SAN pinning, which is similar in concept to LAN pinning, and explain the failure behavior for dynamic and static SAN pinning.

The topics that will be covered in this chapter are as follows:

- Learning about storage connectivity options
- Overview of FC and iSCSI storage
- Storage connectivity design considerations
- FC switching mode
- FC port channel and trunking
- Configuring VSAN and zoning
- Configuring FCoE

# Learning about storage connectivity options

Storage access is a crucial configuration for UCS solutions providing raw storage for both virtualized and non-virtualized servers. Most UCS deployments run virtualized environments where virtual workloads leverage many advanced features of centralized storage accessible through FC, FCoE, and iSCSI protocols. Most UCS blade servers provide very limited direct-attached internal storage space sufficient for installing hypervisors locally and leveraging centralized storage for all virtual servers.

Raw storage is available in three different categories. We will now briefly introduce these main raw storage categories:

- **Direct-attached storage** (**DAS**): This is the storage available inside a server and is directly connected to the system through the motherboard. The cost and performance of this storage depends upon the disks and RAID controller cards inside the servers. DAS is less expensive and is simple to configure; however, it lacks the scalability, performance, and advanced features provided by high-end storage.
- **Network-attached storage** (**NAS**): This storage is usually an appliance providing filesystem access. This storage could be as simple as an NFS or CIFS share available to the servers. Typical NAS devices are cost-effective devices without very high performance but with very high capacity with some redundancy for reliability. NAS is usually moderately expensive, simple to configure, and provides some advanced features; however, it also lacks scalability, performance, and advanced features provided by SAN.
- **Storage area network** (**SAN**): This storage provides remote raw block-level storage to the connected servers. This type of storage provides maximum reliability, expandability, and performance. The cost of SAN is also very high compared to the other two storage options. SAN is the most resilient, highly scalable, and high performance storage; however, it is also the most expensive and complex to manage.

FC and iSCSI are the two main protocols for SAN connectivity. FC has its own standards and protocols provided by IEEE whereas iSCSI runs on top of standard Ethernet protocols. Both FC and iSCSI encapsulate **Small Computer System Interface** (**SCSI**) protocol commands.

iSCSI storage can be connected either with Fabric Interconnect or through network switches to provide enterprise storage capacity to compute servers. UCS Servers can access the iSCSI storage similar through both software and hardware based iSCSI initiator that can be easily created through service profiles on Cisco VICs.

Alternative options for massive storage requirement can be fulfilled by connecting recently launched Cisco UCS S3260 dual node storage servers to Fabric Interconnect as discussed in the first chapter. Each server is capable of providing 600 TB data storage and can be expanded upto 3 PB with multiple servers connected to it. The S3260 can be best fit for the scale-out storage requirements of any enterprise.

# Overview of FC and iSCSI storage

Both FC and iSCSI are used to encapsulate SCSI protocol commands for storage. We will briefly discuss SCSI first.

## Overview of SCSI

SCSI (pronounced as *scuzzy*) is an industry standard protocol for attaching various I/O peripherals such as printers, scanners, tape drives, and storage devices. The most common SCSI devices are disks and tape libraries.

SCSI has evolved from parallel, daisy-chained SCSI to **serially attached SCSI (SAS)**. Older parallel SCSI specifications are defined as Ultra-1, Ultra-2, Ultra-3, Ultra-320, and Ultra-640, whereas the new SAS specifications are defined as SAS 1.0, 2.0, and 3.0. These specifications differ in speed and other performance enhancements. SCSI hard disks are superior in terms of performance and reliability as compared with ATA (PATA and SATA) drives. SCSI drives are commonly used in enterprise-grade SANs because of their reliability and speed.

In the SAN world, SCSI is the core protocol to connect raw hard disk storage with the servers. In order to control remote storage with the SCSI protocol, different technologies are used as wrappers to encapsulate these commands. These primarily include FC and iSCSI. In the following sections, we'll briefly review these technologies.

## Overview of Fibre Channel

The SCSI protocol was initially used inside computers to connect hard disks at a higher speed. Later, SANs were built where storage was separated from the computers and consolidated. The FC protocol provided the infrastructure to encapsulate the SCSI traffic and provided connectivity between computers and storage. FC operates at speeds of 2, 4, 8, and 16 Gbps.

FC consists of the following:

- **Hard disk arrays**: They provide raw storage capacity
- **Storage processors**: They manage hard disks and provide storage LUNs and masking for the servers
- **FC switches** (also known as **fabric**): They provide connectivity between storage processors and server HBAs
- **FC host bus adapters**: They are installed in the computer and provide connectivity to the SAN

FC identifies infrastructure components with **World Wide Numbers** (**WWNs**). WWNs are 64-bit addresses, which uniquely identify the FC devices. Like MAC addresses, they have bits assigned to vendors to identify their devices. Each end device (such as an HBA port) is given a **World Wide Port Number** (**WWPN** or **pWWN**) and each connectivity device (such as a fabric switch or multiport HBA) is given a **World Wide Node Number** (**WWNN**).

An FC HBA, used for connecting to a SAN, is known as an **initiator**, and an FC SAN, providing disks as LUNs, is known as a **target**.

The FC protocol stack is different from Ethernet or TCP/IP protocols. Hence, it has its own learning curve for professionals with a networking and systems administration background.

# Overview of iSCSI

The **Internet Small Computer System Interface** (**iSCSI**) is SCSI over IP that sends SCSI commands using the TCP/IP protocol suite. This means that the SCSI commands are encapsulated on top of IP, which commonly runs on Ethernet. FC SANs typically have a very high cost because the FC equipment is specialized. In comparison, iSCSI provides a cost-effective alternative to FCs because of the low cost of Ethernet equipment; also, the abundance of Ethernet experts, as compared to FC, keeps the administration costs low. Earlier iSCSI was subject to lower performance due to the noisy nature of TCP/IP, causing higher protocol overload. Over the years, iSCSI performance and efficiency has improved. In fact, with the latest 10 Gbps implementation and future 40 Gbps/100 Gbps implementation with **Data Center Bridging** (**DCB**), it is now a serious competitor to FC.

iSCSI consists of the following:

- **Hard disk arrays**: They provide raw storage capacity.
- **Storage processors**: They manage hard disks and provide storage LUNs and masking for the servers.
- **Ethernet switches**: They provide connectivity between storage processors and server HBAs.
- **iSCSI host bus adapters**: They are installed in a computer and provide connectivity to the SAN. Most operating systems provide software implementation of iSCSI in order to utilize the regular Ethernet NICs, eliminating the need for hardware iSCSI HBAs.

# Overview of Fibre Channel over Ethernet (FCoE)

Ethernet is widely used in networking. With some advancement such as DCB and **Priority Flow Control** (**PFC**) in Ethernet to make it more reliable for the data center, FC is now also implemented on top of Ethernet. This implementation is known as FCoE.

In FCoE, fabric switches can be replaced with standard Ethernet switches, which are more cost effective. Also, the future development road map for Ethernet provides much higher speeds (40 Gbps and 100 Gbps) as compared to a native FC. There is rapid adoption of FCoE in the market and chances are that FCoE will completely replace the native FC implementation in the future.

# Storage connectivity design considerations

UCS storage physical connectivity has a slightly different design consideration as compared to LAN physical connectivity.

The following are some design considerations for SAN connectivity:

- Northbound storage physical connectivity does not support vPCs like LAN connectivity, where you can have cross-connected vPCs for redundancy.
- Depending on the storage type, port channeling or trunking is possible to combine multiple storage uplink ports that provide physical link redundancy.
- Redundancy of storage resources is handled by the storage itself and varies from vendor to vendor including active-active, active-passive, **Asymmetric Logical Unit Assignment** (**ALUA**), and vendor specific implantations such as EMC PowerPath.
- Storage can be connected through northbound Cisco Nexus, MDS or third-party fabric switches. This is the recommended configuration for better scalability and performance.
- It is possible to connect storage directly to UCS Fabric Interconnects, which is recommended for small implementations because of FI's physical ports consumption and increased processing requirements. Prior to UCSM Version 2.1, it was necessary to have a northbound Nexus or MDS switch to provide zoning configuration.
- Software configuration including VSANs and zoning is required for providing access to storage resources.

The following diagram provides an overview of storage connectivity. In the following sections, we will go through various storage configurations:

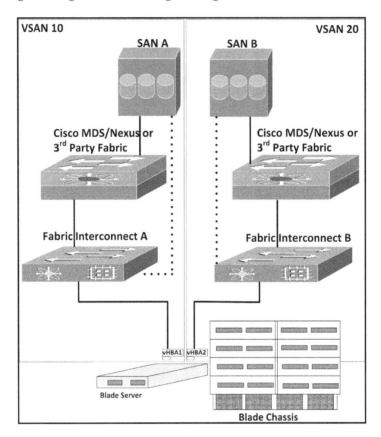

# Learning about the FC switching mode

Similar to LAN connectivity, UCS Fabric Interconnects support two types of switching modes: FC EHM and the FC switching mode. The default switching mode is an end-host mode where UCS appears as a number of hosts attached to the upstream switch. This is also known as **N-Port Virtualization** (**NPV**) and requires an NPIV-capable fabric switch for providing the fiber login services.

The other option available is the native FC switching mode where UCS Fabric Interconnect appears as a native FC fabric switch. Switching between FC modes is a disruptive process and hence should be arranged in a scheduled maintenance window.

In order to configure or verify the end-host mode for the Fabric Interconnects, perform the following steps:

1. Log into UCS Manager.
2. Click on the **Equipment** tab in the navigation pane.
3. In the **Equipment** tab, click on **Fabric Interconnect A** (as shown in the following screenshot).
4. The **Status** area in the work pane shows the current **FC Mode** configuration, which is **End Host**.
5. In the **Actions** area of the work pane, the currently configured **FC Mode**, which in this case is **End Host**, will be shown grayed:

A Fabric Interconnect reboot is required in order to change the FC mode from **End Host** to **Switch** and vice versa.

In order to change the **FC Mode** from **End Host** to **Switch**, perform the following steps:

1. Log into UCS Manager.
2. Click on the **Equipment** tab in the navigation pane.
3. In the **Equipment** tab, click on **Fabric Interconnect A** (as shown in the following screenshot).

4. In the **Actions** area of the work pane, the currently configured **FC Mode**, which in this case is **End Host**, will be shown grayed and cannot be selected.

5. Click on **Set FC Switching Mode** in the **Actions** area of the work pane.

6. Click on **Yes** on the pop-up warning message to restart the Fabric Interconnect:

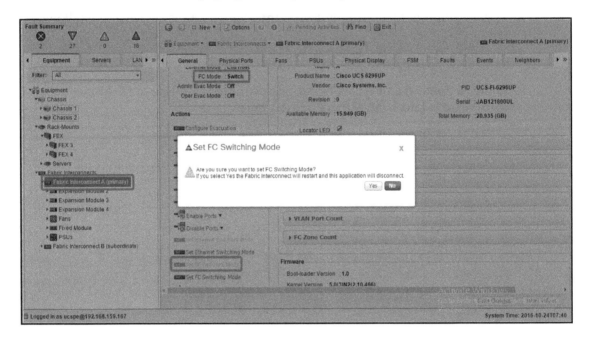

# Configuring the FC ports

By default, all the ports are configured as unified ports until gen 2 but FI 6332-16UP model in gen 3 has first 16 unified ports and FC ports require additional one-time disruptive configuration on both Fabric Interconnects. Fabric Interconnect provides unified port configuration manager that can change the Ethernet port mode to the FC port. You need to plan ahead on the total number of FC ports required for your application, otherwise changing the port mode will require a reboot of Fabric Interconnect in the future. Perform the following steps to configure the FC port for gen 2 FI where gen 3 FI required slider configuration from right to left side for first 16 unified ports with FI 6332-16UP model:

1. Log into UCS Manager.
2. Click on the **Equipment** tab in the navigation pane.
3. In the **Equipment** tab, click on **Fabric Interconnect A**.
4. In the **Actions** area of the work pane, click on **Configure Unified Ports**.
5. Click on **Yes** on the pop-up warning message to restart the Fabric Interconnect.

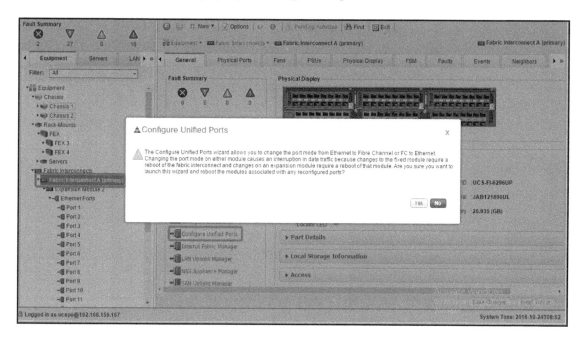

6. **Configure Fixed Module Ports** by dragging the slider (following the Fabric Interconnect screenshot) from the right side to left side depending upon the number of FC ports required.

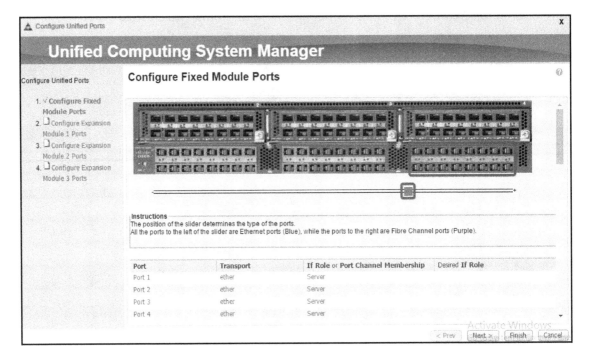

7. Click on the **Next** option to configure the remaining expansion modules if they are available on the Fabric Interconnect.
8. Click on **Finish** to restart the Fabric Interconnect.
9. Click on **Yes** on the pop-up warning message to restart the Fabric Interconnect:

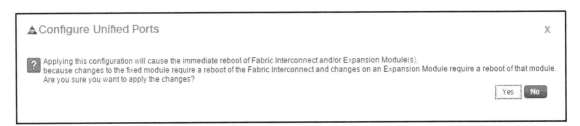

10. Repeat the aforementioned steps for the secondary Fabric Interconnect.

# Configuring the FC uplink port

By default, all FC ports on Fabric Interconnect ports are unconfigured. For FC uplink connectivity, the ports need to be configured as uplink ports in **FC Ports** for each Fabric Interconnect and need to be configured with the correct VSAN (VSANs will be discussed in next section).

To define, change or check the state of a port, expanding the **Fabric Interconnect** inventory from the **Equipment** tab in the navigation pane, perform the following steps:

1. Log into UCS Manager.
2. Click on the **Equipment** tab in the navigation pane.
3. In the **Equipment** tab click on a Fabric Interconnect and expand **FC Ports**.
4. Select one of the FC ports, and its current configuration will be displayed in the right-side working pane.
5. Select the right **VSAN** from the drop-down menu for **VSAN**, under **Properties** in the right-side working pane.

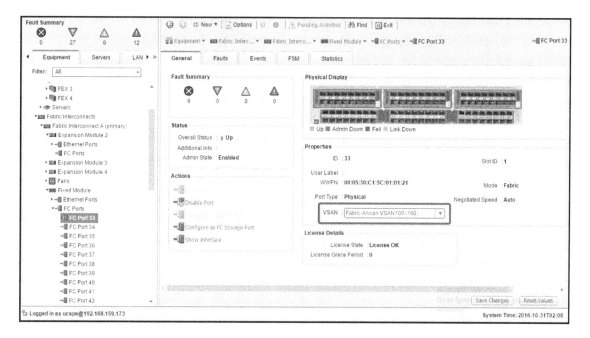

6. Ports can be enabled or disabled from the menu as well.
7. Repeat the same step for the secondary Fabric Interconnect.

# Configuring the FC port channel and trunking

Similar to an Ethernet port channel, a FC port channel or trunk can be created to aggregate multiple physical FC links into a single logical link to provide higher throughput and redundancy. A maximum of 16 uplink ports can be aggregated in a port channel.

Perform the following steps to configure the FC port channel:

1. Log into UCS Manager.
2. Click on the **SAN** tab in the navigation pane.
3. In the **SAN** tab, expand **SAN** and then **SAN Cloud**.
4. Right-click on FC Port Channel and click on **Create Port Channel** as shown in the screenshot.

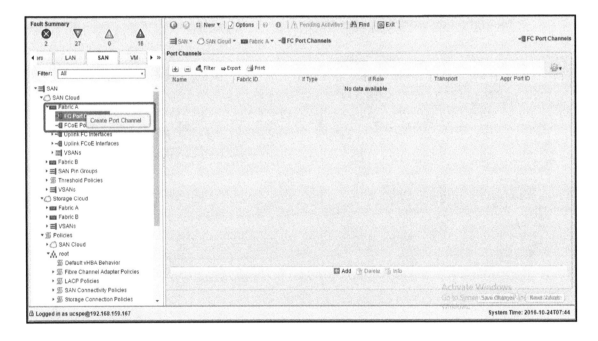

5. In the pop-up window, set the port channel ID and **Name** as shown in the screenshot:

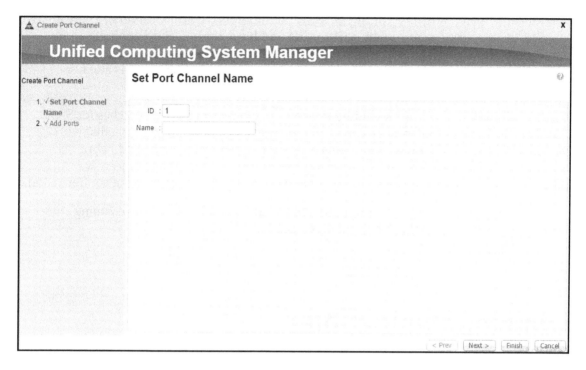

6. Click on **Next**.
7. On the next screen, drag the appropriate ports to the port channel and click on **Add Ports**.
8. Repeat the steps for both VSANs.

# Configuring VSANs and zoning

Storage connectivity not only requires the configuration of connectivity protocols such as FC, FCoE, and iSCSI, but in the case of FC and FCoE SAN connectivity, it is also required to configure zoning to allow access to servers/hypervisors to the SAN LUNs. When using Cisco switches for SAN connectivity, it is also recommended to configure VSANs along with proper zoning. We will now look into zoning and VSANs.

# Learning about zoning

**Zoning** is a conventional SAN security mechanism, which is used to restrict storage access between anticipated targets (typically SANs) and initiators (typically servers). There are two main methods to configure zoning: **soft zoning** and **hard zoning**. Hard zoning is more secure compared to soft zoning and is the preferred zoning method. SAN fabric switches from various vendors might support different zoning configurations, so it is always recommended to consult your SAN admin for proper zoning configuration.

In the previous UCS versions including version 2.0, while using Cisco switches for SAN connectivity, zoning needed to be configured on the northbound MDS or Nexus (with native FC ports) switches which propagates down to the directly connected Fabric Interconnects. So, even though SAN direct connectivity to Fabric Interconnects was possible, northbound MDS or Nexus switches were necessary for the zoning configuration..

 Prior to the UCS 2.1 upgrade, it was not possible to configure zoning directly on the Fabric Interconnects.

# Learning about VSANs

A **VSAN** is a Cisco proprietary security mechanism, which can be compared to VLANs for the networks. VSANs can further increase security for storage and servers by allowing only the physical member ports of storage and servers to physically access each other. As with VLANs, if a port on the same fabric switch is not part of a VSAN, it will not have access to SAN.

There are number of ways that SAN could be connected with UCS servers, which include the following:

- **Cisco FC MDS switches**: MDS switches are Cisco FC SAN connectivity switches. These switches deal with the SAN protocols and are recommended in large-scale environments requiring a dedicated SAN infrastructure.
- **FC module expansion or unified ports in Cisco Nexus switches**: Cisco Nexus 5000 series switches provide FC module expansion to provide FC ports with SAN connectivity. The newer 5500/5600 series switches have unified ports like the Fabric Interconnects, which can be configured as Ethernet, FC, or FCoE. These switches are recommended for medium to large-scale infrastructures.

- **Direct with Fabric Interconnects**: The Fabric Interconnect provides unified ports, which can be configured as Ethernet, FC, or FCoE, and hence storage can be directly attached with the Fabric Interconnects. This is recommended for a small-scale deployment.
- **Third-party fabric switches**: Fabric switches from other vendors, such as Brocade, can also be used to connect storage to Cisco UCS.

# Example configuration - connecting SAN directly to Fabric Interconnects

In our example, we will connect the SAN directly with Fabric Interconnects with zoning configured on FIs. With UCS Version 2.1, it is now possible to configure zoning directly on the Fabric Interconnects using different SAN policies. In our example, we will configure VSANs and zoning directly on the Fabric Interconnects to attach SAN using the FCoE protocol.

The following diagram shows the physical connectivity between the chassis, Fabric Interconnects, and SAN:

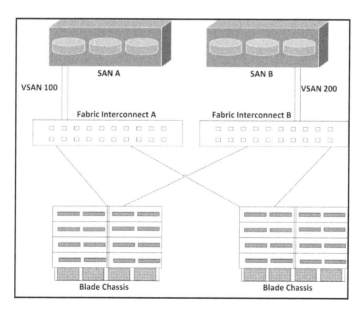

In order to configure VSANs for Fabric Interconnects, perform the following steps:

1. Log into UCS Manager.
2. Click on the **SAN** tab in the navigation pane.
3. In the **SAN** tab, expand **SAN** and then **SAN Cloud**.
4. Right-click on **VSANs** and click on **Create VSAN**.

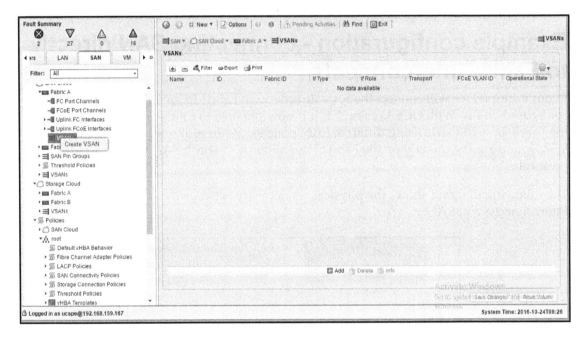

5. In the pop-up window, assign a name to the VSAN.
6. For the **FC Zoning** section, click on the **Enabled** radio button.
7. Attach a zone to **Fabric Interconnect A** or **Fabric Interconnect B**. Unlike common VLAN configuration, VSANs should be should be different for Fabric Interconnect A and B.

8. Assign a **VSAN ID** and its corresponding VLAN ID. The VLAN ID does not need to be the same number as VSAN ID; however, it is a good practice to keep it so. Also, a VLAN ID used for VSAN mapping cannot overlap with that of an Ethernet VLAN.

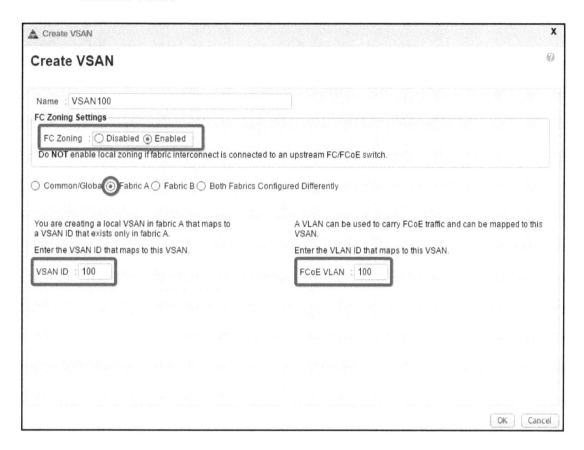

Once VSANs will be created in both Fabric Interconnect, it should be visible as shown in the screenshot.

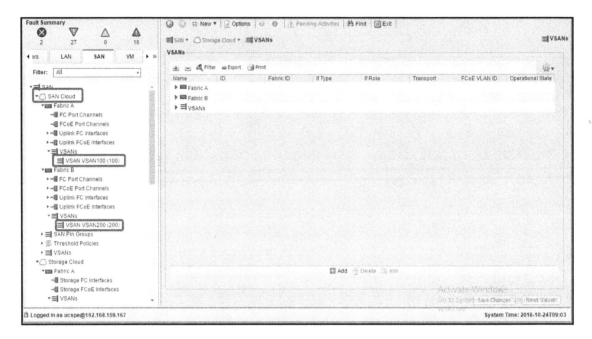

Create the required VSANs and configure ports for VSAN membership. In our example, we created two VSANs for connecting to two separate SAN processes.

Once the physical connectivity is established, the following will configure the zoning for the servers and SAN:

- **Storage connection policies**: These configure the storage connectivity including the WWPN target numbers for the SAN
- **SAN connectivity policies configuration**: This configures vHBAs for the servers and will provide WWPN initiator numbers for them

First, we will configure the storage connection policy by performing the following steps:

1. Log into UCS Manager.
2. Click on the **SAN** tab in the navigation pane.
3. In the **SAN** tab, expand **SAN** and then expand **Policies**.
4. Right-click on **Storage Connection Policies** and click on **Create Storage Connection Policy**.

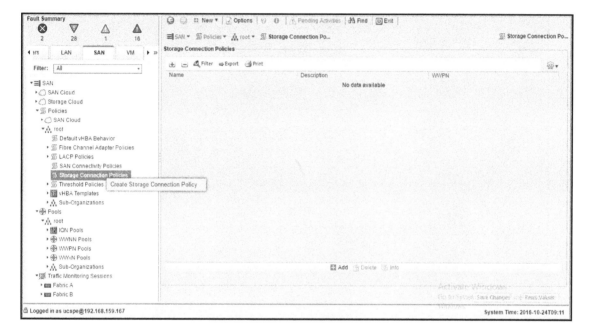

5. In the pop-up window, assign a name to the storage connection policy.
6. Select **Zoning Type**. The recommended and most secure zoning option is the **Single Initiator Single Target**. Consult your storage documentation for zoning recommendations.

7. Click on the + sign to define **FC Target Endpoints**. This is the WWPNs of the SAN and this information will be available from the SAN storage processors.

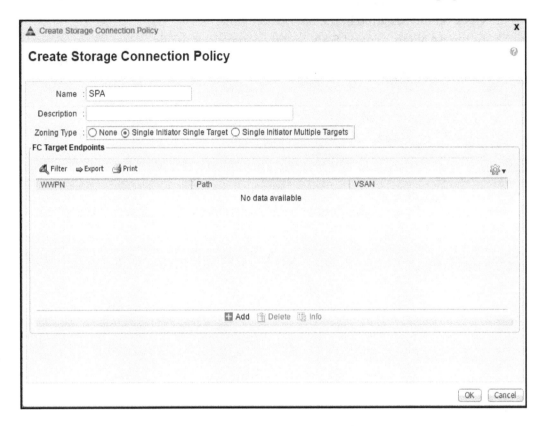

8. On the next screen, manually type the WWPN of the SAN storage processors.
9. Select the Fabric Interconnect **A** or **B** and select a VSAN membership for the storage processors. Click on **OK**:

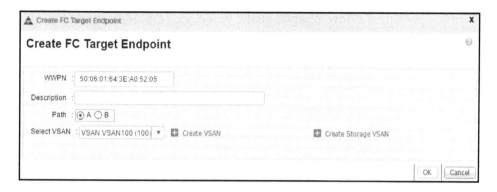

10. Repeat the steps for the second storage processor for the other Fabric Interconnect and VSAN.

Now we will configure the SAN connectivity policy by performing the following steps:

1. Log into UCS Manager.
2. Click on the **SAN** tab in the navigation pane.
3. In the **SAN** tab, expand **SAN** and then expand **Policies**.
4. Right-click on **SAN Connectivity Policies** and click on **Create SAN Connectivity Policy**.

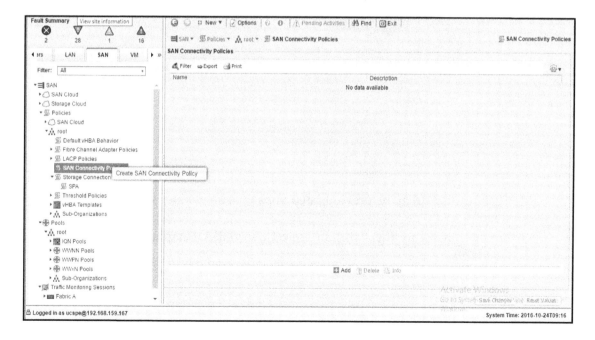

5. In the pop-up window, assign a name to the SAN connectivity policy.
6. Select a predefined WWNN pool for the servers or create a new pool by clicking on the + sign close to **Create WWNN Pool**.
7. Click on **Add** to create vHBAs for the servers. vHBAs can be created in a number of different methods. However, as with vNICs, the recommended method is to create vHBA templates and then use those templates for creating the vHBAs.

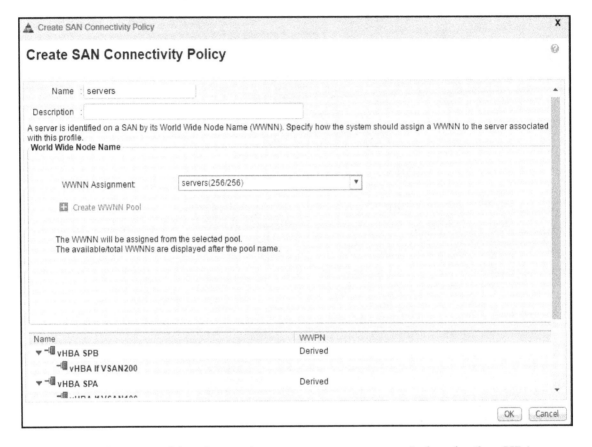

8. Clicking on **Add** in the previous step pops up a new window for the vHBA creation.
9. Provide a name for the vHBA and select **Use vHBA Template** for the creation of the vHBA.

10. Select the required vHBA template and an appropriate **Adapter Performance Profile** for the creation of the vHBAs:

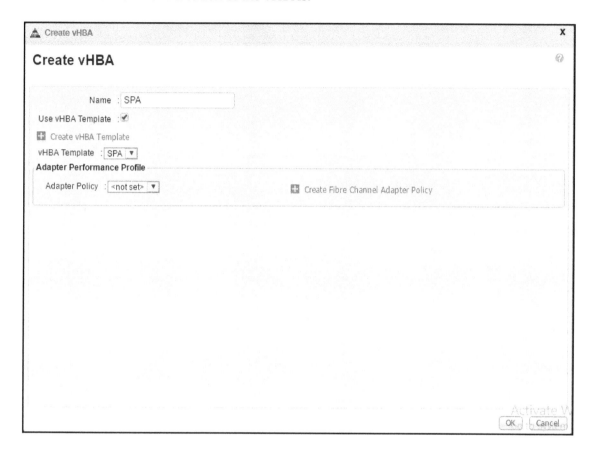

11. New vHBAs will appear in the policy. When this policy is applied during a service profile creation, the vHBAs are automatically created with all configurations for the server:

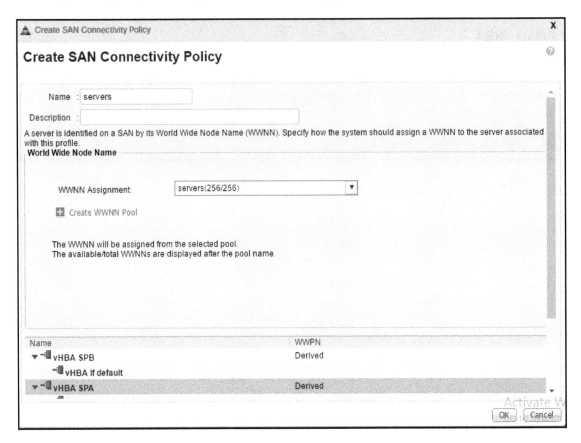

12. Once the SAN connectivity policy is configured, expand it in the navigation pane. In the work pane, click on the **vHBA Initiator Groups** tab and create vHBA initiators for both the vHBAs by clicking on the + sign on the right-hand side of the work pane.

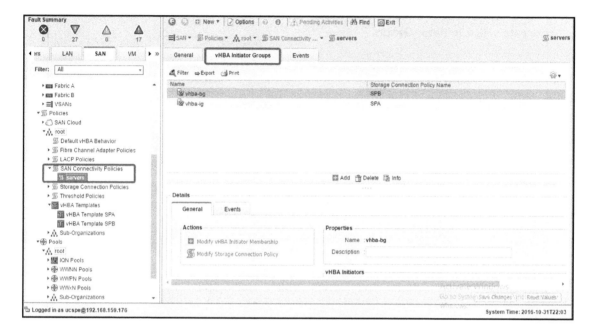

13. In the new window, type a name and a short description for the **vHBA Initiator Group**, and select a **Storage Connection Policy**. Repeat the steps for the other vHBA initiator groups:

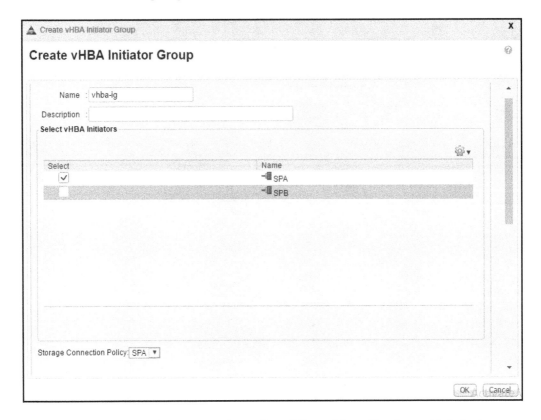

14. New vHBAs will appear in the policy. When this policy is applied during a service profile creation, the vHBAs are automatically created with all configurations for the server.

Zoning is automatically configured for the server vHBAs during the service profile creation using the SAN connectivity policy and storage connection policy. The policies could be applied directly to a service profile or to a service profile template (the procedure for both is the same).

In order to create vHBAs during the service profile or a service profile template creation, perform the following steps:

1. Log into UCS Manager.
2. Click on the **Servers** tab in the navigation pane and click on **Create Service Profile (expert)** or **Create Service Profile Template**.
3. In the third step, where vHBAs for the storage are created, select **Use Connectivity Policy** and click on **Next**:

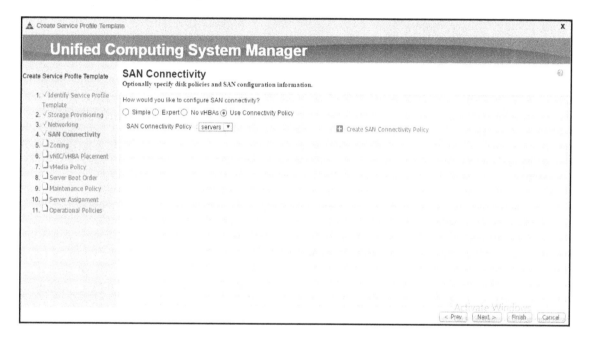

4. This will create the vHBAs for the new server:

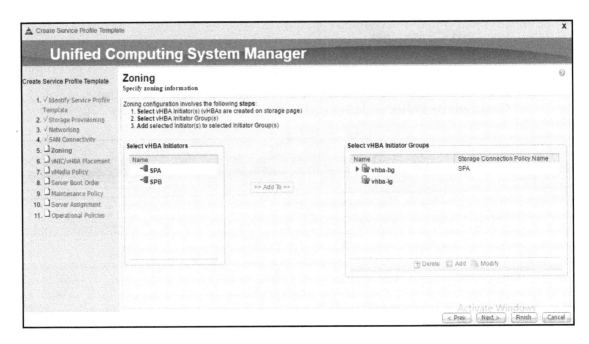

5. Create vHBA initiator groups for both vHBAs.

6. Assign a name to the **vHBA Initiator Group**.

7. Assign the previously created storage connection policy. This will associate the FC target endpoint (storage processor WWPN) and VSAN to the vHBA initiator group.

8. Repeat the same steps for the second vHBA initiator group for the second storage processor and VSAN connectivity.

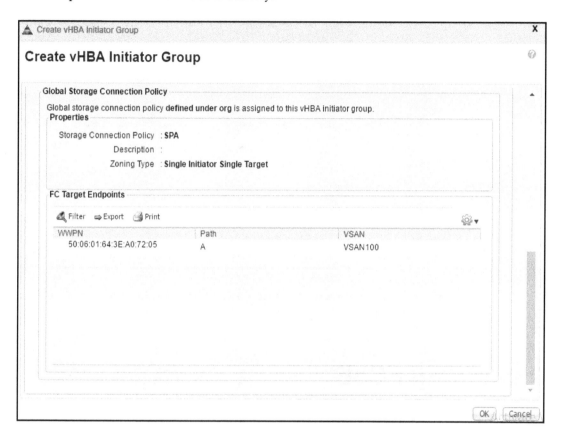

Once the service profile creation is complete, the zoning configuration can be verified by performing the following steps:

1. On the **Servers** tab in the navigation pane, select **FC Zones** from the work pane.

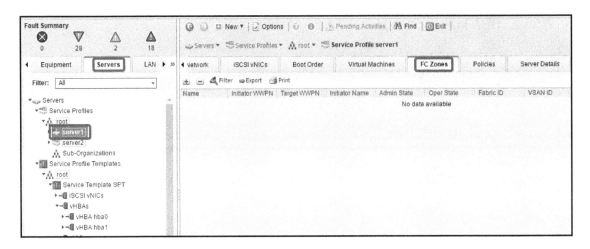

2. Click on the + sign to expand the information which will provide an initiator to target zone mapping:

# Configuring FCoE

FCoE traffic requires dedicated Ethernet VLANs. FCoE VLANs are dedicated during the VSAN configuration. Starting with UCS 2.0 and later, the FCoE VLAN must not conflict with Ethernet VLANs. UCS 2.1 provides FCoE northbound from FI whereas the previous version of FCoE was only possible up to FI where it should be decoded into native FC.

Configuring FCoE involves selecting the Fabric Interconnect unified ports as FCoE ports. To do this, perform the following steps:

1. Log into UCS Manager.
2. Click on the **Equipment** tab in the navigation pane.
3. Expand **Fabric Interconnect** and right-click on any unconfigured unified port and select **Configure as FCoE Uplink Port** or **Configure as FCoE Storage Port**:

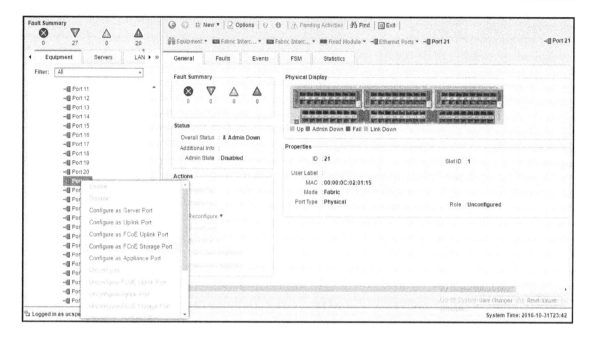

# Manual and automatic uplink pinning

Using the end-host mode (EHM), each server is pinned automatically to an uplink port based on *round-robin algorithm*. Like the Ethernet end-host mode, pin groups can be configured as a static pin group or dynamic pin group. The default configuration is a dynamic pin group.

# Dynamic pin groups

This is the default pin group setting. In dynamic pinning, the Fabric Interconnect automatically binds server vHBAs to uplink Fabric Interconnect FC/FCoE ports.

# Failure response

In case of an uplink failure, server vHBAs are re-pinned to the remaining uplinks of the same Fabric Interconnect. In case of a complete Fabric Interconnect failure, the operating system (Windows, Linux, or hypervisors) relies on its multipath drives (such as MPIO and EMC PowerPath) to re-route I/O for the failed path. If the operating system configuration is missing, FC communication will fail until one FC uplink is restored on the failed Fabric Interconnect.

This behavior is different from the Ethernet automatic re-pinning and is in accordance with the design goals of SAN connectivity.

# Static pin groups

In static pinning, SAN pin groups are defined by the administrator on Fabric Interconnects using UCSM, which can be assigned to vHBAs or vHBA templates. Static pin groups are defined under the **SAN** tab of the UCSM navigation pane. In case of static pinning, if the uplink goes down, automatic re-pinning will not occur.

The steps for creating a static pin group and assigning to a vHBA are as follows:

1. Log into UCS Manager.
2. Click on the **SAN** tab in the navigation pane.
3. In the **SAN** tab, right-click on **SAN Pin Groups** or click on the + sign on the right-hand side to create a new global SAN pin group:

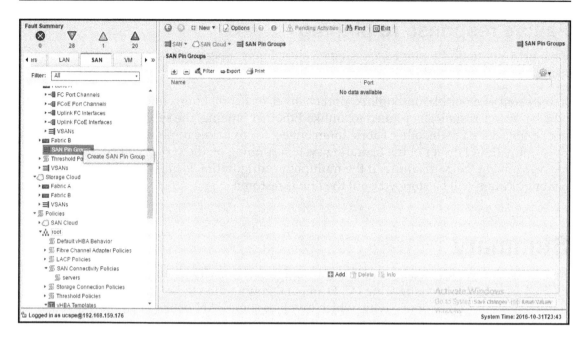

4. In the pop-up window, provide a name for the SAN pin group and bind the interfaces (uplink ports or port channels) to each Fabric Interconnect.

5. Click on **OK** to complete the configuration. A pop-up message will appear to make sure that the selected uplinks are in the same layer 2 network:

## Failure response re-pinning

Each vHBA is statically pinned to a single Fabric Interconnect uplink port or port channel using manual configuration.

In the event of a northbound uplink, port channel, or Fabric Interconnect complete failure to which a server is statically pinned to, unlike Ethernet pinning, the server connection will not be transferred to the other Fabric Interconnect for dynamic re-pinning, and as discussed, the multipath I/O driver of the operating system running on the server will be responsible for recognizing the path failure. If the multipath configuration is missing in the OS, communication will be stopped until the link is restored.

# Summary

In this chapter, we learned about different storage connectivity protocols, including FC and iSCSI. We looked into configuring FC, FCoE, and zoning directly on the Fabric Interconnect's storage connectivity, which involves some SAN policies configuration. iSCSI is SCSI over IP, and requires vNICs and Ethernet for connectivity but no special configuration is required other than what was explained in Chapter 5, *Configuring LAN Connectivity*. Finally, we looked into SAN pin groups which have the same concepts as LAN pin groups, but have a slightly different failure behavior.

In the next chapter, we will look into identity and resource pools, which provide resources such as UUIDs, MAC addresses, WWNN, and WWPN for the service profiles for the servers

# 7
# Creating Identity Resource Pools, Policies, and Templates

Computers and their various peripherals have some unique identities, such as **universally unique identifiers** (**UUIDs**), **media access control** (**MAC**) addresses of **network interface cards** (**NICs**), **World Wide Node Numbers** (**WWNNs**), and **Word Wide Port Numbers** (**WWPNs**) for **host bus adapters** (**HBAs**). These identities are used to uniquely identify a computer system in a network. For traditional computers and peripherals, these identities were burned into the hardware and, hence, couldn't be altered easily. Operating systems and some applications rely on these identities and may fail if these identities are changed. In the event of a full computer system failure or the failure of a computer peripheral with a unique identity, administrators have to follow cumbersome firmware upgrade procedures to replicate the identities of the failed components on the replacement components.

The **Unified Computing System** (**UCS**) platform introduced the idea of creating identity and resource pools to abstract the compute node identities from **UCS Manager** (**UCSM**) instead of using the hardware's burned-in identities. In this chapter, we'll discuss the different pools you can create during UCS deployment and server provisioning. We'll start by looking at what pools are and then discuss the different types of pools, and learn how to configure each of them.

The list of topics that will be covered in the chapter is as follows:

- Understanding identity and resource pools
- Learning to create a UUID pool
- Learning to create a MAC pool
- Learning to create a WWNN pool
- Learning to create a WWPN pool
- Creating IP pools

- Understanding the server pool
- Learning to create server pool membership and qualification policies

# Understanding identity and resource pools

The salient feature of the Cisco UCS platform is stateless computing. In the Cisco UCS platform, none of the computer peripherals consume the hardware's burned-in identities. Rather, all the unique characteristics are extracted from identity and resource pools, which reside on the **Fabric Interconnects** (**FIs**) and are managed using UCSM. These resource and identity pools are defined in an XML format, which makes them extremely portable and easily modifiable. UCS computers and peripherals extract these identities from UCSM in the form of a service profile. A service profile has all the server identities, including UUIDs, MACs, WWNNs/WWPNs, firmware versions, BIOS settings, and other server settings. A service profile is associated with the physical server using a customized Linux OS that assigns all the settings in a service profile to the physical server. In case of server failure, if the failed server needs to be removed and the replacement server has to be associated with the existing service profile of the failed server. In this service profile association process, the new server will automatically pick up all the identities of the failed server and the operating system or applications dependent upon these identities will not observe any change in the hardware. In case of peripheral failure, the replacement peripheral will automatically acquire the identities of the failed component. This greatly improves the time required to recover a system in case of a failure.

Using service profiles with the identity and resource pools also greatly improves the server provisioning effort. A service profile with all the settings can be prepared in advance while an administrator is waiting for the delivery of the physical server. The administrator can create service profile templates that can be used to create hundreds of service profiles; these profiles can be associated with the physical servers with the same hardware specifications. Creating a server template is highly recommended as it greatly reduces the time required for server provisioning. This is because a template can be created once and used for any number of physical servers with the same hardware.

Server identity and resource pools are created using UCSM. In order to better organize, it is possible to define as many pools as needed in each category. Keep in mind that each defined resource will consume space in the UCSM database. It is, therefore, best practice to create identity and resource pool ranges based on the current and near-future assessments.

For larger deployments, it is best practice to define a hierarchy of resources in the UCSM based on geographical, departmental, or other criteria; for example, a hierarchy can be defined based on different departments. This hierarchy is defined as an organization, and the resource pools can be created for each organizational unit. In the UCSM, the main organization unit is root, and further sub-organizations can be defined under this organization. The only consideration to be kept in mind is that pools defined under one organizational unit can't be migrated to other organizational units unless they are deleted first and then created again where required.

The following diagram shows how identity and resource pools provide unique features to a stateless blade server and components such as the mezzanine card:

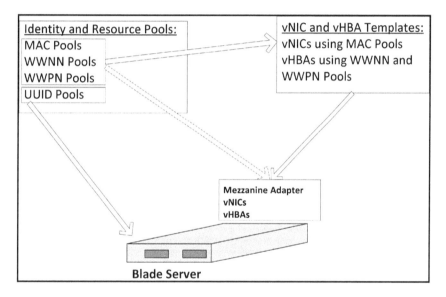

# Learning to create a UUID pool

A UUID is a 128-bit number assigned to every compute node on a network to identify the compute node globally. The UUID is denoted as 32 hexadecimal numbers. In the Cisco UCSM, a server UUID can be generated using the UUID suffix pool. The UCSM software generates a unique prefix to ensure that the generated compute node UUID is unique.

Operating systems including hypervisors and some applications may leverage UUID number binding. The UUIDs generated with a resource pool are portable. In case of a catastrophic failure of the compute node, the pooled UUID assigned through a service profile can be easily transferred to a replacement compute node without going through complex firmware upgrades.

The following are the steps to create UUIDs for blade servers:

1. Log in to UCSM.
2. Click on the **Servers** tab in the navigation pane.
3. Click on the **Pools** tab and expand **root**.
4. Right-click on **UUID Suffix Pools**, and click on **Create UUID Suffix Pool**, as shown in the following screenshot:

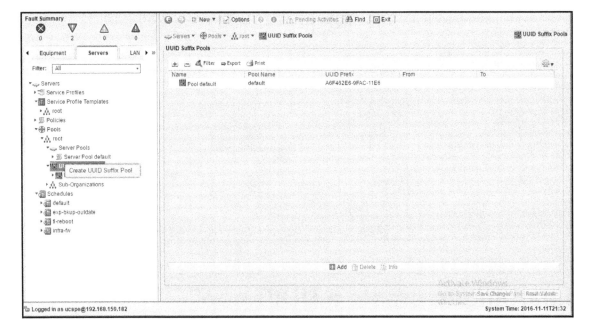

5. In the pop-up window, assign the **Name** and **Description** values to the UUID pool.
6. Leave the **Prefix** value as **Derived** to make sure that UCSM makes the prefix unique.

7. The selection of **Assignment Order** as **Default** is random. Select **Sequential** to assign the UUID sequentially.

8. Click on **Next**, as shown here:

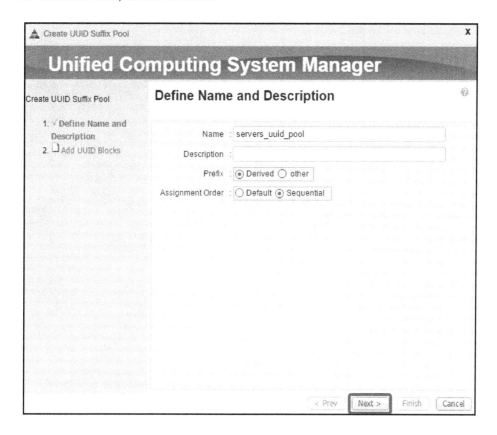

9. Click on **Add** on the next screen.

10. In the pop-up window, change the value for **Size** to create a desired number of UUIDs.

11. Click on **OK** and then on **Finish**, as shown here:

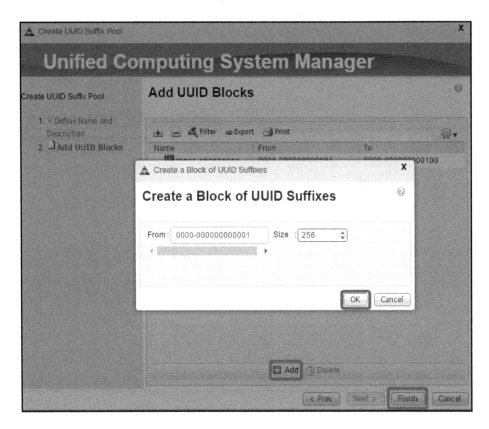

12. In order to verify the UUID suffix pool, click on the **UUID Suffix Pools** tab in the navigation pane and then on the **UUID Suffixes** tab in the work pane:

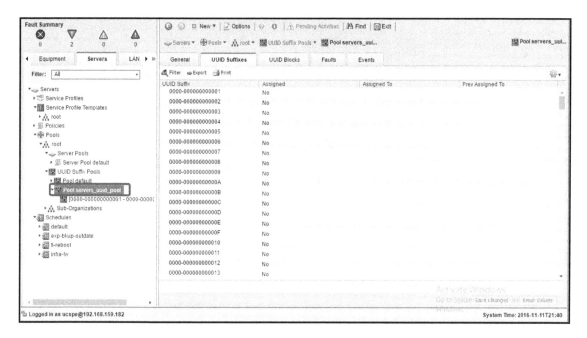

# Learning to create a MAC pool

A MAC is a 48-bit address assigned to the network interface for communication in the physical network. MAC address pools make server provisioning easier by providing scalable NIC configurations before the actual deployment.

The following are the steps to create MAC pools:

1. Log in to the UCSM.
2. Click on the **LAN** tab in the navigation pane.
3. Click on the **Pools** tab and expand **root**.

4. Right-click on **MAC Pools**, and click on **Create MAC Pool**, as shown in the following screenshot:

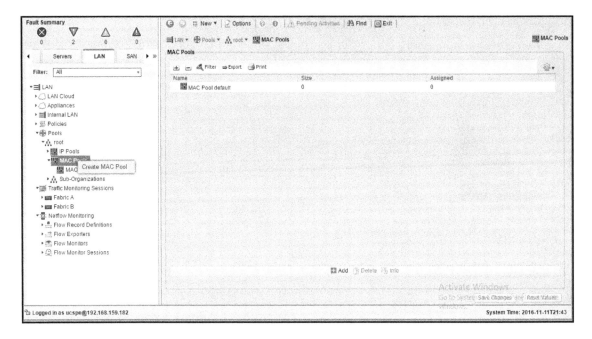

5. The selection of **Default** as the **Assignment Order** value is random. Select **Sequential** to assign the MAC addresses sequentially.

6. Click on **Next**:

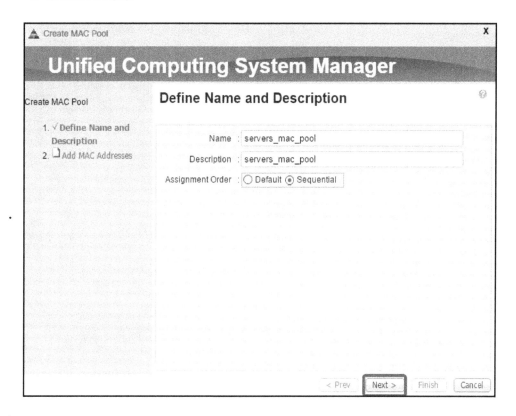

7. Click on **Add** on the next screen.
8. In the pop-up window, change **Size** to create the desired number of MAC addresses.

9. Click on **OK** and then on **Finish**, as shown here:

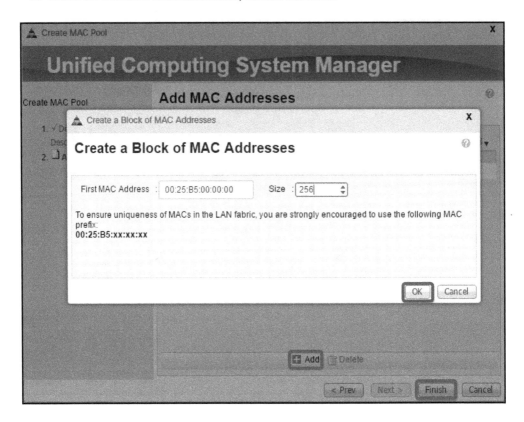

10. In order to verify the MAC pool, click on the **MAC Pools** tab in the navigation pane and then on the **MAC Addresses** tab in the work pane, as shown here:

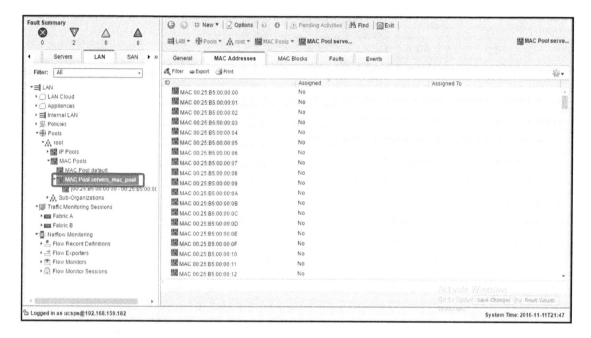

# Learning to create a WWNN pool

A WWNN is a 64-bit address assigned to **Fibre Channel** (**FC**) devices. In UCS, WWNN is assigned to the mezzanine card installed in a blade server because a mezzanine card can have more than one port (vHBA). Each port (vHBA) created from the mezzanine card acquires a unique WWPN. WWPNs are described in the next section.

These are the steps to create WWNN address pools:

1. Log in to the UCSM screen.
2. Click on the **SAN** tab in the navigation pane.
3. Click on the **Pools** tab and expand **root**.

4. Right-click on **WWNN Pools**, and click on **Create WWNN Pool**, as shown in the following screenshot:

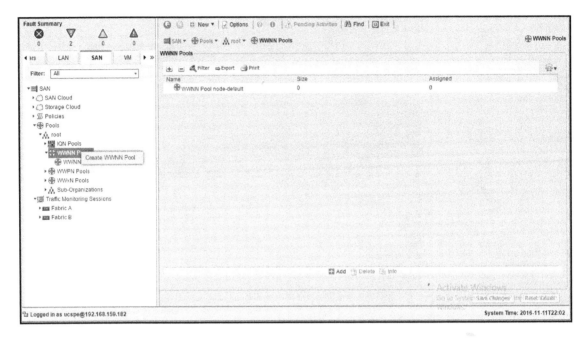

5. In the pop-up window, assign the **Name** and **Description** values to the WWNN pool.
6. The selection of **Default** as the **Assignment Order** value is random. Select **Sequential** to assign the WWNNs sequentially.

7. Click on **Next**:

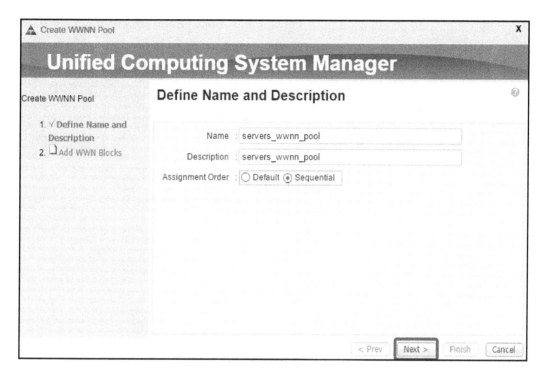

8. Click on **Add** on the next screen.
9. In the pop-up window, change **Size** to create the desired number of WWNN addresses.

10. Click on **OK** and then on **Finish**, as shown here:

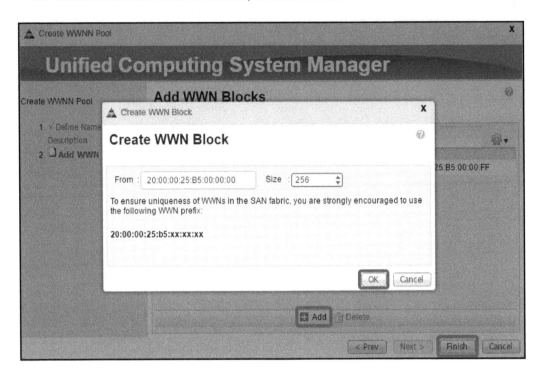

11. In order to verify the WWNN pool, click on the **WWNN Pools** tab in the navigation pane and then on the **Initiators** tab in the work pane, as shown here:

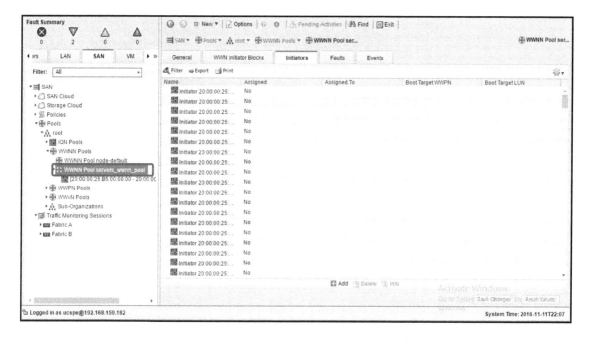

# Learning to create a WWPN pool

Similar in format to WWNNs, a WWPN is a 64-bit address assigned to individual vHBAs in servers. The WWNN for the vHBAs in a blade server is always identical, whereas the WWPN is always unique. Storage zoning is done using the WWPN addresses.

The following are the steps to create WWNN address pools:

1. Log in to the UCSM screen.
2. Click on the **SAN** tab in the navigation pane.
3. Click on the **Pools** tab and expand **root**.

4. Right-click on **WWPN Pools**, and click on **Create WWPN Pool**, as shown in the following screenshot:

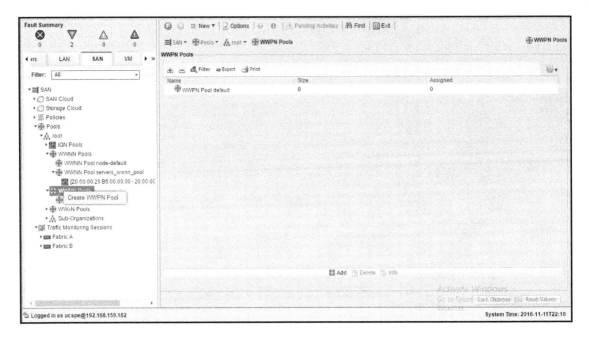

5. In the pop-up window, assign the **Name** and **Description** values to the WWPN pool.
6. The selection of **Default** as the **Assignment Order** value is random. Select **Sequential** to assign WWPNs sequentially.

7. Click on **Next**:

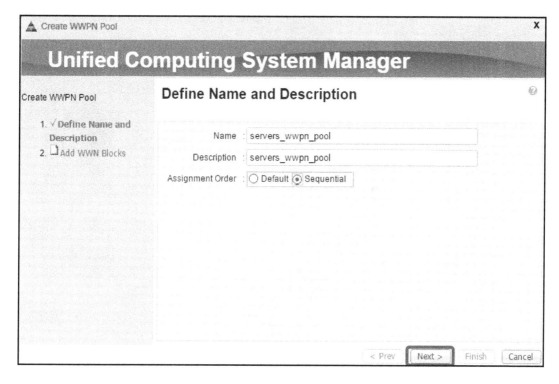

8. Click on **Add** on the next screen.
9. In the pop-up window, change **Size** to create the desired number of WWPN addresses.

10. Click on **OK** and then on **Finish**, as shown here:

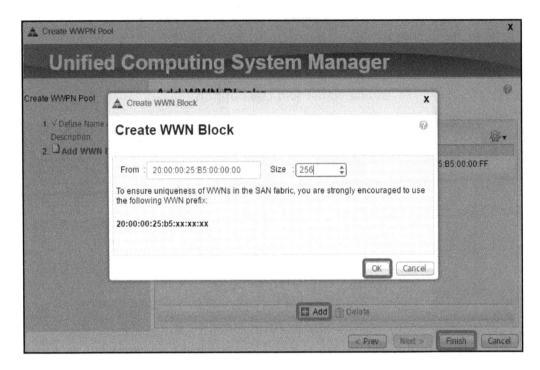

11. In order to verify the WWPN pool, click on the **WWPN Pools** tab in the navigation pane, and click on the **Initiators** tab in the work pane as shown here:

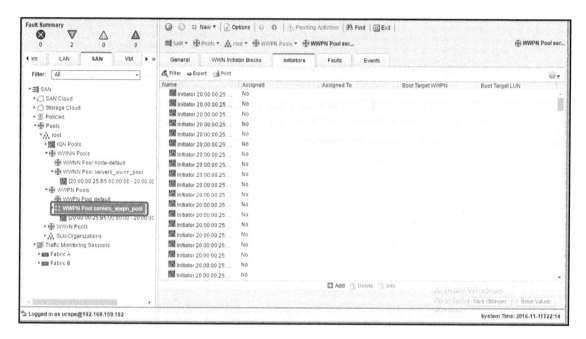

To ensure the uniqueness of WWNN and WWPN pools, only use WWN numbers from 20:00:00:00:00:00:00:00 to 20:FF:FF:FF:FF:FF:FF:FF or from 50:00:00:00:00:00:00:00 to 5F:FF:FF:FF:FF:FF:FF:FF. To ensure the uniqueness of the Cisco UCS WWNNs and WWPNs in the SAN fabric, it is recommended you use the prefix in a pool as 20:00:00:25:B5:XX:XX:XX.

# Learning to create IP pools

IP Pools are the logical IP address that can be assigned to blade servers. There are two kind of IP pools in UCSM.

- **ext-mgmt** pool
- **iscsi-initiator** pool

An **ext-mgmt** pool is collection of IP addresses that are assigned as management interface to blade server. This IP address provide KVM console to manage the server remotely while **iscsi-initiator** pool provide the IP address for accessing the iSCSI storage

The following are the steps to create **ext-mgmt** pool:

1. Log in to the UCSM.
2. Click on the **LAN** tab in the navigation pane.
3. Click on the **Pools** tab and expand **root**.
4. Click on the **IP Pools** tab and expand it.
5. Right-click on **IP Pool ext-mgmt**, and click on **Create Block of IPv4 Addresses**, as shown in the following screenshot:

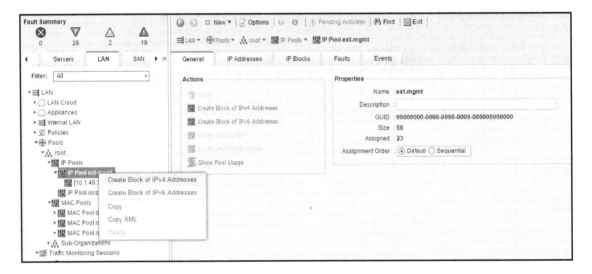

6. Enter the management IP address information in **From** along with range in **Size**, **Subnet Mask** and **Default Gateway** details as shown in the screenshot.
7. Click on **Ok.**

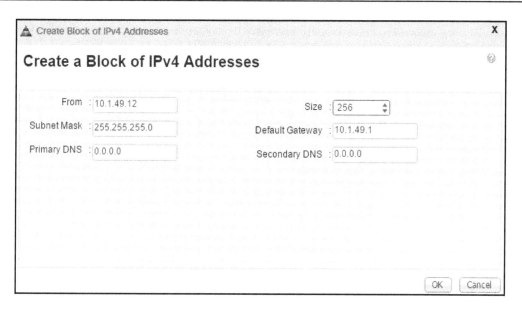

# Making your identity pools meaningful

Although not a requirement, it is beneficial to implement some naming hierarchy when creating MAC, WWNN, and WWPN identity pool addresses. This naming hierarchy could be very helpful in troubleshooting scenarios such as network traces and SAN zoning. We will use an example of a MAC pool to implement a simple naming hierarchy. Using these guidelines, you can create the naming hierarchy for any pool.

Cisco MAC pools have the 00:25:B5:XX:XX:XX format, where 00:25:B5 is the Cisco organizational identifier. Now, we have the other six hexadecimal numbers to implement the naming convention with.

In our example, we will use the following convention. You can always come up with other suitable guidelines according to your environment:

- Use one hexadecimal number to represent your site or location
- Use one hexadecimal number to represent the cabinet where the chassis is located
- Use one hexadecimal number to represent the primary FI
- Use one hexadecimal number to represent the server operating system

In the following example, we can easily identify the server, which is located at the primary site in cabinet **1**, the chassis number (**Ch**) as **3**, and the operating system running on the server as **Windows**:

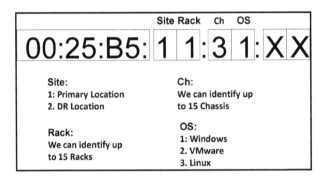

# Understanding server pools

Server pools are used to organize servers based on specific criteria, such as CPU family, amount of RAM, type of mezzanine card, and power. Each server is associated with a unique service profile to receive all the settings. A server pool can be associated with a service profile. UCSM automatically selects an available server in the server pool and associates it with a service profile.

Server pools can be manually populated, or they can be autopopulated using server pool policies. Server pools make the servers available for association with service profiles. It is possible to have a server in more than one server pool at the same time.

In order to create and manually populate the server pool, carry out the following steps:

1. Log in to the UCSM screen.
2. Click on the **Servers** tab in the navigation pane.
3. Click on the **Pools** tab and expand **root**.

4. Right-click on **Server Pools**, and click on **Create Server Pool**, as shown in the following screenshot:

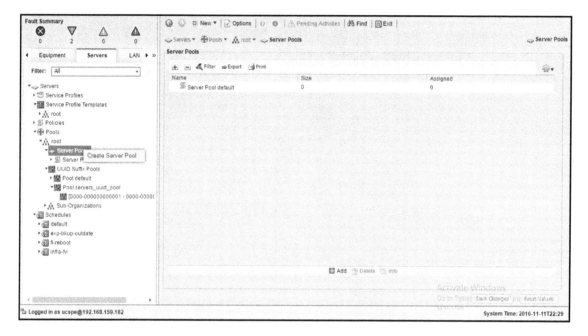

5. In the pop-up window, assign the **Name** and **Description** values to the server pool.

6. Click on **Next**:

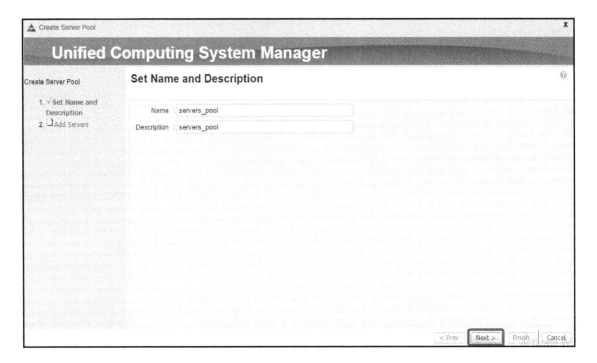

7. Add servers to the pool by selecting the servers provided on the left-hand side and adding them to the list of **Pooled Servers** on the right-hand side.

8. Click on **Finish** after adding servers to the pool:

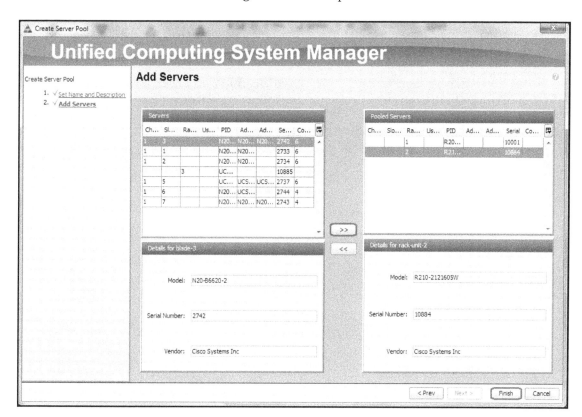

# Learning to create server pool membership and qualification policies

Server pools can be automatically populated with servers that match the specifications based on the defined policy settings using **Server Pool Policy Qualifications** and by applying these qualification policies using **Server Pool Policies** under the **Servers** tab in the navigation pane.

First, we will discuss how to create server qualification policies using the options available in the **Server Pool Policy Qualifications** policy.

The steps to create this policy are as follows:

1. Log in to the UCSM screen.
2. Click on the **Servers** tab in the navigation pane.
3. Click on the **Policies** tab and expand **root**.
4. Right-click on **Server Pool Policy Qualifications**, and click on **Create Server Pool Policy Qualification**, as shown in the following screenshot:

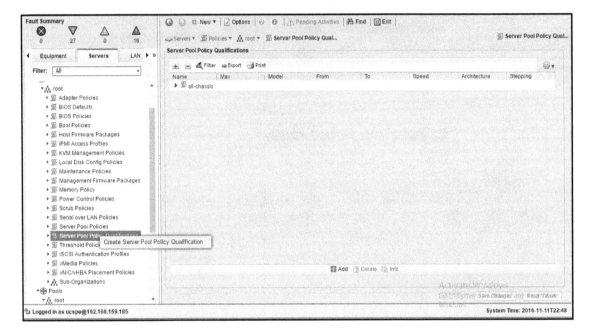

5. In the pop-up window, assign the **Name** and **Description** values to the server pool policy qualifications.
6. In the left-hand pane, click on the options to define the new server pool policy qualifications, as shown in the following screenshot:

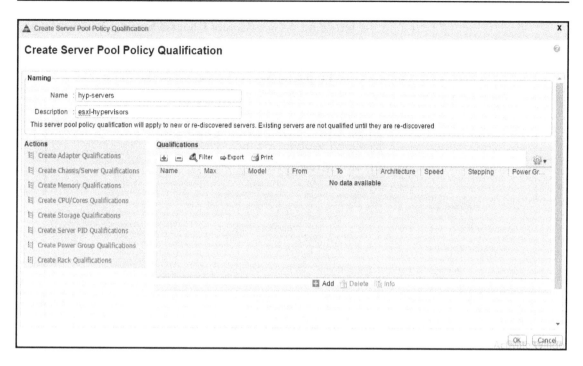

7. The first option in the left-hand pane is **Create Adapter Qualifications**. This setting defines the type of adapter a qualifying server must have. Select the **Type** of the adapter from the drop-down list. It is also possible to select a unique adapter based on the **process identifier** (**PID**) and capacity, which could be from 1 to 65535, as shown in the following screenshot:

8. The second option in the left-hand pane is **Create Chassis/Server Qualifications**. This setting defines the list to select the servers from the chassis. Select the values for **First Chassis ID** and **Number of Chassis**, which is the total number of chassis to be included, starting with **First Chassis ID** as shown in the following screenshot:

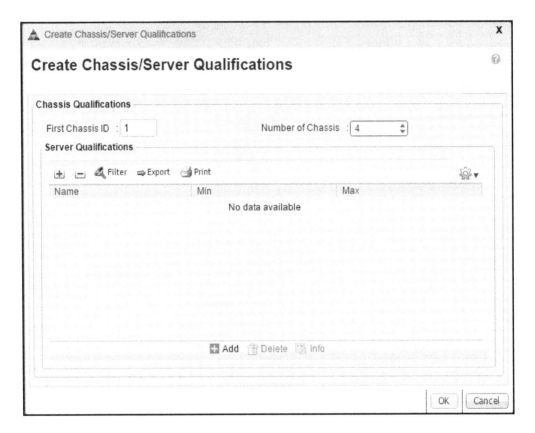

9. Click on the **Add** sign to select the server slots in each qualified chassis.
10. Select the values for **First Slot ID** and **Number of Slots**, which is the total number of server slots to be included, starting with **First Slot ID**.
11. Click on **OK**, as shown in the following screenshot:

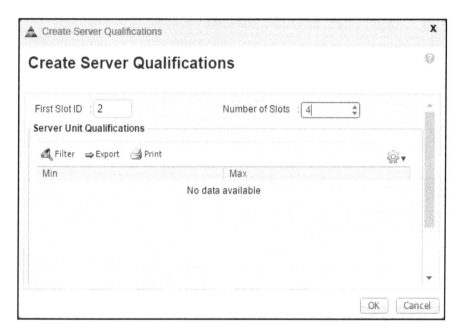

12. The minimum and maximum slot ID will be automatically populated in the previous screen.

13. Click on **OK** to complete the policy creation, as shown in the following screenshot:

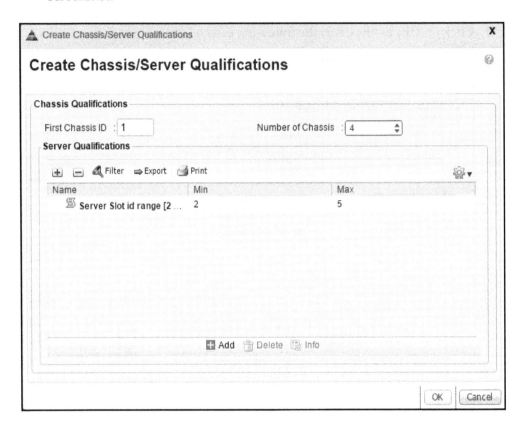

14. The third option is **Create Memory Qualifications**. This option defines the
    memory characteristics of the servers for qualification. The options include clock
    speed **Clock (MHz)**, **Latency (ns)**, minimum and maximum memory size **Min
    Cap (MB)** and **Max Cap (MB)**, data bus **Width**, and data bus width measurement
    **Units**, as shown in the following screenshot:

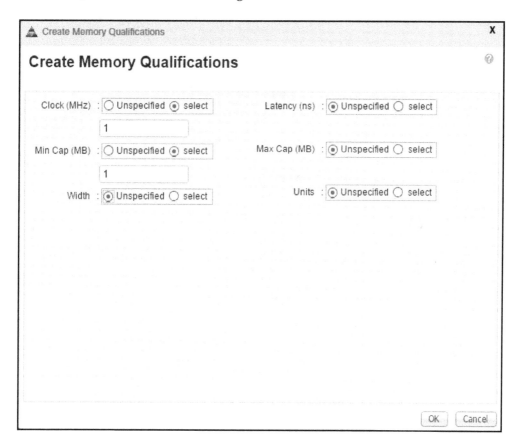

15. The fourth option is **Create CPU/Cores Qualifications**. This option defines the CPU characteristics of the servers for qualification. The options include **Processor Architecture, PID (RegEx), Min Number of Cores, Max Number of Cores, Min Number of Threads, Max Number of Threads, CPU speed (MHz)**, and **CPU Stepping**, as shown in the following screenshot:

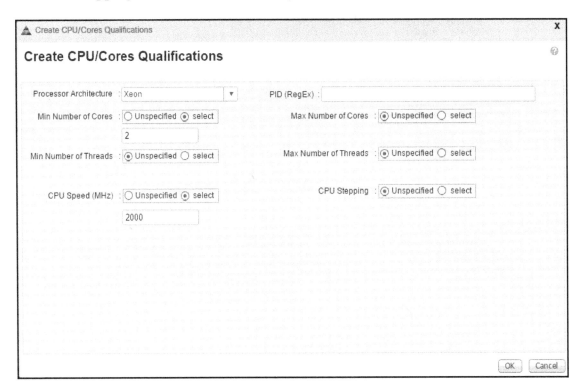

16. The fifth option is **Create Storage Qualifications**. This option defines the storage features of the qualifying servers. The options include the **Diskless** disk status, the **Number of Blocks** value in the disk, **Block Size** (bytes), minimum/maximum storage capacity across all disks **Min Cap (MB)** and **Max Cap (MB)**, minimum storage capacity per disk **Per Disk Cap (MB)**, and number of **Units**, as shown in the following screenshot:

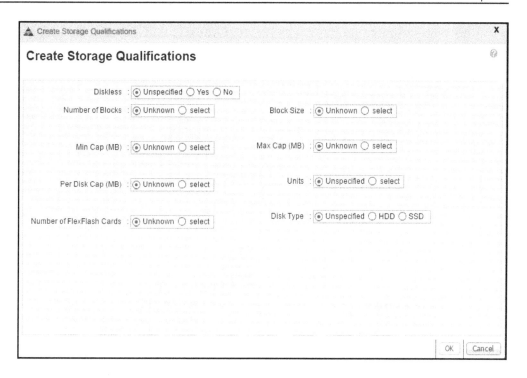

17. The sixth option is **Create Server PID Qualifications**. This is a regular expression string that the server PID must match in order to qualify, as shown in the following screenshot:

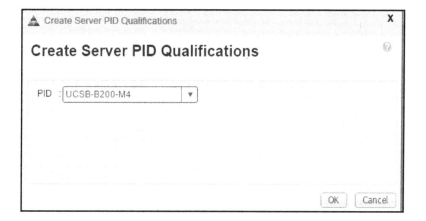

18. The seventh option is **Create Power Group Qualifications**. This policy could match a server based on the server **Power Group** value, as shown in the following screenshot:

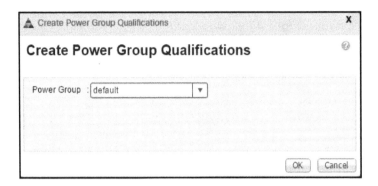

19. The last option is **Create Rack Qualifications**. This option is only applicable if there are some rack-mount servers managed by the UCSM. The **First Slot ID** value is the first server to be included, and the **Number of Slots** value defines the total number of servers to be included starting from the **First Slot ID**, as shown in the following screenshot:

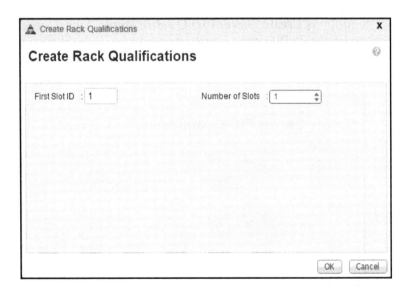

Once we have defined the desired **Server Pool Policy Qualification** policies, we can use the **Server Pool Policies** tab to associate qualifying servers to be automatically added to an already created empty server pool.

In the following example, we will create a CPU qualification policy and assign it to a server pool:

1. Log in to the UCSM screen.
2. Click on the **Servers** tab in the navigation pane.
3. Click on the **Policies** tab and expand **root**.
4. Right-click on **Server Pool Policy Qualifications**, and then click on the **Server Pool Policy Qualifications** option.
5. In the pop-up window, assign the **Name** and **Description** values to the **Server Pool Policy Qualifications** policy.
6. In the left-hand navigation pane, click on the **Create CPU/Core Qualifications** policy to define the CPU features for the qualifying servers. We created a CPU qualification policy, as shown in the following screenshot:

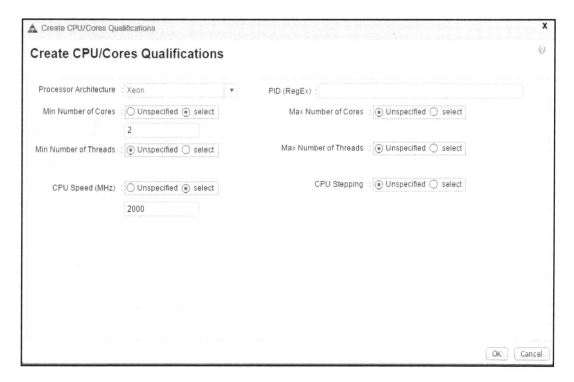

7. Click on **OK** to finish the creation of the **Server Pool Policy Qualifications**.

8. Right-click on **Server Pool Policies** in the navigation pane, and click on **Create Server Pool Policy**.

9. In the pop-up window, assign the **Name** and **Description** values to it. Select the **Target Pool** value from the drop-down menu, which is already defined, and the **Qualification** policy already created in step 6 (in this case, **CPU**), as shown in the following screenshot:

# Summary

In this chapter, we learned about creating different identity and resource pool options available with the UCS platform. We learned that by leveraging identity and resource pools, the UCS platform makes server deployments highly scalable, flexible, and portable. Well-organized resource and identity pools in UCS not only provide security and role-based access for larger organizations based on geographical, departmental, or any other criteria, but are also the basic building blocks for contemporary multi-tenancy cloud-service environments.

So far, we have learned about LAN configuration, SAN configuration, server policies, and identity and resource pools, which are the building blocks for creating service profiles. In the next chapter, we will use LAN configuration, SAN configuration, server policies, and vNIC/vHBA templates and identity and resource pools to configure the service profiles that abstract all the necessary configurations for stateless physical blade servers.

# 8

# Creating and Managing Service Profiles

The Cisco UCS service profile provides the necessary platform for abstracting fundamental building blocks such as BIOS settings, firmware, storage, and networking settings for the servers. Combined with the simplified architecture and reduced infrastructure management, service profiles provide the stateless nature of Cisco UCS platforms. A service profile provides all identities and configurations to a UCS server necessary for the installation of the operating system, making the system unique on the network.

In the previous chapters, we learned about different components of UCS solutions including LAN configuration, SAN configuration, and identity and resource pools creation. These individual components provide all the resources and configurations to a blade server in the form of service profiles.

In this chapter, we'll explain the role of service profiles in the UCS platform. We'll look into creating various policies for the UCS server's configuration. We'll discuss the difference between standard and expert mode service profiles. Finally, we'll take a deep dive into creating service profiles as well as service profile templates and show the granular configuration options of each.

The list of topics that will be covered in the chapter are as follows:

- Overview of service profiles
- Different ways of creating a service profile
- Creating a service profile template
- Configuring the server BIOS policy
- Configuring the adapter policy
- Configuring the scrub policy

- Configuring the QoS policy
- Configuring the local disk policy
- Configuring IPMI
- Walking through the service profile creation-expert mode

# Overview of service profiles

A service profile is the principle feature of the UCS platform that enables stateless computing. Service profiles radically improve server provisioning and troubleshooting. Servers can be provisioned in software even before the delivery of physical hardware; in case of hardware failure, it can be replaced by associating the existing software service profile of the failed server without going through any painstaking firmware upgrade procedures.

UCS Manager abstracts a service profile from the configurations available under the following categories:

- **Identity and resource pools**: As explained in `Chapter 7`, *Creating Identity Resource Pools, Policies, and Templates,* identity and resource pools provide silos for computing node-unique characteristics such as MAC addresses, WWNs, and UUIDs. These identities uniquely recognize systems on the network. UCS servers abstract these physical identities from software pools available from UCS Manager instead of using burned hardware identities.
- **Service policies**: Service policies, which will be explained later in this chapter, provide different configurations for the UCS servers including BIOS settings, firmware versions, adapter policies, scrub policies, IPMI policies, and so on.
- **Templates**: Templates provide the pre-configured settings that can be reused for rapid deployment of servers such as vNIC, vHBA, and service profile templates. vNIC or vHBA templates provide the customized configuration of network adapter and host bus adapter that can be recalled to create multiple interfaces for any server where a service profile template can be used to create multiple service profiles with desired identities, resource pools, and policies. A service profile combines information and features abstracted from identity and resource pools, server policies, and vNIC/vHBA templates. It is a software entity residing in UCS Manager that provides a complete server role when associated with a stateless physical hardware server. Service profile information and association is depicted in the following diagram:

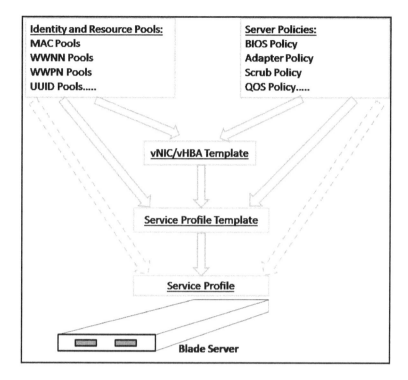

The preceding diagram shows how a service profile provides all features and identities to the physical server by extracting those identities, resources, and policies from different configurations in the form of templates, pools, and policies. It is possible to create a service profile directly from pools and policies; however, it is recommended to create service profile templates, which could be applied to any number of similar servers, reducing the management effort.

# Different ways of creating a service profile

Cisco UCS Manger provides the following three options for creating a service profile:

- Creating a basic service profile
- Creating a service profile expert mode
- Creating a service profile from a service profile template

These service profile creation methods provide various levels of abstraction, flexibility, and scalability in terms of features and configuration options. We will discuss each option in detail.

# Creating a basic service profile

This is the most basic and rarely used option for creating a service profile using the burned-in physical identities. A service profile configuration is completed on a single page wizard providing a basic server configuration. This option can be used to configure a server quickly without applying many advanced policies. For production environments, this option is seldom applicable for server configurations.

Perform the following steps to configure the service profile using this method:

1. Log in to UCS Manager.
2. Click to expand the **Servers** tab in the navigation pane.
3. Click to expand the **Service Profiles** tab and expand **root**.
4. Right-click on **root** and on the pop-up menu that appears, click on **Create Service Profile**:

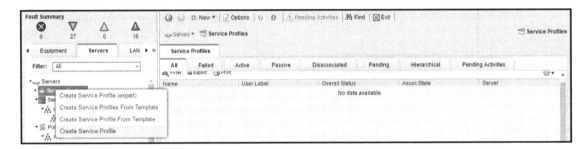

5. In the pop-up screen, provide a **Name** and a short **Description** to the service profile.
6. Create two Ethernet vNICs, two storage vHBAs, select a boot order, and provide a service profile association on the next page.

7. Click on **OK**, which completes the service configuration as shown in the screenshot:

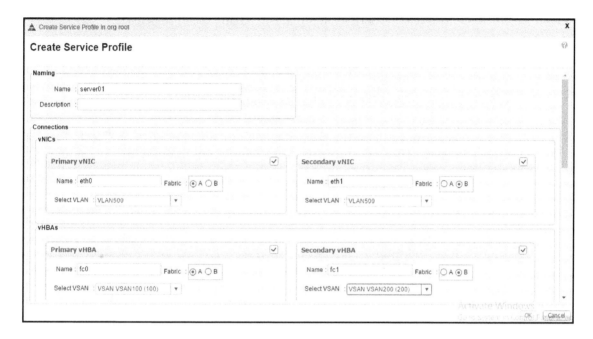

The primary and secondary boot device configuration with server association (optional):

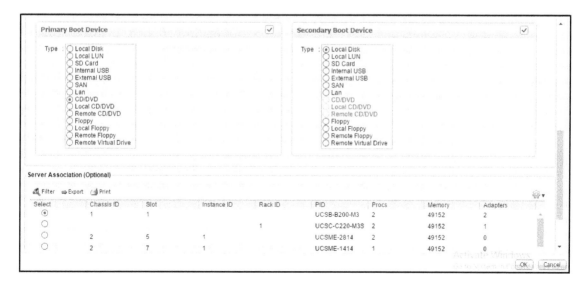

# Creating a service profile in the expert mode

Creating a service profile in the expert mode utilizes all UCS features and creates a rich service profile with abstracted identities, templates, and advanced policies.

Perform the following steps to configure the service profile using the expert mode:

1. Log in to UCS Manager.
2. Click to expand the **Servers** tab in the navigation pane.
3. Click on the **Service Profiles** tab and expand **root**.
4. Right-click on **root** and on the pop-up menu that appears, click on **Create Service Profile (expert)**. This will start a wizard to configure different options, as shown in the following screenshot:

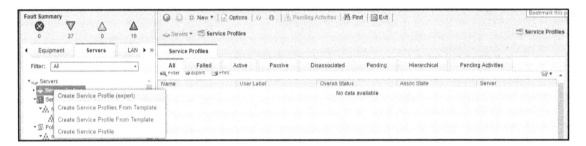

5. Provide a **Name** and a short **Description** to the service profile. On the same screen, also select a **UUID pool** for assigning a unique identity to the server or click on the + sign to create a new UUID pool if needed. Click on **Next**.
6. On the subsequent screens, configure processor features, vNICs, vHBAs, storage zoning, boot order, maintenance policy, and operational policies, and finally associate the profile with the server:

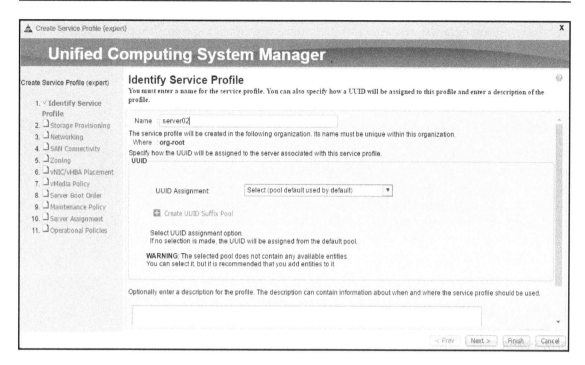

7. We will provide details of the expert mode service profile creation steps, which we have briefly described here, in a subsequent section in this chapter after explaining how to configure various policies.

# Creating a service profile from a service profile template

A service profile template is an excellent feature of UCS Manager which assists in provisioning multiple physical servers with similar hardware configuration through a single profile source. A template can be configured once for each type of server in the environment and can be used to create multiple service profiles for the physical servers with the same specifications very quickly.

The procedure to create service profile templates follows the same steps as creating a service profile in the expert mode. In production environments, a service profile template is highly recommended as it facilitates consistent server provisioning with ease and also reduces the chances of human errors occurring due to repeated manual profile creation steps.

We will provide detailed procedures for creating and applying a service profile template in the final section of this chapter after explaining how to configure policies and providing a walkthrough of service profile creation using the expert mode.

# Configuring policies

UCS Manager allows creation of a number of policies that can be consumed by service profiles associated with servers. When applied through the association of a service profile, these policies provide the necessary features and configurations to the physical servers. Policies can be configured for BIOS configuration, firmware versions, adapter configuration, QoS configuration, local disk configuration, boot order configuration, server data scrubbing, server power utilization, and other operational and maintenance configurations.

# Configuring the server BIOS policy

BIOS policy lets you configure a server's BIOS settings including CPU, memory, PCI cards, and other options. Perform the following steps to configure the BIOS settings policy:

1. Log in to UCS Manager.
2. Click to expand the **Servers** tab in the navigation pane.
3. Click to expand the **Policies** tab and expand the **root** tab.
4. Right-click on **BIOS Policies** and on the pop-up menu that appears, click on **Create BIOS Policy**:

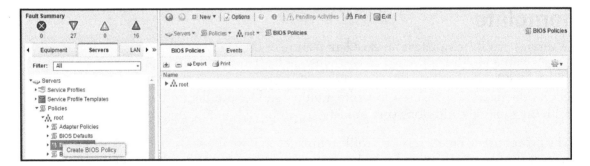

5. In the pop-up screen on the **Main** tab, assign a value for **Name**, and click on the **Reboot on BIOS Settings Change** checkbox if the server needs to reboot automatically on any BIOS change. It is also recommended to properly configure the maintenance policy in order to achieve the desired reboot response from the server.

6. Cisco suppresses the POST messages with a Cisco splash screen. It is recommended to make **Quiet Boot** as **disabled** in order to see boot messages.

7. **POST Error Pause** should be **enabled** if it is required to pause the system in the event of a critical error. If this setting is **disabled**, the system will try to boot up.

8. The **Resume Ac On Power Loss** field settings show self-explanatory power state settings.

9. If **Front Panel Lockout** is **enabled**, it will block the power and will reset buttons on the front panel of the server; now, the server can only be rebooted or powered on or off from the CIMC. Click on **Next**.

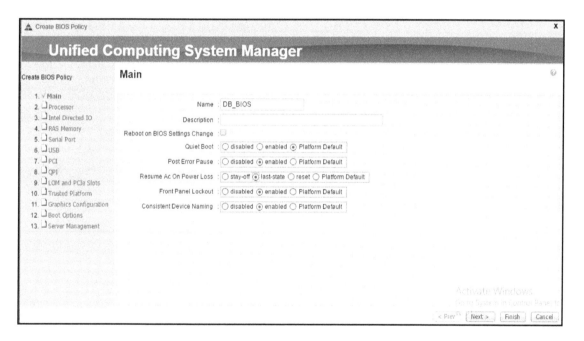

10. The next screen shows the **Processor** settings. A number of CPU settings are available, and it is recommended to check the operating system platform related best practices for CPU settings. As a general recommendation for virtualization, enable **Virtualization Technology (VT)** and disable **Turbo Boost**, **Enhanced Intel Speedstep**, and all C-States. **Turbo Boost** with **Enhanced Intel Speedstep** and **Processor C State** manages CPU power consumption by slowing down or stopping the CPU cores, which may not be handled accurately by the OS. Again, always consult the OS platform recommendation.

11. Click on **Next**:

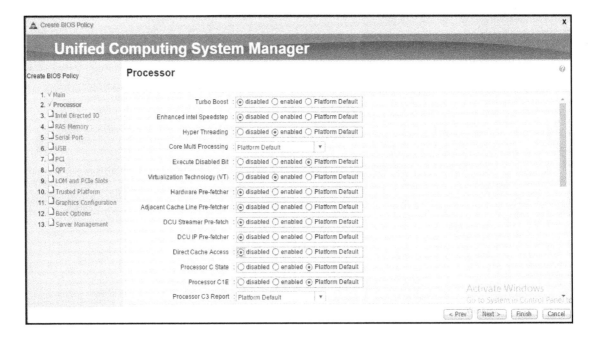

12. **Intel Directed IO** settings are pertinent to the processor features used to facilitate virtualization tasks. Configure the recommended settings for your hypervisor platform or leave it as **Platform Default**:

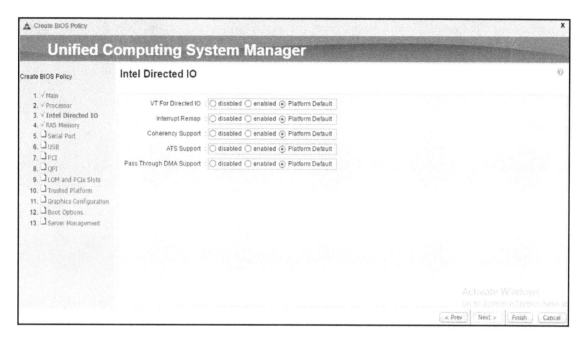

13. **RAS Memory** is a configuration for the memory. Memory RAS configuration options include the following:

- **maximum performance**: System performance is optimized
- **mirroring**: System reliability is optimized by using half the system memory as backup
- **lockstep**: For similar DIMM pairs, the **lockstep** mode minimizes memory access latency
- **sparing**: System reliability is enhanced with reserved memory providing redundancy in case of memory module failure

- The other two memory configuration options are NUMA (also known as Non Uniform Memory Access) and low voltage **LV DDR Mode**:

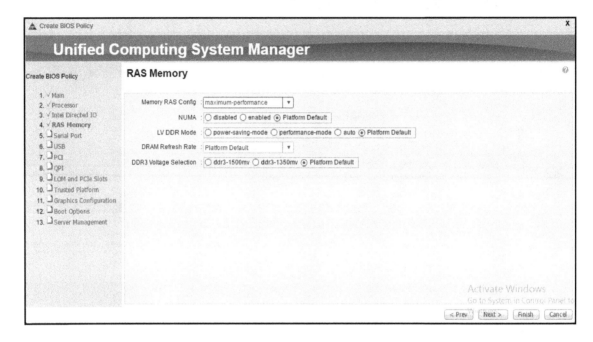

14. The **Serial Port** configuration enables or disables a server serial port:

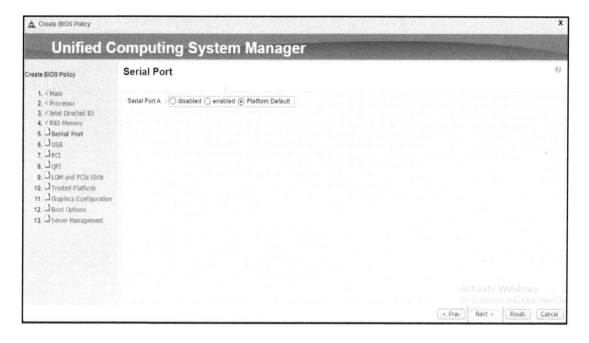

15. The **USB** configuration provides options for the server USB ports:

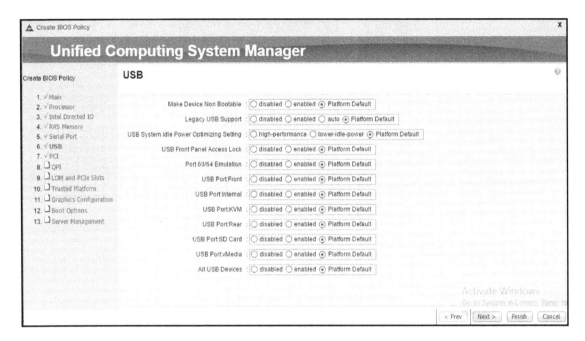

16. The **PCI** configuration checks the operating system requirements for the configuration details or leaves it as **Platform Default**:

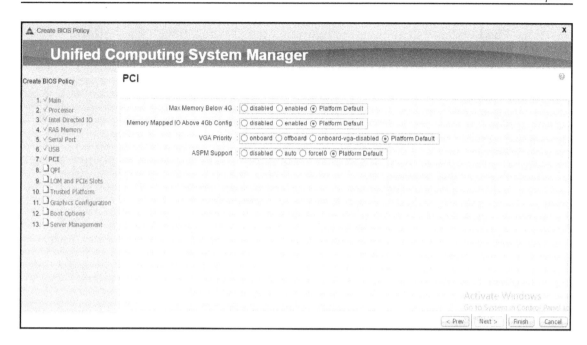

17. The **QPI** configuration can also be left with the **Platform Default** setting to automatically use the default settings for the server platform:

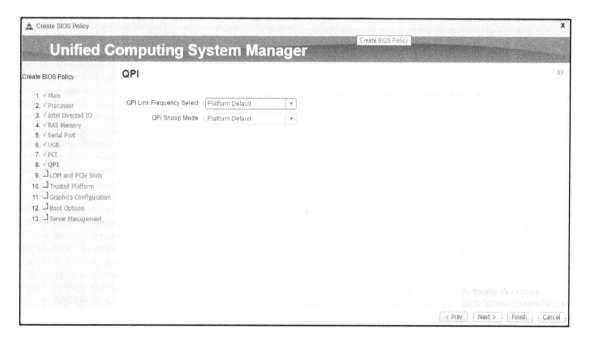

18. The **LOM and PCIe Slots** configuration can also be left with the **Platform Default** setting to automatically use the default settings for the server platform:

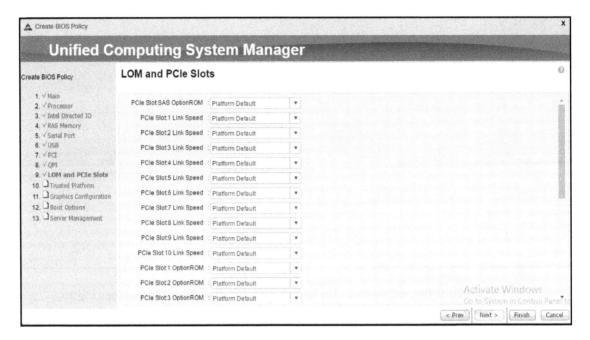

19. The **Trusted Platform** configuration can also be left with the **Platform Default** setting to automatically use the default settings for the server platform:

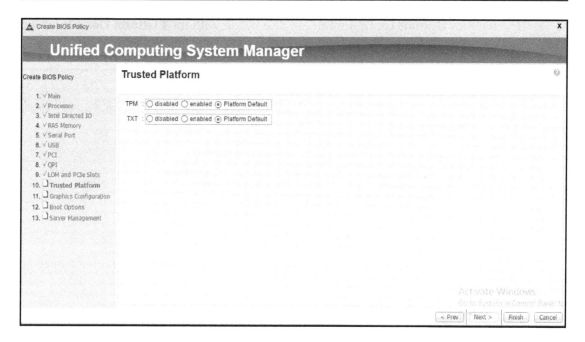

20. The **Graphics Configuration** can also be left with the **Platform Default** setting to automatically use the default settings for the server platform:

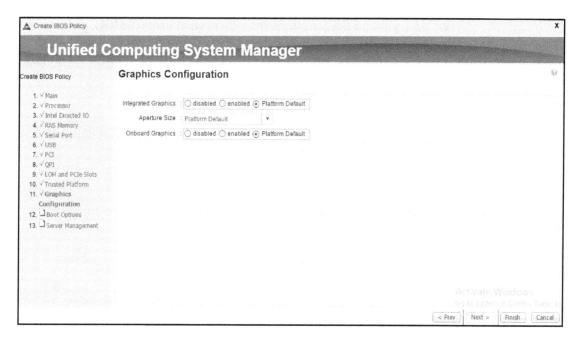

21. The **Boot Options** configuration can also be left with the **Platform Default** setting to automatically use the default settings for the server platform:

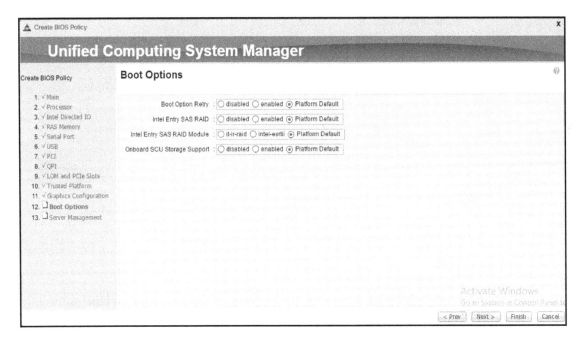

22. The **Server Management** BIOS options provide **system error (SERR)**, **processor bus parity error (PERR)**, **OS Boot Watchdog Timer**, and server **Console Redirection** configurations. Again, these settings can be left as **Platform Default** if you are unsure about the configuration:

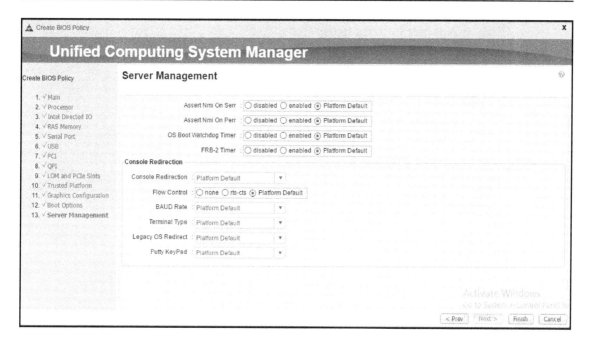

23. Click on **Finish** to complete the BIOS settings.

 UCS Manager also provides BIOS Defaults Policy, which can be configured to provide platform-default settings for each server's BIOS.

# Configuring adapter policies

UCS has some predefined adapter policies for the most popular operating systems, including the hypervisors. The settings in these predefined policies are for optimal adapter performance. Separate adapter policies for Ethernet adapters, Fibre Channel adapters, and iSCSI adapters are available. Select the appropriate policy for the OS/hypervisor. Perform the following steps to configure adapter policies:

1. Log in to UCS Manager.
2. Click to expand the **Servers** tab in the navigation pane.
3. Click on the **Policies** tab and expand **root**.

4. Click on **Adapter Policies** to expand and select the appropriate policy:

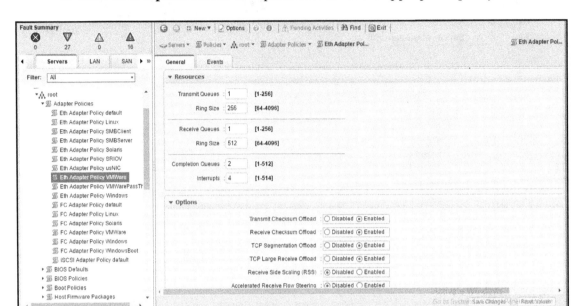

# Configuring scrub policies

A **scrub** policy defines the behavior of a server when it is disassociated from a service profile in terms of BIOS settings and the installed OS on the server. A scrub policy could be very useful for erasing servers for security compliance:

1. Log in to UCS Manager.
2. Click to expand the **Servers** tab in the navigation pane.
3. Click on the **Policies** tab and expand **root**.
4. Right click on **Scrub Policies** and when the pop-up menu appears, click on **Create Scrub Policy**.
5. Assign a **Name** and a short **Description** to the scrub policy.
6. Set **Disk Scrub** to **Yes**, if it is required to erase all data from the server hard disk, otherwise leave it as **No**.

7. Set **BIOS Settings Scrub** to **Yes** if it is required to serve BIOS, otherwise leave it as **No**.

8. Set **FlexFlash Scrub** to **Yes**, if it is required to erase all data from the server flash, otherwise leave it as **No**:

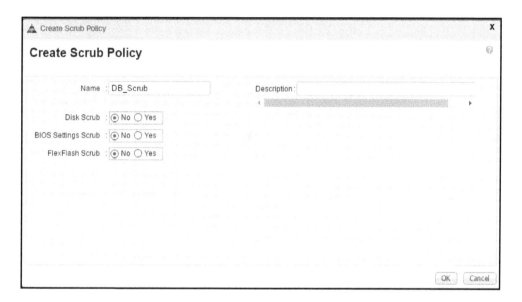

# Configuring QoS policies

The **Quality of service** (**QoS**) policy can be configured to implement network traffic prioritization based on the importance of the connected network; for example, you can implement different QoS policies for application traffic and management traffic. In the following example, we will configure a QoS policy with platinum priority with the help of the following steps:

1. Log in to UCS Manager.
2. Click to expand the **LAN** tab in the navigation pane.
3. Click on the **Policies** tab and expand **root**.

4. Right-click on **QoS Policies**, and on the pop-up menu that appears, click on **Create QoS Policy**:

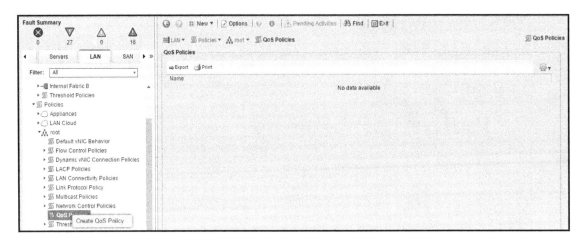

5. Assign a name to the QoS policy.
6. Select **Platinum**, **Gold**, **Silver**, or **Bronze** for vNIC priorities but do not select **Best Effort** which is reserved. Select **FC** for Fibre Channel vHBAs.
7. **Burst (Bytes)** determines the traffic burst size. The default is **1040**, the minimum is **0**, and the maximum is **65535**.
8. The **Rate** field determines the average rate of traffic, and the default is **line-rate**, which should not be changed.
9. The **Host Control** field defines whether UCS controls the class of service or no; if checked the end host provides CoS values:

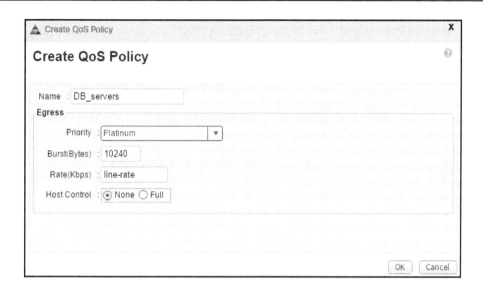

# Local disk configuration policies

This policy is used for local disks' RAID configuration. Based on the number of local disks and RAID controller model, different RAID options include 0, 1, 5, 6, and 10. Perform the following steps to configure this policy:

1. Log in to UCS Manager.
2. Click to expand the **Servers** tab in the navigation pane.
3. Click on the **Policies** tab and expand **root**.
4. Right-click on **Local Disk Config Policies**, and on the pop-up menu that appears, click on **Create Local Disk Configuration Policy**:

5. Assign a **Name** and a short **Description** to the local disk configuration policy.
6. Select a **RAID** level from the pop-up menu.
7. Select the **Protect Configuration** checkbox in order to preserve the local disk configuration even if the service profile is disassociated.

Flex Flash state is disabled by default. If you want to install the SD cards in the servers, these configurations need to be enabled to get detected:

# Maintenance policies

The maintenance policy is a very important policy that controls the server's response to any changes in the service profile. Many service profile changes need a reboot of the server to take effect. It is therefore recommended to configure this policy with user acknowledgment settings for production environments so that servers can be rebooted in a controlled change management window.

Following are the steps to create a maintenance policy.

1. Log in to UCS Manager.
2. Click to expand the **Servers** tab in the navigation pane.
3. Click on the **Policies** tab and expand **root**.
4. Right-click on the **Maintenance Policies** tab and on the pop-up screen that appears, click on **Create Maintenance Policy**:

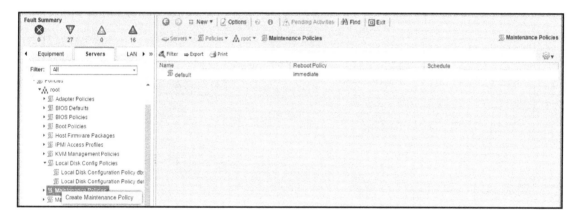

5. Assign a **Name** and a short **Description** to the maintenance policy.

6. Setting a value for **Reboot Policy** is critical. **Immediate** means the server will be instantaneously rebooted for changes that require a reboot, which is not a recommended setting for production servers. **User Ack** means that any change that requires a server reboot will be held until the user's acknowledgement. This setting allows scheduling a maintenance window and rebooting the server following proper procedures. **Timer Automatic** allows you to schedule a maintenance window and automatically reboot the server at a specific time without an administrator's intervention:

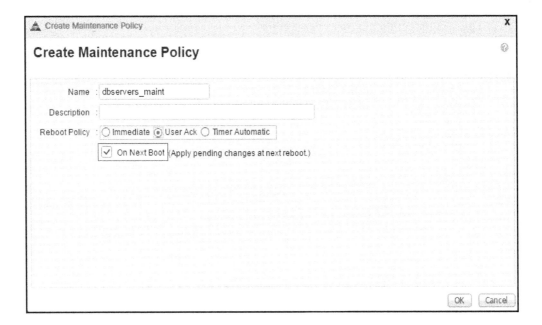

# Configuring IPMI

The **Intelligent Platform Management Interface** (**IPMI**) is open standard technology for monitoring the server's hardware sensors. IPMI runs directly on the **baseboard management controller** (**BMC**). It is, therefore, necessary to create an IPMI profile with a username, password, and the desired level of access, which could be read-only or read/write, and assign the IPMI profile to the blade server for direct management using IPMI commands.

Perform the following steps to configure the IPMI profile:

1.  Log in to UCS Manager.
2.  Click to expand the **Servers** tab in the navigation pane.
3.  Click on the **Policies** tab and expand the **root** tab.
4.  Right-click on **IPMI Access Profiles** and on the pop-up menu that appears, click on **Create IPMI Access Profile**:

5. Assign a **Name** and a short **Description** to the IPMI access profile, and select the **Enable** option for the **IPMI Over LAN** config. Click on the + sign to create the IPMI users under the **IPMI Users** section:

# Configuring the Host Firmware policy

**Host Firmware Packages** is used to upgrade the firmware version of all UCS components. It is one single policy that can be assigned to the service profile or the service profile template to upgrade all the components at the same level. While upgrading or downgrading UCS firmware, it is always recommended to follow the latest UCS Firmware management guide.

Cisco UCS Firmware Management Guide is available at following link:
`http://www.cisco.com/c/en/us/td/docs/unified_computing/ucs/ucs`
`-manager/GUI-User-Guides/Firmware-Mgmt/3-1/b_UCSM_GUI_Firmware`
`_Management_Guide_3_1/b_UCSM_GUI_Firmware_Management_Guide_3_`
`1_chapter_01.html`

Perform the following steps to configure the Host Firmware Package:

1. Log in to UCS Manager.
2. Click to expand the **Servers** tab in the navigation pane.
3. Click on the **Policies** tab and expand the **root** tab.
4. Right-click on **Host Firmware Packages** and on the pop-up menu that appears, click on **Create Host Firmware Package**:

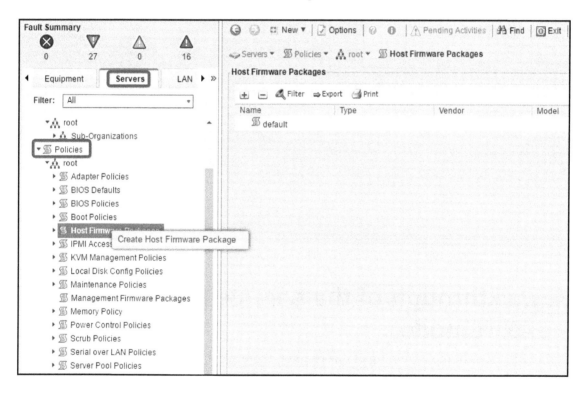

5. Assign a **Name** and a short **Description** to the host firmware package, and select the **Simple or Advanced** config option. Simple configuration will allow selection of the package level at blade, rack, and M-Series and then automatically upgrade all the components where advanced configuration will provide more flexibility to select the package level for each component in the UCS:

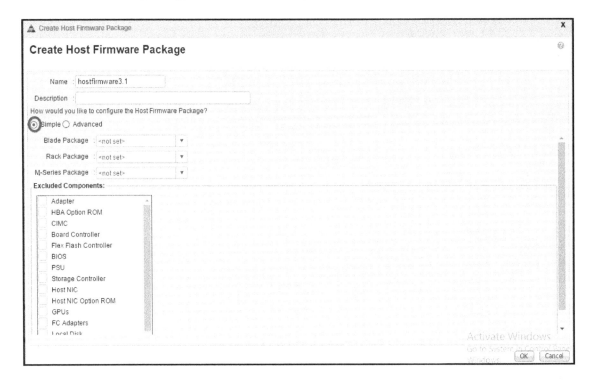

# A walkthrough of the service profile creation - expert mode

As we discussed at the beginning of this chapter, there are three methods to create a service profile. The quickest method is to create a basic service profile using a single configuration page. This method, however, does not make use of advanced UCS features such as policies and templates and therefore, a basic profile is not recommended for production servers. For production environments, it is recommended to use the expert mode creation method for service profiles that leverage advanced UCS features, and provide a detailed identity to the servers where this service profile is applied.

It is highly recommended to create service profile templates using the expert mode so that, in the future, servers with similar specifications can be added without a lot of administrative effort. We will now walk through the service profile creation—the expert mode—using the identity and resource pools along with policies. Note that the sections and steps discussed are similar for the creation of both the service profiles in the expert mode and service profile templates. Service profile expert mode or service profile template creations are lengthy processes. We will explain these steps according to the sections in the configuration wizard. Perform the following steps to configure the service profile using the expert mode method.

# Identifying the service profile

In the first section, provide a **Name** and identify a UUID pool for the server identity. Perform the following steps to do so:

1. Log in to UCS Manager.
2. Click on the **Servers** tab in the navigation pane.
3. Click to expand the **Service Profiles** tab and expand **root**.
4. Right-click on **root** and on the pop-up menu that appears, click on **Create Service Profile (expert)**.

5. Assign a **Name** and a short **Description** to the service profile and select an already created UUID pool. If a UUID pool does not exist, click on the + sign to create a new UUID pool:

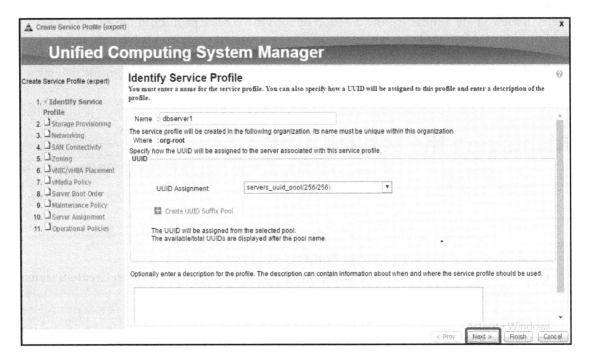

6. Click on **Next** to continue to storage provisioning.

# Configuring the storage provisioning

Now we will configure the storage provisioning, which includes a local disk storage policy. You may create a local storage policy based on your requirements. The steps are as follows:

1. After configuration of UUID, click on **Next**.
2. Now configure a local storage, which may use an existing local disk configuration policy.
3. In this example, we will be selecting an existing **Local Disk Configuration Policy** for the configuration of local storage, and if a policy does not exist, we can create a new policy by clicking on the + sign. In this example, we assigned a pre-configured local disk configuration policy named **dbservers-raid1** for RAID configuration of local disks:

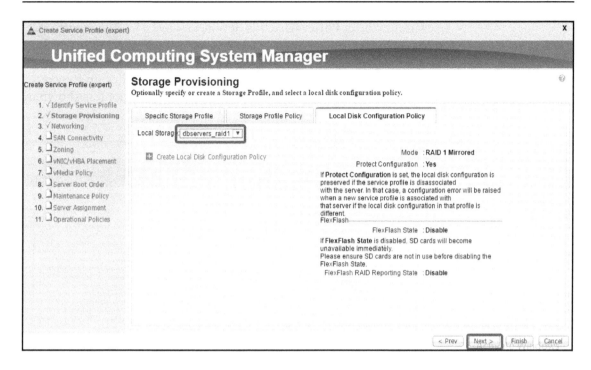

# Configuring the networking settings

Perform the following steps to configure the networking settings:

1. On the **Networking** page, configure the networking settings. You may select or create a new dynamic vNIC connection policy. There are multiple options available for the network configuration:

   - **Simple**: The **Simple** option will create two vNICs. Existing VLAN IDs can be assigned to the vNICs or VLAN IDs can be created using the + sign.

   - **Expert**: The **Expert** mode can be used to create any number (depending upon the mezzanine card model) of vNICs and iSCSI adapters. vNICs can be configured manually or vNIC templates can also be created.

   - **No vNICs**: No vNICs will be created. vNICs can be added to a service profile later.

   - **Hardware Inherited**: This option creates two vNICs using the burned-in identities. This is the same as creating vNICs in a basic service profile creation.

- **Use Connectivity Policy**: Use this option to select a LAN connectivity policy.

2. We will utilize the **Expert** mode in our example configuration. Click on **Expert** from the LAN connectivity. This option will change the page options as shown in the following screenshot:

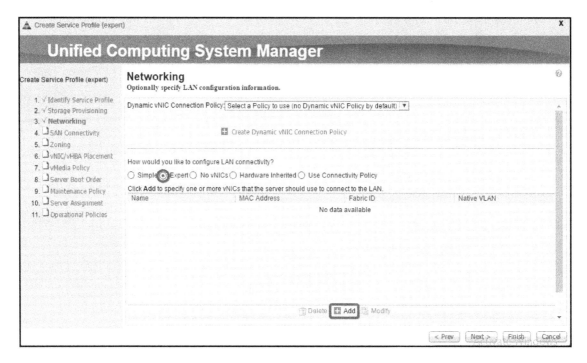

3. Click on the + sign to add a new vNIC.
4. On the pop-up page, you may either manually create the vNIC by assigning a MAC address pool, fabric ID, VLAN membership, and various policies such as the QoS and adapter policy, or use an existing vNIC template if a vNIC template already exists. If a vNIC template does not exist, you can quickly create a new vNIC template by clicking on the + sign on the same page.

5.  In this example, we will use an existing vNIC template, refer to `Chapter 5`, *Configuring LAN Connectivity*, that discusses the procedure to create vNIC template. Click on the checkbox **Use vNIC Template**:

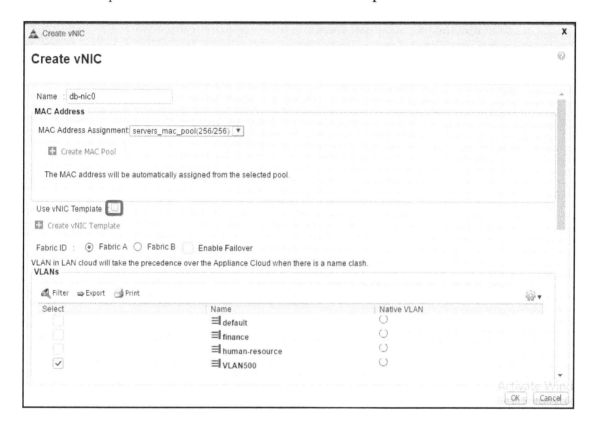

6. Clicking on the checkbox will change the screen. On the next screen, assign a **Name** to vNIC, select an existing vNIC template to abstract vNIC configuration, or create a new vNIC template by clicking on the + sign. You can also assign an existing **Adapter Policy** for traffic optimization or create a new adapter policy, as shown in the following screenshot:

7. Repeat steps 3 to 6 in order to create as many vNICs as you require:

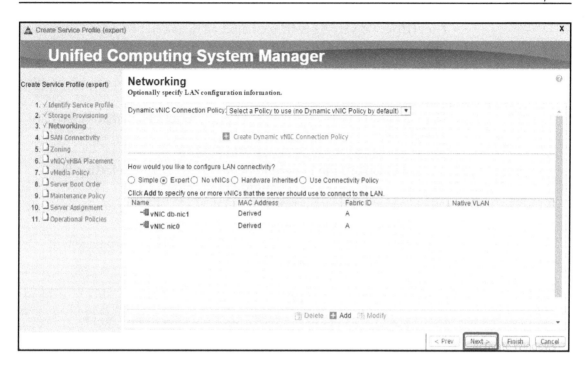

It is recommended to select different primary Fabric Interconnects for data connectivity while creating vNIC templates, which ensures load distribution for data traffic

# Configuring the SAN connectivity

Now we will configure the storage, which includes both local storage and SAN connectivity vHBAs. The steps are as follows:

1. On the **SAN Connectivity** page, configure vHBAs. Similar to vNICs, there are the following multiple options for creating vHBAs:
    - **Simple**: The **Simple** option will create two vHBAs. Existing VSAN IDs can be assigned to the vHBAs or VSAN IDs can be created using the + sign. You also need to assign a WWNN pool or create an new WWNN pool using the + sign.
    - **Expert**: The **Expert** mode can be used to create any number (depending upon the mezzanine card model) of vHBA adapters. vHBAs can be configured manually or vHBA templates can also be created.

- **No vHBA**: No vHBAs will be created. vHBAs can be added to a service profile later.
- **Hardware Inherited**: This option creates vHBAs using the burned-in identities. This is the same as creating vHBAs in a basic service profile creation.
- **Use Connectivity Policy**: Use this option to select a SAN connectivity policy.

2. In this example, we will use the **Expert** mode to create vHBAs. Selecting the **Expert** mode will change the screen configuration options.
3. Select an existing WWNN pool for WWNN number assignments or create a new WWNN pool by clicking on the + sign.
4. Click on the + sign near **Add** to create a new vHBA. A new pop-up page will provide options for configuring the vHBA:

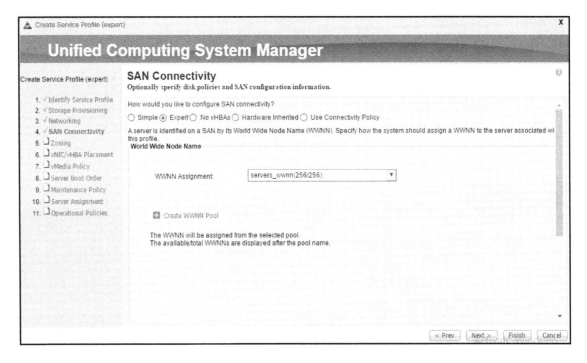

5. On the pop-up page, you may either manually create the vHBA by assigning a WWNN address pool, fabric ID, VSAN membership, and various policies such as the QoS and adapter policy, or use an existing vHBA template. You can also quickly create a new vHBA template by clicking on the + sign on the same page.

6. In this example, we will use an existing vHBA template, refer to `Chapter 6`, *Configuring SAN Connectivity*, that discuss the procedure to create vHBA template. Click on the **Use vHBA Template** checkbox:

7. Clicking on the checkbox will change the screen. On the next screen, assign a **Name** to vHBA, select an existing vHBA template to abstract the vHBA configuration, or create a new vHBA template by clicking on the **+** sign. You can also assign an existing **Adapter Policy** for traffic optimization or create a new adapter policy.

8. Repeat steps 7 to 10 to create more vHBAs for the service profile.

9. In this example, we configured two vHBAs. You may configure the required number of vHBAs as per the requirements of your environment. Click on **Next** after the vHBAs creation.

# Configuring zoning

On the **Zoning** page, configure the zoning information only if the storage is directly connected with the FIs (an option for small environments). In most environments, storage is not directly connected to the FIs and is either connected through MDS or Brocade switches, in which case zoning is configured on the storage fabric. Proceed with zoning configuration on the FI only if storage is locally connected. The page shows vHBAs (initiators) on the left-hand side of the pane and zones (initiator groups) information on the right-hand side of the pane. Select each vHBA (initiator), and add it to an existing zone vHBA initiator group by clicking on the **>>Add To >>** sign:

Previous versions of UCS Manager supported default zoning. Default zoning allows using a single zone for all vHBAs, which is not the recommended setting from a security perspective. UCSM 2.1 does not support default zoning.

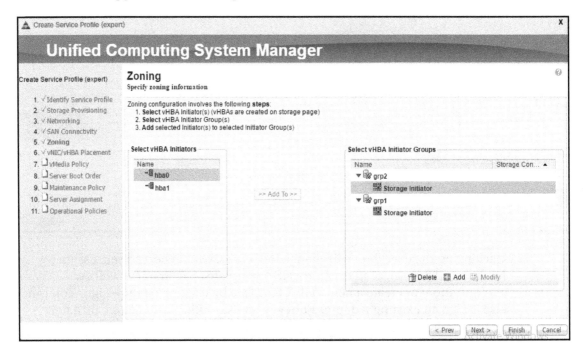

# vNIC/vHBA placement

On the **vNIC/vHBA Placement** screen, the vNIC/vHBA placement order is configured. The default configuration is the **Let System Perform Placement** order. Other options include using a placement policy or manually ordering the placement of vNICs and vHBAs. Click on the + sign to create a new placement policy if needed:

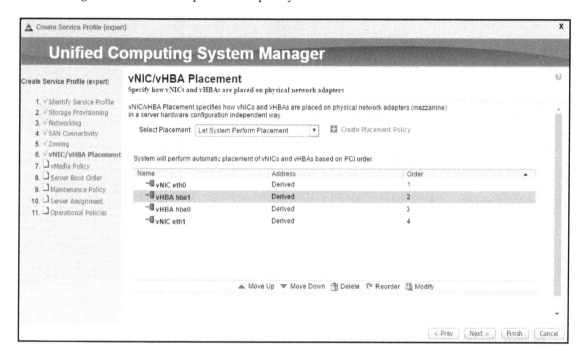

# vMedia policy configuration

The vMedia policy allows you to map the remote server ISO image through scripting or programming. Normally you mount the ISO image during the installation of a server to boot from it; the same thing can be achieved through vMedia policy. Click on **Create vMedia Policy** if needed:

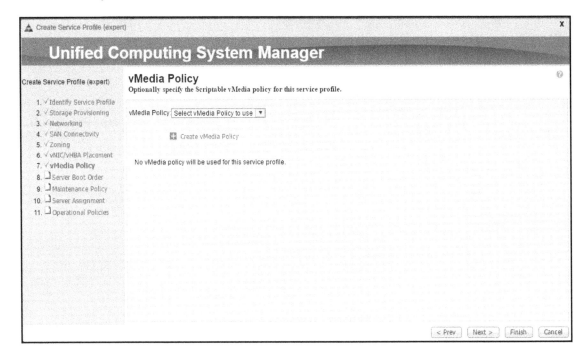

Name the **vMedia Policy** and click on **Add vMedia Mount Point**:

# Server boot order configuration

The next configuration is of **Server Boot Order**. An existing boot policy can be used to populate the boot sequence, or a new boot policy can also be created by clicking on the + sign. It is also possible to manually create the boot sequence by double-clicking on the boot devices available on the left-hand side of the pane. When manually populated, the boot devices order can also be changed using the move up and down buttons at the bottom of screen. In this example, we have used the preconfigured **default Boot Policy**:

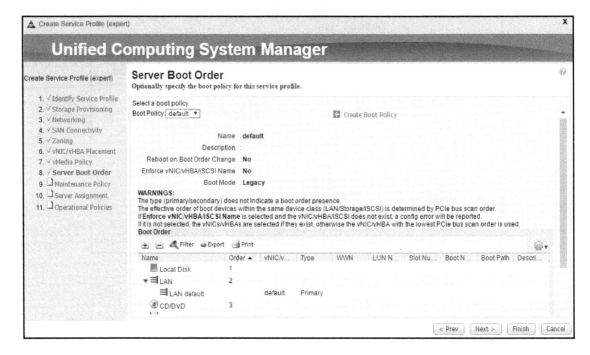

# Configuring a SAN boot policy

In many environments, it is common practice to use diskless servers, and boot the hypervisor or OS directly from SAN. UCS makes it very simple to configure a SAN boot policy for direct SAN boot. Make sure you have already configured appropriate vHBAs, and perform the following steps to configure a SAN boot policy for the server:

1. In the **Server Boot Order** tab of template configuration wizard, click on the + sign beside **Create Boot Policy**:

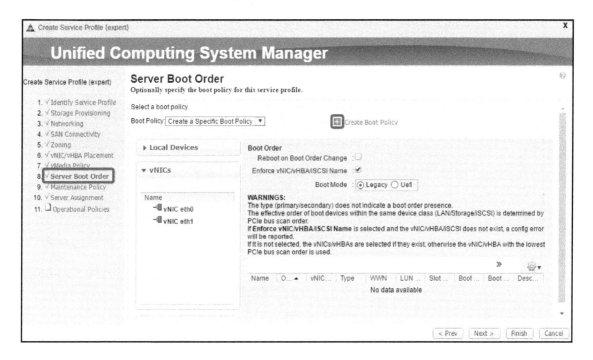

2. On the next pop-up window, provide a **Name** and **Description** for the new policy, expand the vHBAs section, and click on **Add SAN Boot**:

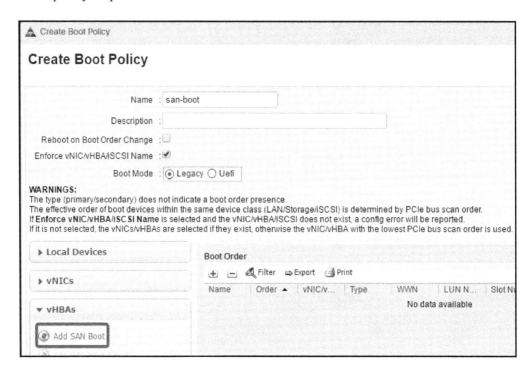

3. On the pop-up window, provide the name of the appropriate vHBA configured. Repeat the steps for primary and secondary vHBAs:

4. After adding vHBAs, **Add SAN Boot Target**, which was initially grayed out, will be highlighted. Click on **Add SAN Boot Target**:

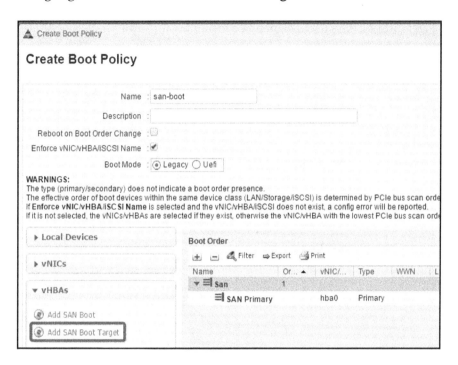

5. On the pop-up window, add values for **Boot Target LUN**, **Boot Target WWPN**, and **Type** as **Primary** or **Secondary**. Contact the SAN administrator to get the appropriate information about the boot LUN designated for the SAN boot:

# Configuring the server maintenance policy

The next configuration is the **Maintenance Policy** selection. If no preconfigured policy is selected, the default policy is used, which is configured for immediate reboot after any change. Options for a maintenance policy are to select an existing maintenance policy or create a new one by clicking on the + sign. For production environments, it is strongly recommended to create a maintenance policy with the user acknowledge setting. With this maintenance policy, UCS Manager prompts a user to acknowledge the reboot. Hence, the server can be easily scheduled for a reboot during the planned maintenance window. In this example, we are using an existing maintenance policy which has the user acknowledge setting. At the bottom of the screen, the maintenance policy configuration is displayed, which in this example is **User Ack**:

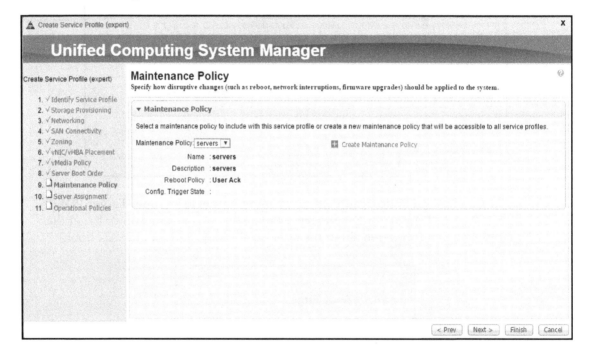

# Associating service profiles

Perform the following steps to associate the service profiles with the server pools:

1. On the **Server Assignment** screen, you can assign the service profile to a server pool if a server pool already exists or you can create a new server pool for assignment by clicking on the **+** sign. It is also possible to not put the server in any pool, and a service profile can be manually associated with a physical server. The second option is to select a server specification based on a **Server Pool Qualification** policy, such as CPU and RAM for a server pool membership:

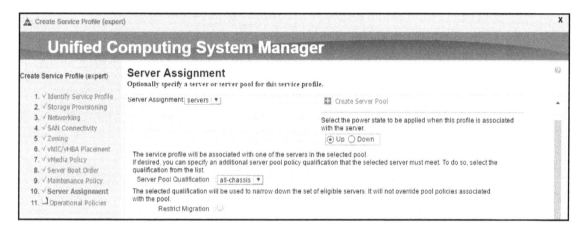

2. The third option available on the **Server Assignment** page is the selection of the host firmware package. Use the **+** sign to create a host firmware package if it has not been created already:

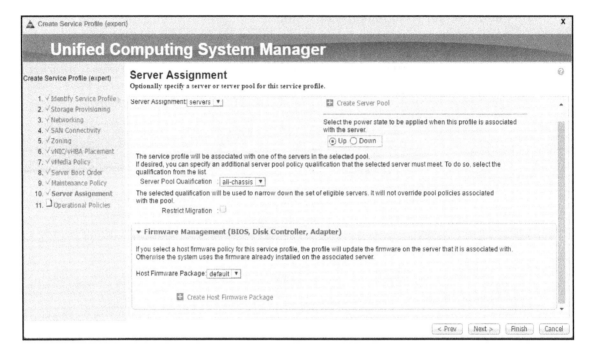

# Operational policies

The last page is the **Operation Policies** page and has a number of configurations. Policies that are configured on this page are as follows:

- **BIOS Configuration**: Configure BIOS settings
- **External IPMI Management Configuration**: IPMI configuration
- **Management IP Address**: Configure a static IP or an IP Pool
- **Monitoring Configuration (Thresholds)**: Configure monitoring thresholds
- **Power Control Policy Configuration**: Configure Blade Power control
- **Scrub Policy**: Configure data scrub settings

Now we will configure the operational policies one-by-one:

1. The first policy is the **BIOS Configuration** policy. You may select an existing
   BIOS policy or you can create a new BIOS policy by clicking on the + sign. If no
   BIOS policy is selected, default values from BIOS defaults of the platform will be
   used:

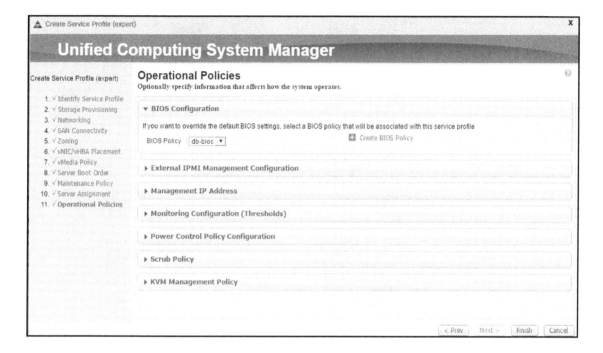

2. The next policy is the IPMI and Serial over LAN (SoL) configuration. Select an existing IPMI user access profile or create a new IPMI access profile by clicking on the + sign. If serial over LAN redirection for the server is required, configure a new SoL policy or select an existing one:

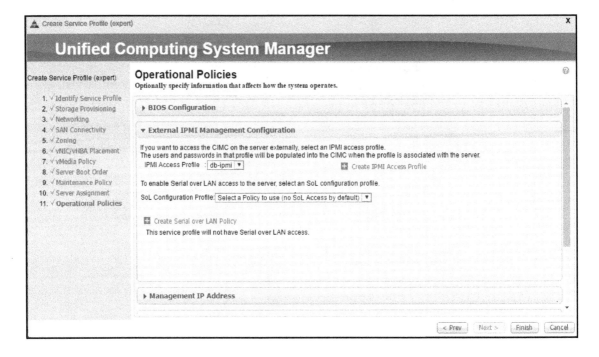

3. The next policy is **Management IP Address**. It is possible to create a management IP pool and IPs will be automatically assigned to the servers. The other option is to assign a static IP to the server management console. In this example, we selected the **Static** option for the **Management IP Address Policy** field:

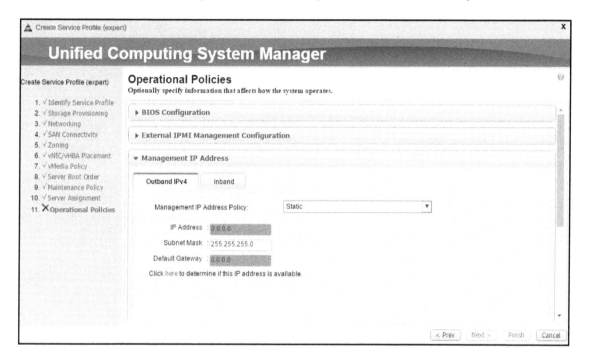

4. The next configuration is **Monitoring Configuration (Thresholds)**. It is possible to create a customized threshold policy with granular settings for server components. Mostly, a **default** policy is recommended, so this configuration can be skipped:

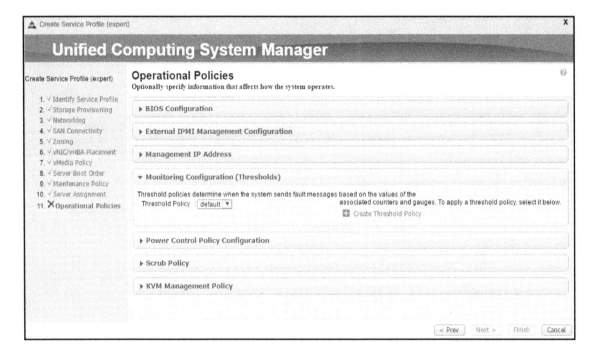

5. The next configuration is **Power Control Policy Configuration**, which determines the power allocation for the server. Typically, this policy can also be skipped unless it is a situation where power management is required. The **default** setting provides maximum power to the blades. For the server's power control, it is possible to create a new power policy or use an existing one:

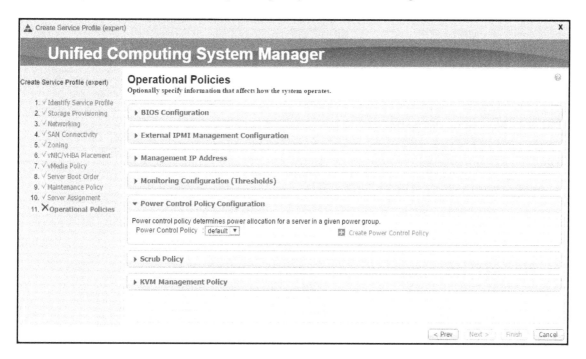

6. The last operational policy configuration is the selection of the server **Scrub Policy**. The options are to select an existing scrub policy or create a new scrub policy by clicking on the + sign:

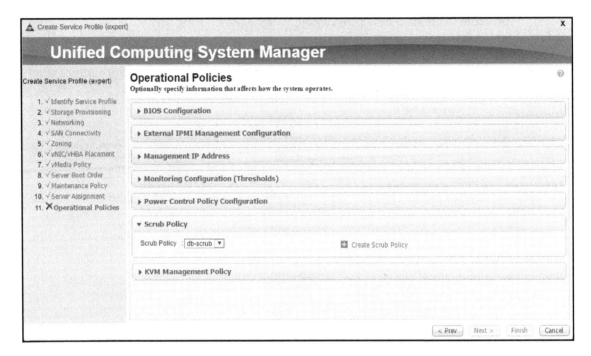

7. The last **KVM Management Policy** configuration is the selection of the vMedia encryption policy. The options are to select an existing KVM management policy or create a new KVM management policy by clicking on the + sign:

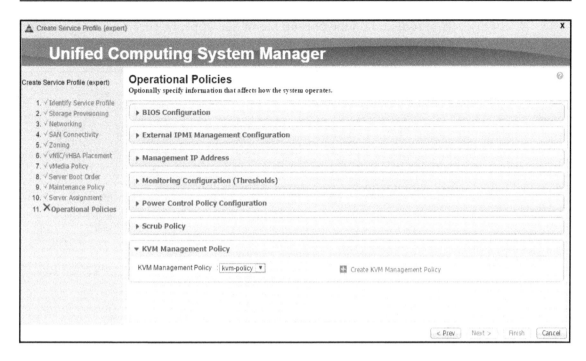

8. Click on **Finish** to complete the service profile configuration.

# Creating and applying a service profile template

UCS service profile template creation is an excellent feature. Service profile templates can be created once and deployed to any number of servers with similar hardware specifications. The procedure for creating a service profile template is exactly the same as the procedure for creating a service profile template in the expert mode. Only the initial steps are different compared to the service profile in the expert mode and are shown in the following:

1. Log in to UCS Manager.
2. Click to expand the **Servers** tab in the navigation pane.
3. Click on the **Service Profiles Template** tab and expand **root**.

4. Right-click on **root** and on the pop-up menu that appears, click on **Create Service Profile Template**:

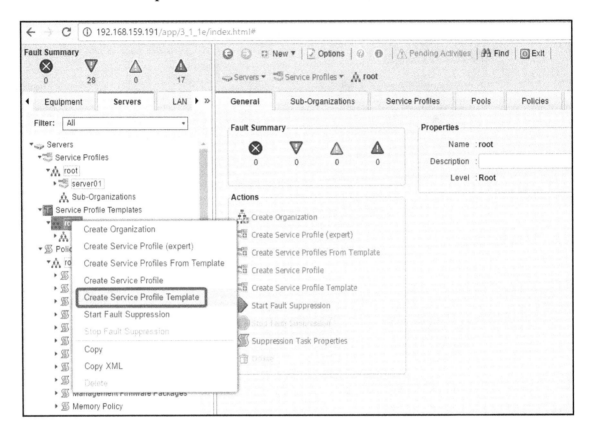

The next steps are exactly the same as we followed while creating the service profile in the expert mode. Once the template has been configured, it can be used to create any number of service profiles using minimal effort. Perform the following steps to configure a service profile from an existing service profile template:

1. Click on the **Servers** tab in the navigation pane.
2. Click on the **Service Profiles** tab and expand **root**.
3. Right-click on **root** and on the pop-up menu that appears, click on **Create Service Profiles From Template**:

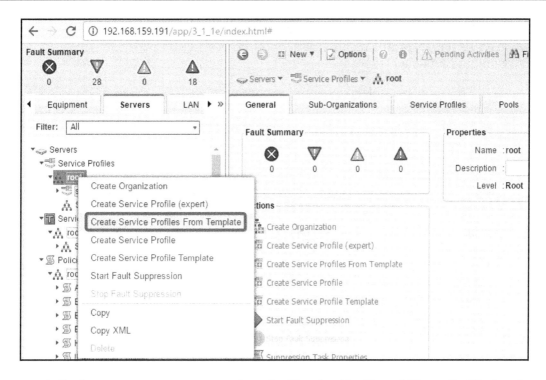

4. In the pop-up screen, enter values for **Naming Prefix** and **Name Suffix Starting Number** to create a name for the new service profile, and select **Service Profile Template** from the list of available templates:

If you are using previous versions of UCS Manager, including version 2.0, pay special attention to the service profile naming, as service profiles created with previous versions of UCSM cannot be renamed.

It is now possible to rename a service profile after its creation in UCSM version 2.1. In previous versions, it was not possible to rename a service profile, other than by deleting and recreating with appropriate profile names.

# Service profiles cloning

Service profile is created for any server, its name cannot be changed. Cloning of service profile can help to create a replica of the same server with a new name. A new service profile can be created from an existing server profile by cloning the similar configuration and parameters for all resource identities, pools, and policies. However, a cloned service profile will have its own identities from the same pool.

# Summary

In this chapter, we first acquired an understanding of the service profile and looked into various service profile creation options. We learned that the expert mode service profile creation provides advanced configuration features, and also learned that creating service profile templates facilitates rapid server provisioning. Then we looked into various policies that can be configured and, later on, assigned them to blade servers through service profiles. We looked at policies such as BIOS, Adapter, Scrub, and QoS. Finally, we did a walkthrough of service profile creation using the expert mode, and utilized different UCS policies and settings to create a service profile that can be associated to a physical blade server, to provide the server with all configurations necessary for proper operation. We utilized the knowledge gained throughout the previous chapters and created a service profile that can provide the server with all the necessary characteristics.

In the next chapter, we will be looking into some common management tasks for managing and monitoring components, and advanced tasks such as role-based access control, authentication using external LDAP/AD, and multitenant environment considerations.

# 9
# Managing UCS through Routine and Advanced Management

In this chapter, we'll cover some of the most common and advanced management tasks you'll perform with UCS Manager. These tasks include licensing extra ports, starting up, shutting down, blade power controls, locator LED, logging, the Call Home feature, organizational structure, role-based access, and configuring permissions in a multitenant environment. These routine management and operational tasks are crucial to understand in order to effectively design and administer Cisco UCS.

The tasks covered in this chapter do not fall into a single category and hence, are not located under a single tab in the UCS GUI navigation pane. Most of the tasks are found in miscellaneous categories under the **Admin** tab in the navigation pane, but other tasks are found on other tabs. For example, licensing configuration is under the **Admin** tab in the navigation pane, but the option to get the host ID of the Fabric Interconnect is under the **Equipment** tab of the navigation pane. It is therefore necessary that you become very familiar with the UCS Manager GUI in order to find the pertinent information or configuration.

The topics that will be covered in this chapter are:

- Licensing Cisco UCS Fabric Interconnect
- Startup and shutdown of Fabric Interconnects
- Controlling blade server power
- Status and locator LEDs
- Configuring logging
- Configuring Cisco Call Home
- Organizational structure in UCS Manager

- Role-based access control
- Permissions in multitenancy

# Licensing Cisco UCS Fabric Interconnect

Cisco UCS Fabric Interconnect comes with default port licenses that are factory installed. Additional licenses can be purchased during the initial procurement (these licenses will also be factory installed) or licenses can be purchased later after delivery.

Each Fabric Interconnect provides the following licenses preinstalled:

- **Cisco UCS 6248**: 12 unified ports enabled with preinstalled licenses. Expansion modules provide eight licenses, which can be utilized on the expansion module or the main Fabric Interconnect.
- **Cisco UCS 6296**: 18 unified ports enabled with preinstalled licenses. Expansion modules provide eight licenses, which can be utilized on the expansion module or the main Fabric Interconnect.

- **Cisco UCS 6332**: Eight ports enabled with preinstalled licenses. These eight ports can be broken into *8 x 4 = 32* 10 G port licenses to connect with Cisco UCS chassis and upstream switches.
- **Cisco UCS 6332-16UP**: 12 ports enabled with preinstalled licenses. Expansion modules provide eight licenses, which can be utilized only on the expansion module and four licenses for Fabric Interconnect fixed ports.

In order to purchase extra port licenses, you need to provide the host ID of the Fabric Interconnect to Cisco.

Use the following procedure to get the Fabric Interconnect host ID:

1. Log in to UCS Manager.
2. Click to expand the **Equipment** tab in the navigation pane.
3. In the **Equipment** tab, click to expand **Fabric Interconnects**.
4. In the **Properties** area of the **General** tab in the work pane, note down the **serial number** (**SN**) of Fabric Interconnect.

It is imperative to always have the same number of licenses on both Fabric Interconnects configured in **high availability** (**HA**).

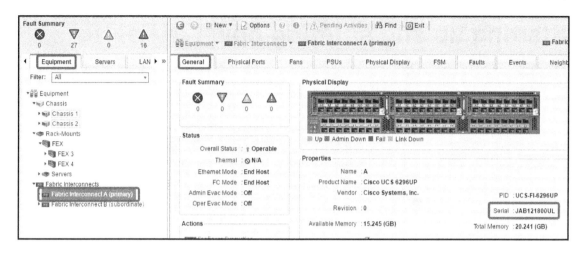

Once the license file is received from Cisco, it can be installed on Fabric Interconnect using the UCS Manager GUI under the **Admin** tab or CLI, using the following steps:

1. In the navigation pane, select **License Management** under the **Admin** tab.
2. Select the **General** tab under the **Fabric Interconnect A** tab (as shown in the following screenshot) in the work pane and select the **Download License Files** tab.
3. In the pop-up window, browse for the **Local File System** of the PC running the UCS Manager GUI session or provide details of the **Remote File System** for **FTP**, **TFTP**, **SCP**, or **SFTP** sessions.
4. Repeat this task for all the licenses for both Fabric Interconnects.

# Starting up and shutting down of Fabric Interconnects

UCS Fabric Interconnects are designed for continuous operation. In a production environment, there is no need to shut down or reboot Fabric Interconnects. Therefore, there is no power button on UCS Fabric Interconnects. In order to shut down UCS Fabric Interconnect, you are required to pull the power cable manually. Another option could be using smart PDUs that provide a remote control for the power of the electrical outlet.

In some rare cases, if it is necessary to reboot Fabric Interconnect, use the following procedure:

1. Log in to Fabric Interconnect using SSH.
2. Issue the following two commands:

```
FI # connect local-mgmt
FI # reboot
```

# Controlling blade server power

The UCS blade server chassis has a maximum of four power supplies. Each power supply is 2,500 watts. Under normal conditions, UCS always has enough power to run all blade servers in the chassis. If required, power to each blade server can be capped. This may be required in a disaster situation where a limited amount of power is available.

When manual blade-level power capping is configured in the global cap policy, you can set a power cap for each blade server in a Cisco UCS domain.

Use the following procedure to enable the global manual power policy:

1. Log in to UCS Manager.
2. Click to expand the **Equipment** tab in the navigation pane.
3. In the main **Equipment** tab, click to expand **Equipment**.
4. Select **Global Policies** from the **Policies** tab in the work pane.

5. In the **Global Power Allocation Policy** area, select **Manual Blade Level Cap** for the **Allocation Method**:

Once the global power policy is enabled for **Manual Blade Level Cap**, use the following procedure to allocate power to each blade:

1. Log in to UCS Manager.
2. Click to expand the **Equipment** tab in the navigation pane.
3. In the **Equipment** tab, click to expand **Chassis**.
4. Expand the **Servers** tab and select **Server 1** in the navigation pane.
5. In the **General** tab of the selected server in the work pane, select **Power Budget** for the server.

6. Select **Enabled** and define the power value for the blade in watts.

Power capping only goes into effect if there is insufficient power available to the chassis to meet the demand. If there is sufficient power, the server can use as many watts as it requires.

# Status and locator LEDs

The following physical components of UCS have status and locator LEDs:

- UCS chassis
- Blade server
- UCS Fabric Interconnect

Status provides the overall operational state of the equipment and can be very useful in initial diagnostics. The status of a UCS component is available in the work pane in the top-left corner under the **Fault Summary** area.

Locator LEDs, on the other hand, can be turned on in order to physically identify the equipment and are very useful for onsite troubleshooting. Suppose one of the Fabric Interconnects or one of the blade servers is faulty, you may help an onsite technician to physically identify (and maybe replace) the faulty components if the locator LED is remotely turned on by the administrator from UCSM.

Please perform the following procedure for looking up the UCS component status and turning on/off the locator LED:

1.  Log in to UCS Manager.
2.  Click to expand the **Equipment** tab in the navigation pane.
3.  In the **Equipment** tab, click to expand **Chassis**.
4.  In the **Status** area of the work pane, the operational status of Fabric Interconnect is shown.
5.  Click on **Turn on Locator LED** in the work pane. This option is also available if you right-click on **Chassis**.
6.  Click on **OK** on the pop-up message to confirm your action:

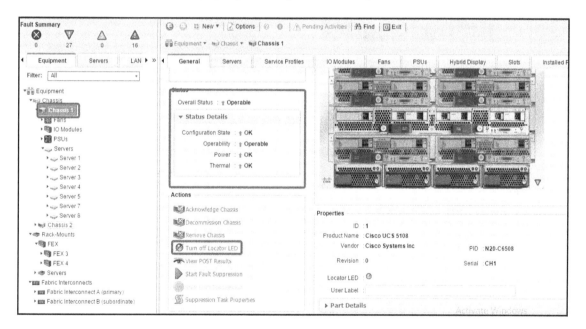

The preceding screen shows the **Status** of the selected chassis. It also shows the option of turning on the locator LED. Once turned on, the locator LED will turn gray in UCS Manager and the text will change to **Turn off Locator LED**; now, the locator LED can be turned off from the same location:

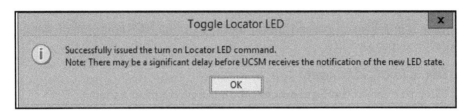

 The locator LED is a vivid blue color LED. The status LED is green or orange depending the equipment state.

# Configuring logging

There are three major categories of the information collected by UCS Manager. These logs are accessible through the **Admin** tab in the navigation pane.

Perform the following procedure to access the logs:

1. Log in to UCS Manager.
2. Click to expand the **Admin** tab in the navigation pane.
3. In the **Admin** tab, click on **Faults, Events and Audit Log** to expand its content.
4. Click on the individual expanded tabs in the navigation pane or individual horizontal tabs in the work pane to expand the details of each category:

    - **Faults**: The **Faults** tab shows all the faults occurring on all UCS components. Individual faults are shown for each component when you are in the *components* view and this tab provides details of all the faults:

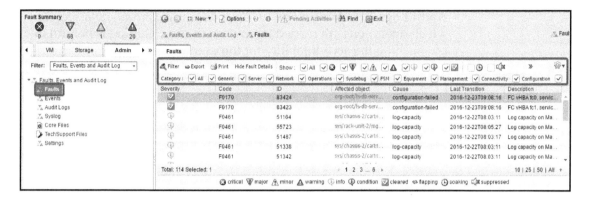

You may check or uncheck individual categories to filter the results.

- **Events**: Events are all the operations happening on all components such as a port configuration, a service profile association, and a VLAN configuration:

- **Audit Logs**: The **Audit Logs** tab provides the *audit trail*, detailing which operations are carried out by which user. This log is helpful in establishing the accountability for the user actions:

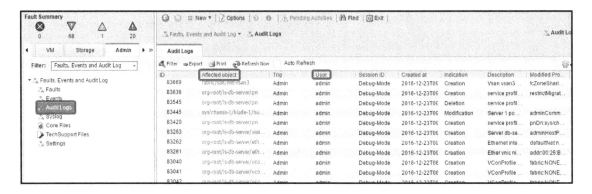

By default, the **Faults, Events and Audit Log** is stored on the local UCS Fabric Interconnect. The default log settings are as shown in the following screenshot:

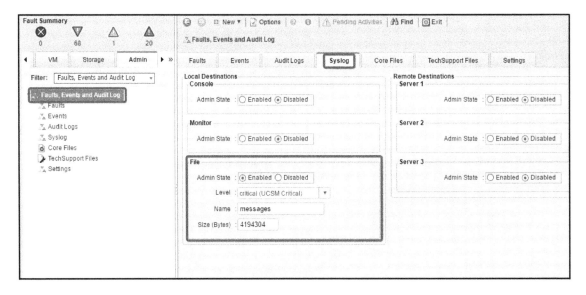

The default setting is to save all messages to a local file on Fabric Interconnect. In the **Level** section under **Local Destinations**, select the lowest message level and all the messages before that level will be automatically displayed.

It is also possible to show log messages on the **Console** or **Monitor** areas. The configuration option is the same; select the lowest level message and all messages before that level will be automatically displayed.

The following recipe shows how to direct the log message to the console:

1. Log in to UCS Manager.
2. Click on the **Admin** tab in the navigation pane.
3. In the **Admin** tab, click on **Faults, Events and Audit Log** to expand its content.
4. Click on individual expanded tabs in the navigation pane or individual horizontal tabs in the work pane to expand the **Syslog** category.

In the work pane, under the **Console** area, click on **Enabled** to enable the **Admin State**. Select the message with the desired lowest state using one of the three radio buttons: **Emergencies**, **Alerts**, or **Critical**:

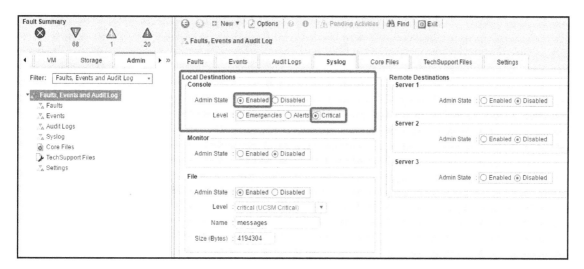

It is also possible to configure three remote syslog servers for the collection of UCS logs. Syslog servers centralize the log collection.

Please use the following procedure to configure a remote syslog server:

1. Log in to UCS Manager.
2. Click on the **Admin** tab in the navigation pane.
3. In the **Admin** tab, click on **Faults, Events and Audit Log** to expand its content.
4. Click on the individual expanded tabs in the navigation pane or individual horizontal tabs in the work pane to expand the **Syslog** category.

5. In the work pane, in the **Remote Destinations** area, click on **Enabled** to enable the **Admin State**.
6. Select the message with the desired lowest state using the drop-down menu for the messages. The previous level messages will be automatically included.
7. Configure the **Hostname (or IP Address)** for the remote syslog server and select the **Facility** level:

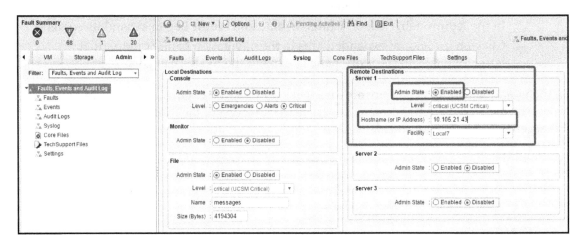

# Configuring the Cisco Call Home feature

The Call Home feature enables configuration of e-mail alert notifications for UCS errors and faults. The e-mail notifications can be configured for Cisco TAC (predefined) (this is known as **Smart Call Home**) or any other internal recipient such as members of the technical team or NOC engineers. This feature can be used to send a page message or an e-mail, or to generate a case with the Cisco **Technical Assistance Center** (**TAC**).

When Call Home is configured, UCSM executes the appropriate CLI `show` command and the command output is attached to the message for Call Home messages.

Call Home messages are delivered in the following three formats:

- **Short text format**: This provides a short description (one or two lines of the fault) that is suitable for pagers
- **Full text format**: This provides the complete message with detailed information
- **XML format**: The XML format provides detailed information helpful in troubleshooting the issue and is used for communication with the Cisco TAC team

In the following example, we will configure Cisco Smart Call Home for UCS Call Home, which will send the alert e-mails directly to Cisco TAC and to a network engineer:

1. Configure **Contact Information** with the following details:
   - **Contact**
   - **Phone**
   - **Email**
   - **Address**
2. In the work pane, on the **General** tab, click on **On** under the **Admin** area **State** The screen will be extended for further configuration. **Configure Switch Priority and Throttling.**
3. Click on **Call Home** under **Communication Management**.
4. In the **Admin** tab, click on **Communication Management** to expand its content.
5. Click on the **Admin** tab in the navigation pane.
6. Log in to UCS Manager.
7. Configure the Cisco ID. The following information should be available from the CCO account:
   - **Customer ID**
   - **Contract ID**
   - **Site ID**
8. Configure the **From** e-mail address for the sender of the e-mail along with the **Reply To** e-mail address.

9. Configure the SMTP Server with Host (IP Address or Hostname) and Port settings.

10. Click on the **Profiles** tab in the work pane and edit the predefined **Profile CiscoTAC-1**:

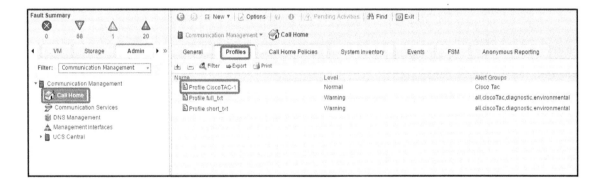

11. Add the e-mail recipient `support@cisco.com` by clicking on the **+** sign in the pop-up window. The default e-mail format setting for the Cisco TAC profile is **Xml** and it cannot be changed. The severity level, however, can be changed:

12. In the **Profiles** tab, edit the other predefined **Profile full_text** and add the e-mail recipient. The default e-mail format is clear text and is grayed out. The severity level of messages can also be changed.

Apart from the predefined profiles, it is possible to create new profiles. Creating a new profile provides customization options such as the severity level, mail format, and alert groups for all fields.

For the Smart Call Home feature, you will receive an e-mail confirmation from the Cisco TAC team for completing the configuration.

# Organizational structure in UCS Manager

The UCS organizational structure provides hierarchical configuration of the UCS resources. An organization can be created for policies, pools, and service profiles. The default organization for each category is **root**. Based on the requirement, multiple sub-organizations can be created under the root organization. It is also possible to create a nested sub-organization under another sub-organization. The hierarchical configuration into sub-organizations has the following benefits:

- **Role-based Access Control (RBAC)**: For large setups, it is often necessary to delegate operational management to a team of professionals, and often with limited level of access to the resource, according to the role of the individual. Creating a sub-organization and mapping appropriate user roles provides excellent security privileges and nonrepudiation.
- **Multitenancy**: For service providers, a sub-organization's configuration provides the logical access isolation for the various clients who are sharing the physical UCS components. Unique resources to each tenant can be assigned related to the organizational structure. Combined with the RBAC configuration, a tenant's access privileges can be restricted to their organization only.

Please perform the following procedure for creating a sub-organization under **Pools**. The procedure for creating sub-organizations under the navigation pane is similar, and once a sub-organization is created under any tab, it will be available under all categories and resources:

1. Log in to UCS Manager.
2. Click on the **Servers** tab in the navigation pane.
3. On the **Servers** tab click on **Pools** to expand its content.
4. Right-click on **root** under **Pools** and click on **Create Organization**:

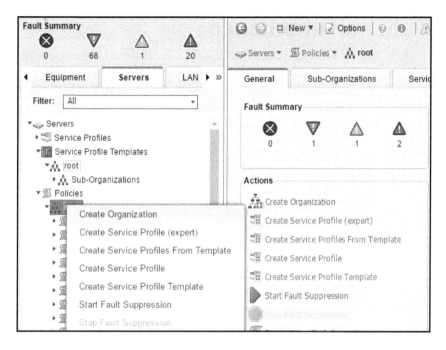

5. In the pop-up window, provide a **Name** and **Description** to the new organization and click on **OK**:

6. The new sub-organization will be created under the **root** organization.

# Organizational inheritance

The policies, pools, and other resources configured under the root organization are available to all sub-organizations. Root is the parent organization for all sub-organizations. The resources configured under the sub-organizations at the same level are not shared among the other sibling sub-organizations. A sub-organization under another sub-organization shares the resources of the parent.

# RBAC

UCS RBAC provides granular control over the user security privileges. Combined with UCS organizations, RBAC delegates and controls the user access privileges according to the role and restricts user access within an organization boundary defined for the tenant in case of multitenancy.

Access privileges provide the users with the capability to create, modify, or delete a specific type of configuration. UCS provides some predefined roles and it is also possible to create custom roles based on requirements. The **roles** are a collection of different privileges. Hence, roles can be assigned to users according to their job requirements. For example, there's a built-in role called **read-only** that provides only read privileges to the user. This role can be assigned to any user to whom you do not want to provide any configuration capability.

In UCS, a user's authentication can be configured from various resources including the following:

- Local user
- LDAP (Active Directory, OpenLDAP, and so on)
- RADIUS
- TACACS+

# Active Directory integration

We will now configure the AD/LDAP authentication integration for UCS. We will integrate UCS Manager to the Microsoft Active Directory domain controller. On the AD side, appropriate user groups should be created that can be used to provide mapping to UCS roles that provide privileges to the AD authenticated users accordingly.

Perform the following procedure to enable Active Directory authentication:

1. Log in to UCS Manager.
2. Click on the **Admin** tab in the navigation pane.
3. On the **Admin** tab, click on **User Management** to expand its content.
4. Click on **LDAP** in the navigation pane and click on **Create LDAP Provider** in the work pane:

5. In the pop-up window, provide the following AD configuration details:
   1. Provide a DNS hostname or IP of the domain controller.
   2. Type in `lowest-available` in the **Order** field.
   3. Provide the **distinguished name** (**DN**) of the user with read and search permissions in the Active Directory in the **Bind DN** field. It is recommended to use the normal user or service account with read permissions only and not an administrator account for **Bind DN**.
   4. Provide a specification location of the AD where the search should start in the **Base DN** field. You may start from the root of the AD for smaller organizations. For a large AD implementation, it is recommended to start the search from the OU where the AD users/groups are located.
   5. Type `389` in **Port** and leave **Enable SSL** unchecked for regular communication without SSL or check **Enable SSL** with the appropriate AD port.
   6. Type `sAMAccountName=$userid` into the **Filter** field.
   7. Leave the **Attribute** field blank.

8. Type in a password for the bind user configured in step 3 and reconfirm the password. Type in a Timeout value in seconds:

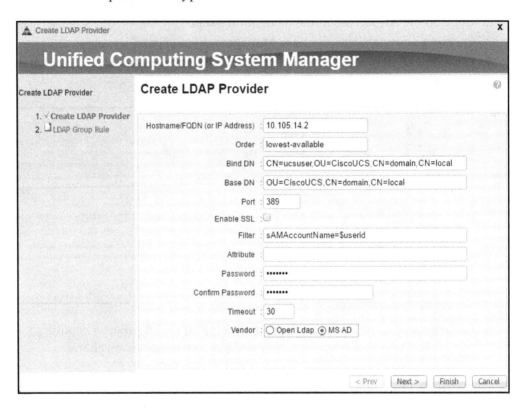

9. Click on **Next** and configure **Group Authorization** by clicking on the **Enable** button.
10. Leave the other two settings, **Group Recursion** and **Target Attribute**, with the default values.
11. Click on **Finish**.
12. Repeat the steps for the other domain controllers:

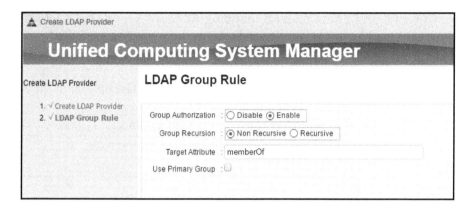

6. Create an LDAP provider group adding all domain controllers in the provider group and perform the following steps:

   1. Click on **LDAP** in the navigation pane and click on **Create LDAP Provider Group** in the work pane.

   2. In the pop-up window, assign a **Name** for the **LDAP Provider Group**.

   3. Select domain controllers in the left-hand side pane and click on **>>** to add them to the group.

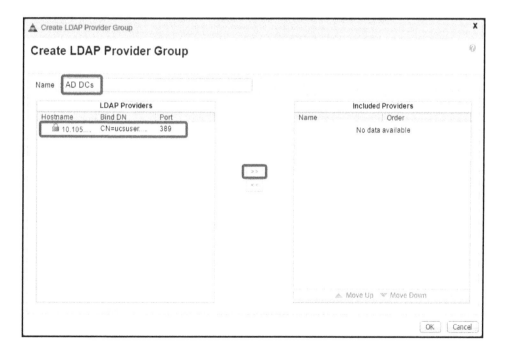

7. Create an LDAP group map for mapping AD users/groups to UCS local roles in order to provide access privileges. Perform the following steps to do so:

    1. Click on **LDAP** in the navigation pane and click on **Create LDAP Group Map** in the work pane.

    2. In the pop-up window, type in the **LDAP Group DN** of the AD user group to be mapped to a local role.

    3. Select the local UCS role from the **Roles** field.

    4. Repeat the same procedure for adding all the roles.

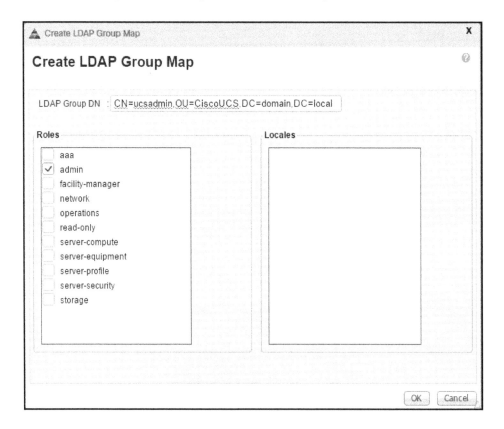

    5. The next screenshot shows an example of some LDAP groups mapped to UCS roles. You can create different LDAP groups and map them to UCS local roles as per your environment:

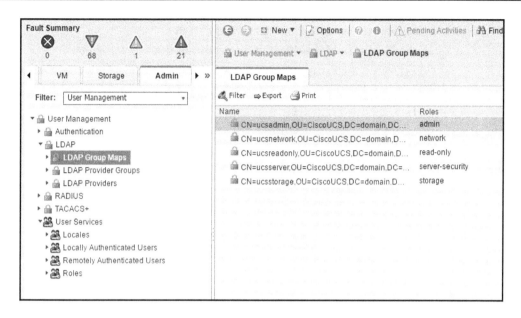

8. The last step for the Active Directory configuration is to define the authentication domain for UCS Manager:

1. Expand **Authentication** in **User Management** and right-click on **Authentication Domains** to create a new domain:

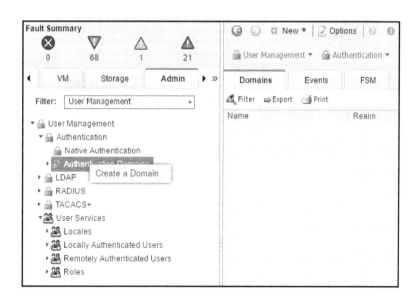

2. In the pop-up window, assign a **Name** to the domain.
3. In the **Realm** field, select the **Ldap** radio button.
4. Select value for **Provider Group** from the drop-down menu and select **OK**:

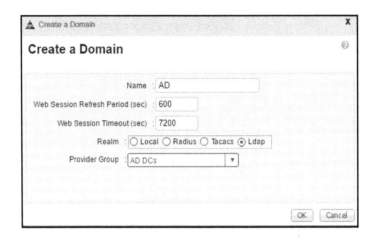

# Predefined roles

UCS provides a number of predefined roles. These roles combine and provide different privileges as per organizational/team role roles of individual users. The built-in roles are as follows:

- **aaa**: This role provides the member with full access to a user configuration, roles assignment, and **Authentication, Authorization, and Accounting (AAA)** configuration and provides the read access to the rest of the system.
- **admin**: This role provides the member *complete* control of the UCSM. The default local admin account has this role by default, which cannot be changed.
- **facility-manager**: This role provides the member with full access to power management operations through the **power-mgmt** privilege and provides read access to the rest of the system.
- **network**: This role provides the member full access to the Fabric Interconnect infrastructure and network security operations and provides read access to the rest of the system.
- **operations**: This role provides the member full access to systems logs, including the syslog servers and faults, and provides read access to the rest of the system.

- **read-only**: This role provides the read-only access to the system configuration with no privileges to modify the system state.
- **server-compute**: This new role, introduced in UCS 2.1, provides somewhat limited access to the service profiles. For example, a user cannot change vNICs or vHBAs configurations.
- **server-equipment**: This role provides full access to physical-server-related operations and provides the read access to the rest of the system.
- **server-profile**: This role provides full access to logical server related operations and provides the read access to the rest of the system.
- **server-security**: This role provides full access to server-security-related operations and the read access to the rest of the system.
- **storage**: This role provides full access to storage operations and provides the read access to the rest of the system.

It is also possible to create user-defined roles based on design requirements by adding the new role and assigning required individual privileges.

# About UCS locales

UCS locales define the location of the user in the UCS organization hierarchy. A user without a locale assignment has access to the root organization. This means that the user has access to all sub-organizations. Locales can be mapped to the sub-organization, restricting the user access within the scope of the sub-organization. Locales can be created and then the user can be mapped to locales.

Perform the following steps to create a locale and restrict some users access to a sub-organization:

1. Log in to UCS Manager.
2. Click to expand the **Admin** tab in the navigation pane.
3. On the **Admin** tab, click on **User Management** to expand **User Services**.

4. Right-click on **Locales** in the navigation pane and click on **Create Locale**:

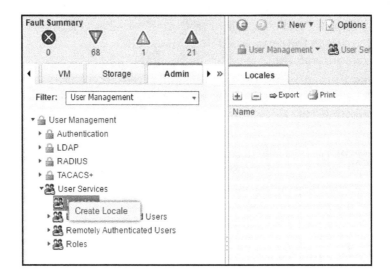

5. Assign a **Name** for the locale and click on **Next**:

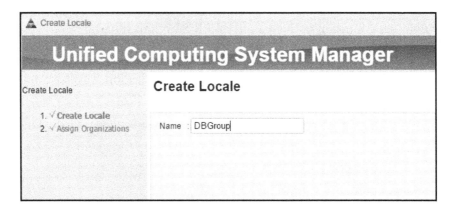

6. Expand **Organizations** in the left-hand side pane and select the locale in the right-hand side pane:

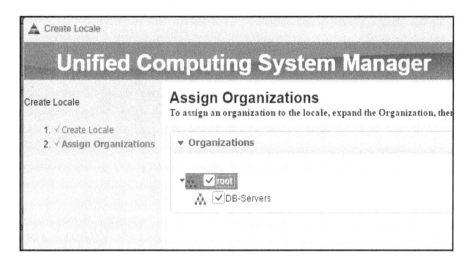

7. Click on **Finish**.

The new locale will be available which can be used by any locally or remotely authenticated users. Once the locale is assigned to the users/groups, the access will be limited to the sub-organization.

To assign a locale to remote Active Directory authenticated users/groups, perform the following procedure:

1. Log in to UCS Manager.
2. Click on the **Admin** tab in the navigation pane.
3. On the **Admin** tab, click on **User Management** to expand the **LDAP** content.
4. Select the existing AD group and double-click on it to edit the settings.

5. A new option in the locale will be available which can be assigned:

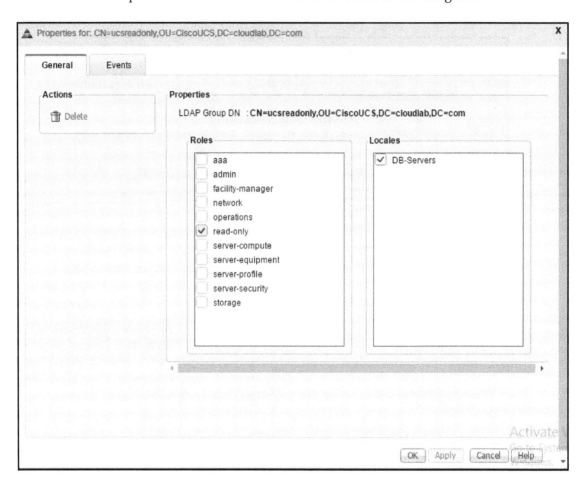

The UCS Manager **admin** user, which is configured as part of the initial configuration, can be used to log in to UCS Manager if the LDAP authentication is not available by selecting local authentication on the UCSM login screen.

# Permissions in multitenancy

Multitenancy is a requirement for service providers. A service provider can provide access to multiple tenants within the same UCS infrastructure with logical security isolation between tenants so that the resources provided to one tenant cannot be tampered with by another.

UCS multitenancy can be achieved with the following:

- Creation of a sub-organization for each tenant
- Creation of locales to restrict user access to individual sub-organization

For example, we will create two tenants: tenant one and tenant two.

Follow the steps defined in the *Organizational structure in UCS Manager* section of this chapter and create two tenants. Two organizational units defined as **Tenant1** and **Tenant2** are shown in the following screenshot:

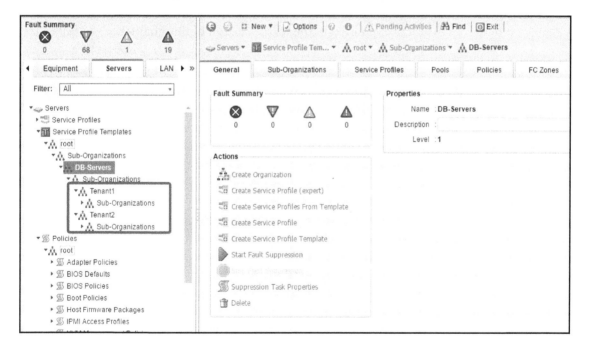

Follow the steps explained in the *RBAC* section of this chapter to create two locales for the sub-organizations for the tenants:

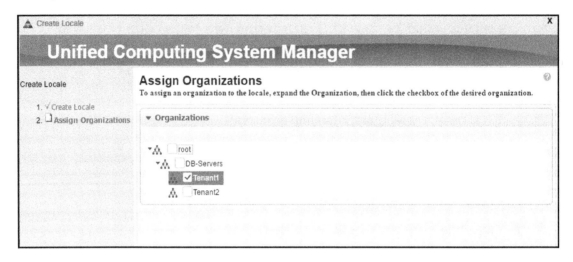

Create and map local users as explained in the *RBAC* section of this chapter:

# Summary

In this chapter, we learned about the miscellaneous and most common tasks along with some advanced management tasks you need to perform with UCS Manager. We started looking at how to obtain and configure extra port licenses for Fabric Interconnects. We learned that UCS Fabric Interconnects are designed for continuous operation and hence do not have a power button. It is however possible to reboot Fabric Interconnect, but only from CLI. We learned about a corner case requirement in a DR situation for how to control blade power usage. We learned about looking into the status messages and turning on/off the locator LEDs available on blades, blade chassis, and Fabric Interconnects. We covered what the default logging setting is and how we can configure a remote syslog server. We configured the Call Home feature which can be used to inform/alert UCS management teams and Cisco TAC.

Finally, we learned about how we can configure organizational structure and RBAC in UCS. We configured an external authentication using the LDAP configuration for Microsoft Active Directory and also mapped users to UCS locales. Combining user authentication, organization structure, and locales, it is possible to configure permissions for multitenant environments. UCS organizational design and the RBAC configuration provide the required security for authentication, authorization, and accountability to UCS in large-scale or multitenant UCS deployments where delegation of accesses with user nonrepudiation is required.

In the next chapter, we will learn about the integration of Cisco UCS within virtualized environments, mostly with VMware vSphere, which is the dominant hypervisor deployed in production environments, and we will also look at the Cisco Nexus 1000V distributed virtual switch.

# 10
# Virtual Networking in Cisco UCS

The Cisco Nexus 1000V switch is a virtual machine that acts as an access switch. It is an intelligent software switch implementation based on IEEE 802.1Q standard for VMware vSphere environments, running the Cisco NX-OS software operating system.

The Nexus 1000V switch is a distributed layer 2 switch that is implemented as a virtual softswitch and runs Cisco's NX-OS. Any network administrator familiar with NX-OS software can easily manage Nexus 1000V without learning new operating system skillsets. It provides similar CLI and functionality to physical Nexus switches. With Nexus 1000V, network admins can manage both physical and virtual network infrastructure with better visibility, control, and it is easier to troubleshoot.

In this chapter, we will cover the following topics:

- Knowing about VN-Link
- Using the NX-OS
- Development of Nexus 1000V through VSUM
- Nexus 1000V components
- VEM and VSM implementation
- VEM data plane
- VSM control plane
- Nexus 1000V and physical switches
- VSUM deployment
- Communication between VSM and VEM

# Learning about VN-Link

VN-Link network services are available in VMware vSphere environments with the Nexus 1000V switch. Basically, it is a set of features and capabilities that enables VM interfaces to be individually identified, configured, monitored, migrated, and diagnosed so that they are consistent with the current network operational models. It replicates an operational experience similar to using a cable to connect an NIC with the network port of an access-layer switch.

# Using the NX-OS

The Nexus 1000V switch offers the same Cisco NX-OS capabilities as the Nexus switch, which includes the following:

- **High availability**: Stateful failover is possible through synchronized, redundant VSMs
- **Management**: Standard management tools such as CLI, SNMP, XML API, and CiscoWorks **LAN Management Solution** (**LMS**) can be used

# Changes in the data center

Moving from the physical to virtual, applications, network policies, and the **network administrator** (**NA**) and **server administrator** (**SA**) roles are getting continuously overlapped, where the network edge is now virtual and has moved into the host, that is, the ESXi server. This changes the distinct boundary between the SA and NA roles.

Where physical machines were once just plugged into a switch, and the switch port configured by a network administrator, the SA can now create and deploy multiple hosts in a fraction of the time. And while the host life cycle has changed significantly, the same management policies need to apply in both cases, which means that access lists, VLANs, port security, and many more parameters need to be consistent. The challenge for SAs is to take advantage of the flexibility of virtualization while conforming to organizational policy.

The challenge for NAs is to maintain control over the network traffic and the access ports that are running over hardware that they don't directly control. Have a look at the following diagram for more details:

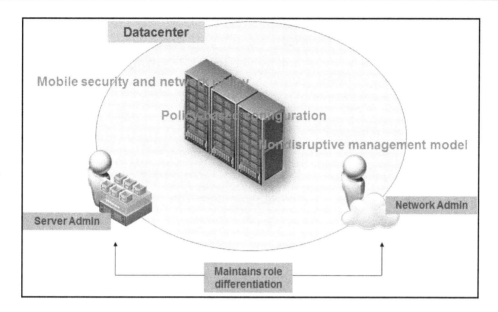

Specific benefits of the Nexus 1000V switch that help address these challenges are as follows:

- **Policy-based configuration**: This signifies a real-time configuration of network, storage, and security services. SA's efficiency and flexibility can be rapidly improved using the policy-based configuration as it introduces a VM-centric management.
- **Mobile security and network policy**: When you perform a live migration such as vMotion, it moves the policy as well with the VM for a persistent network. In that way, vMotion won't affect the VM traffic counters.
- **Nondisruptive management model**: Management and operations can come together in a single line for VMs' connectivity in the data center. Operational consistency and visibility is well maintained throughout the network.

# Role differentiation

**Nexus 1000V** (**N1KV**) offers flexible collaboration between the server, network, security, and storage teams while supporting organizational boundaries and individual team autonomy. Essentially, it ensures that the traditional boundary between the SA and NA roles is maintained.

# Role issues

There is the added complication of VM life cycles moving from months/years to weeks/days. So basically, port management is increasingly difficult. Have a look at the following diagram for more details:

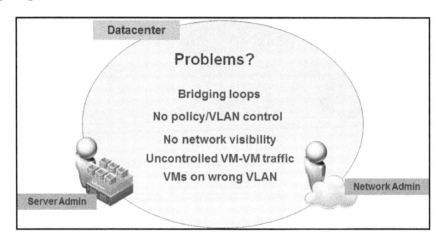

The following are some major problems with role issues:

- VMs can result in bridging loops on the network
- VMs could be on the wrong VLANs
- No insight into VM to VM communication is available
- The network admin has no visibility or policy/VLAN control

# Development of Nexus 1000V

N1KV was developed jointly by VMware and Cisco. As such, it is certified by VMware to be compatible with VMware vSphere, vCenter, ESXi, and many other vSphere features.

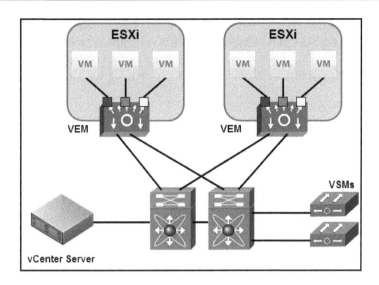

# Virtual Ethernet interfaces

Cisco N1KV, when enabled for VN-Link, operates on the basis of **Virtual Ethernet** (**vEth**) interfaces. Once enabled for VN-Link, it maintains network configuration attributes, such as security and statistics for a given virtual interface across mobility events. vEth interfaces are comparable to physical network access ports. A mapping gets created between each vEth interface and the corresponding vNICs on the VM. You may ask me why you would need vEth interfaces. The main advantage of using these is that they can follow vNICs when VMs move to other ESXi hosts. Once you set up a VN-Link on N1KV switches, it enables transparent mobility of VMs across different ESXi hosts and physical access-layer switches, and it does so by virtualizing the network access port with vEth interfaces.

# Learning about port profiles

Port profiles are nothing but a collection of interface configuration commands (the same as physical switches) that can be dynamically applied at either physical or virtual interfaces on Cisco N1KV. So, as an effect, if you make any change to a given port profile it will be propagated immediately to all the ports that have been associated with it. For troubleshooting in a port profile, you have the flexibility to define a collection of attributes, such as VLAN, **private VLAN** (**PVLAN**), ACL, port security, NetFlow collection, rate limiting, QoS marking, and even remote-port mirroring, but only through **Encapsulated Remote SPAN** (**ERSPAN**).

VN-Link can be implemented as a Cisco **distributed virtual switch** (**DVS**), running entirely in software within the hypervisor layer (N1KV) or in devices that support **network interface virtualization** (**NIV**), eliminating the requirement for software-based switching within hypervisors (Cisco UCS).

# Nexus 1000V components

N1KV consists of VSMs and VEMs. While VEMs are software elements that reside inside the hypervisor, running as a part of the VMware ESXi kernel. The VEM acts like a line card to VSM and provides packet forwarding and other functions for virtual machines. Whereas VSM is deployed as a virtual appliance and provides control to manage multiple VEMs and virtual machine traffic steering. Have a look at the following diagram for more details:

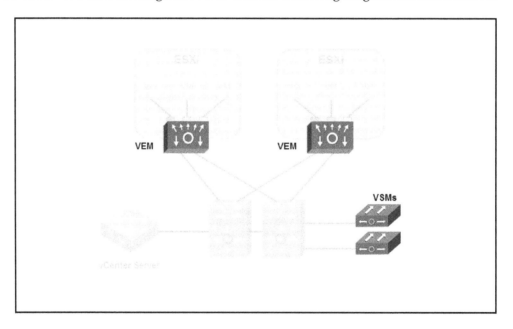

The highlighted components in the preceding diagram are explained in the following sections.

# The Virtual Ethernet Module

The **Virtual Ethernet Module** (**VEM**) runs as a part of the VMware ESXi kernel. It uses the VMware **vNetwork Distributed Switch** (**VDS**) API to provide advanced networking capabilities to VMs.

The VEM provides advanced networking functions, such as QoS, security features, and monitoring features, by taking configuration information from the VSM.

# The Virtual Supervisor Module

Multiple VEMs create a single logical switch layer to the **Virtual Supervisor Module** (**VSM**). The VSM maintains configuration and pushes down the configuration to the VEMs. The administrator has the ability to define configurations on all VEMs being managed by the VSM from a single interface.

 The VSM can reside on a host that has exclusive network connectivity through Cisco N1KV. It can, therefore, manage its own network connectivity.

# VEM implementation

The following are some important features of VEM:

- It is a virtual line card
- It is embedded in the vSphere host (hypervisor)
- It provides each VM with dedicated switch ports
- It is the switch in every host

Here, we run the ESXi package manager to show the VIB file used to implement the VEM. If you list the processes, you will also see the **VEM data path agent** (**vemdpa**) that communicates with the VSM (running in the user mode).

Finally, the hypervisor driver (running in the kernel mode) performs packet switching.

 vCenter can operate without too much regard for the VEM. Typically, the only reason to go there (via SSH) is for troubleshooting purposes.

The *esxupdate* utility is no longer supported, but we can use it here to illustrate a point.

# VSM implementation

The VSM acts as a control plane for the N1KV solution, that is, it is responsible for the vCenter communication, programming, and management of VEMs. Unlike the VEM, which is a code running in the hypervisor, it is actually a VM on an ESXi server. It can also be deployed on a dedicated hardware appliance, such as Nexus 1010. VSMs are typically deployed as **high availability (HA)** pairs. Have a look at the following diagram for more details:

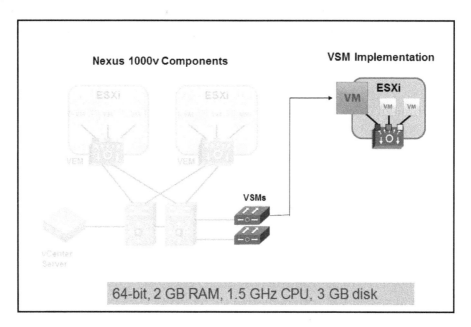

Please note that we can't have one VSM on hardware appliance Nexus 1110 and the other on the ESXi VSM. Both VSMs should be either on hardware appliance or on ESXi hosts:

- Control plane controls multiple VEMS
- Virtual machine running NX-OS

# VEM data plane

There is a 1:1 mapping between hypervisor and VEM. VEM replaces the virtual switch by performing the following functions:

- Advanced networking and security
- Switching between directly attached VMs
- Uplinking through physical NICs

You can install only one version of VEM on an ESXi host at any given point in time. Please have a look at the following diagram for more details:

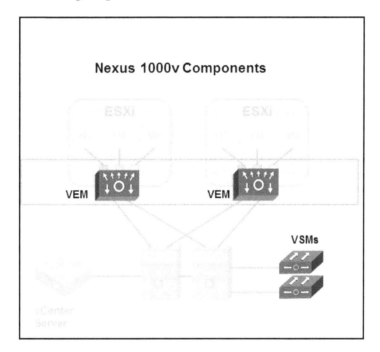

# VEM functions

The following are the various functions of VEM:

- Advanced networking and security
- Switching between directly attached VMs
- Uplink to the rest of the network

Unlike conventional Nexus switches, each line card has its own **media access control** (**MAC**) table that goes through the same process as conventional switches:

- **Ingress**: Traffic that comes inbound towards the interfaces of the N1KV switch
- **L2 lookup**: A process that handles the packets after the parser engine has parsed the initial packet delivery
- **Egress**: Traffic goes out of the interfaces of the N1KV switch

# VSM control plane

A VSM can be deployed either as a standalone or as an active/standby HA pair. The pair can be protected through VMware DRS anti-affinity rule to be hosted on different ESXi. It controls the VEMs and performs the following functions for the Cisco N1KV system:

- Configuration
- Management
- Monitoring
- Diagnostics
- Integration with the VMware vCenter

The following diagram explains the various N1KV components and their relationship. Essentially, it explains the relationship between a VSM and VEM:

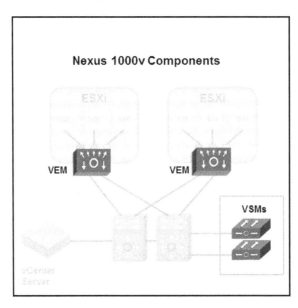

# Nexus 1000V and physical switches

The VEM corresponds to a line card in a conventional physical switch, while the VSM corresponds to a supervisor engine.

## The physical switch chassis

In a hardware switch, the physical wiring that connects the **Supervisor Engine** (**SE**) and the individual line cards is known as the **backplane**. This is incorporated into the switch chassis. There are numerous types of modular switches, which will have different configurations depending on their functions. However, all switches will have an SE and typically some Ethernet line cards.

## Line cards

Other line cards include **advanced integrated services modules** (**AISMs**) that include firewall services, content switching, **Intruder Detection System** (**IDS**), and **Wireless and Network Analysis Modules** (**WNAM**).

Cisco N1KV uses local VEM instances to switch the traffic between VMs. Each VEM also interconnects the local VM with the rest of the network through the upstream access-layer network switch. VSM never forwards the packets. It runs the control plane protocols and configures the state of each VEM accordingly.

## The N1KV backplane

The backplane function here is performed by the physical uplink switches, that is, the organization's network infrastructure. The number of line cards supported then is not determined by the physical capacity of the chassis, but by the VSM. Currently, up to 64 VEMs are supported by a single VSM or an HA pair.

 Obviously, you're limited to the type of cards that are feasible using this model. However, there are ways to enhance the functionality of N1KV using an appliance, which allows other modules such as a firewall and **Network Access Module** (**NAM**). Nexus 1110 is one such appliance.

In N1KV VSM, there are two module slots. Either module can act as active or standby. As an effect, the first ESXi host will automatically be assigned to module 1. The ports to which the virtual NIC interfaces connect are virtual ports on Cisco N1KV, where they are assigned a global number. Have a look at the following diagram for more details:

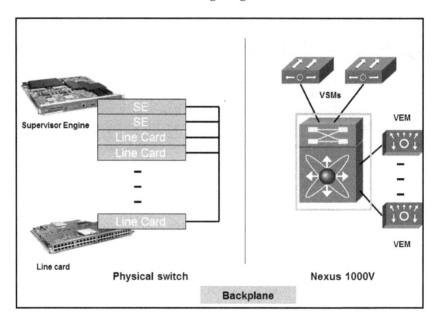

With the challenges presented by virtualization to the demarcation between host and network, N1KV allows the necessary collaboration between NAs and SAs.

Internal fabric helps the supervisors and line cards to communicate in a physical switch. On a similar note, N1KV uses external fabric that is provided by the upstream switches in the physical infrastructure.

The physical switch's backplane helps line cards to forward traffic to each other. However, N1KV does not have a backplane, thus a VEM cannot directly forward packets to another VEM. So it has to forward the packet via some uplink to the external fabric, which then switches it to the destination.

Each VEM in Cisco N1KV is designed in order to prevent loops in the network topology, as using the **Spanning-Tree Protocol** (**STP**) will deactivate all but one uplink to an upstream switch, hence preventing full utilization of the uplink bandwidth.

You can bundle the uplinks in a host in a port channel for load balancing and HA.

# Nexus and vPath

Cisco vPath allows you to deploy network services, like in a physical switch. It is embedded in every VEM. Essentially, it provides intelligent packet steering, which means that policy lookup is decoupled from enforcement. For example, with the **Virtual Security Gateway (VSG)**, which is a virtualized Cisco firewall, once a policy decision is made at the VSG for a particular flow, it's up to vPath now to implement that policy for each packet in that flow, thereby freeing up the VSG.

The vPath is enabled at a port-profile level. When VSG policies are configured, flow is evaluated against the policy by the VSG, and then the policy decision is pushed for implementation to vPath. It stores that decision only for the duration of that flow. Once there is a **Reset (RST)** event or **Finish (FIN)** flag, the flow entry is removed from the vPath table. There is also an activity timer, which can terminate sessions.

FIN and RST are TCP control bits (flags). FIN indicates that the client will send no more data, while RST resets the connection. **Virtual Wide Area Application Services (vWAAS)** is Cisco's WAN optimization technology, used to improve application delivery in cloud environments. Have a look at the following diagram for more details:

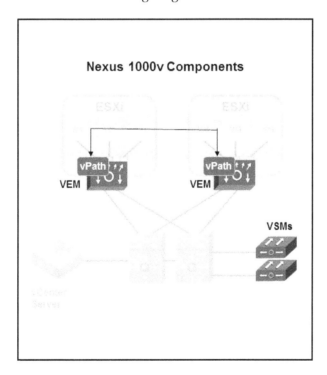

# Performance advantages using vPath

vPath also provides performance advantages. Since only the initial packets of a flow need to go to the VSG, there is less packet steering going on. Subsequent policy enforcement is done by the local N1KV VEM in the kernel mode, so you get better performance overall.

HA is available, but if the service that vPath is directing to fails (for example, in the case of a firewall service where both firewalls are down), there is the option of failing *closed* or *open*. It can stop all traffic, or can be configured to let everything through.

# Deploying VSM

Cisco has simplified the VSM deployment with **Virtual Switch Update Manager** (**VSUM**), a virtual appliance that can be installed on VMware ESXi hypervisor and registered as a plugin with VMware vCenter. VSUM enables the SA to install, monitor, migrate, and upgrade Cisco Nexus 1000V in high availability or standalone mode. With VSUM, you can deploy multiple instances of Nexus 1000V and manage them from a single appliance. VSUM only provides layer 3 connectivity with ESXi hosts. For layer 2 connectivity with ESXi, you still have to deploy Nexus 1000V VSM manually and need to configure L2 mode in basic configuration.

# VSUM architecture

VSUM has two components: the backend as a virtual appliance and frontend as GUI integrated into VMware vCenter Server. The virtual appliance will be configured with an IP address similar to VMware vCenter management IP address subnet. Once a virtual appliance is deployed on the ESXi, it establishes the connectivity with VMware vCenter Server to access the vCenter and hosts.

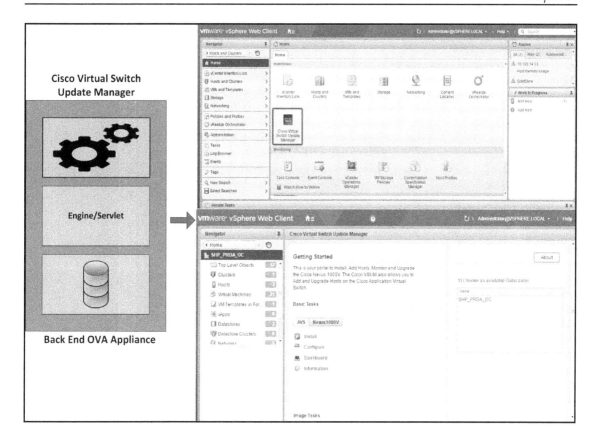

# VSUM and VSM installation

The VSM deployment will be divided into two parts: first, installation of VSUM and registering as a plugin with VMware vCenter; second, importing the Nexus 1000V package into VSUM and then deploying Nexus 1000V through the VSUM GUI interface.

For installing and configuring Cisco VSUM, you require one management port group, which will communicate with vCenter. However, Nexus 1000V VSM will require two port groups, control and management. You can use just one VLAN for all of these, but it is preferred to have them configured with separate VLANs.

Download the Nexus 1000V package and VSUM at
`https://software.cisco.com/download/type.html?mdfid=282646785&flowid=42790` and
then use the following procedure to deploy VSUM and VSM:

1. Go to vCenter, click on the **File** menu, and select **Deploy OVF Template**.
2. Browse to the location of the VSUM OVA file and click on **Browse...** to install the required OVA file, and click on **Next**, as shown in the following screenshot:

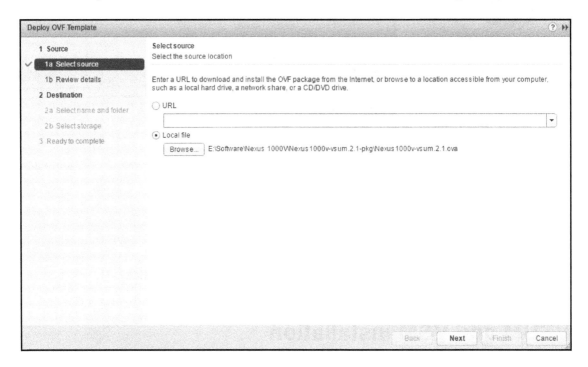

3. Click on **Next** twice.
4. Click on **Accept** for the **End User License Agreement** page and then click on **Next**.

5. Specify a name for the VSUM and select the data center where you would like it to be installed. Then click on **Next**, as shown in the following screenshot:

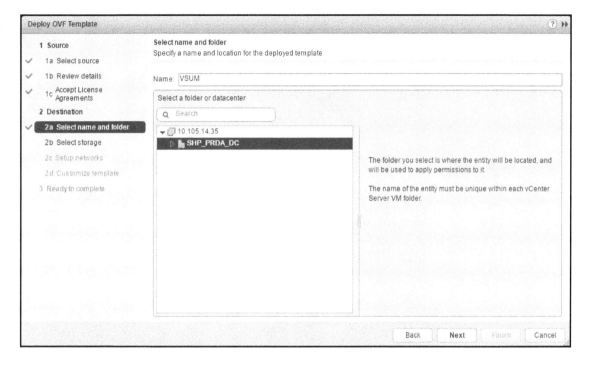

6. Select the **Datastore** object to install the VSUM.
7. Choose **Thin Provision** for the virtual disk of VSUM and click on **Next**.

8. Under the **Destination** network page, select the network that you had created earlier for **Management**. Then, click on **Next**, as shown in the following screenshot:

9. Enter the management IP address, DNS, vCenter IP address, username and password values, as shown in the following screenshot:

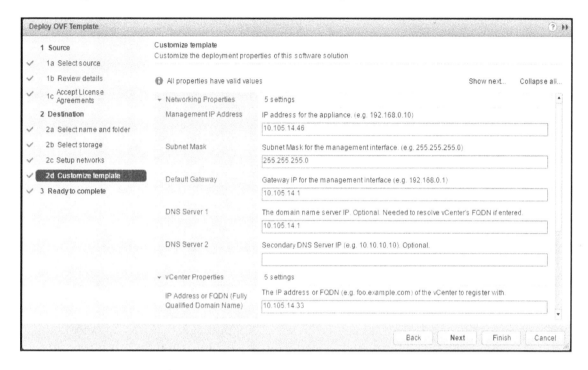

10. A summary of all your settings is then presented. If you are happy with these settings, click on **Finish**.

11. Once VSUM is deployed in the vCenter, power on the VM. This will take 5 minutes for installation and registration as a vCenter plugin. To view the VSUM GUI, you need to log in to vCenter Server again to activate the VSUM plugin:

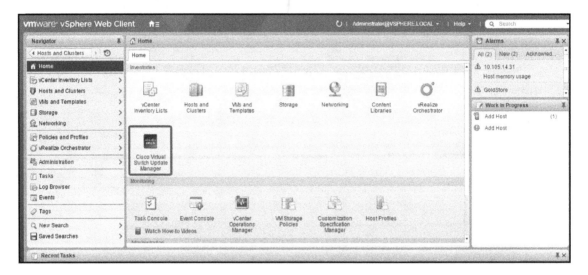

12. Click on **Cisco Virtual Switch Update Manager** and select the **Upload** option under **Image Tasks**. Upload the Nexus 1000V package, that was downloaded earlier under **Upload switch image**. This will open **Virtual Switch Image File Uploader** and select the appropriate package:

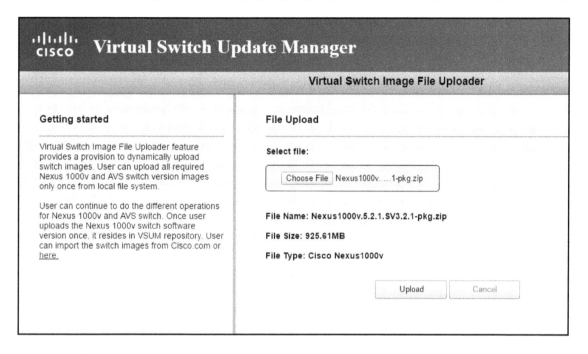

13. Once the image is uploaded, this will display under **Manage Uploaded switch images**.

14. Click on the **Nexus 1000V** tab under **Basic Tasks**, and click on **Install** and select the desired data center:

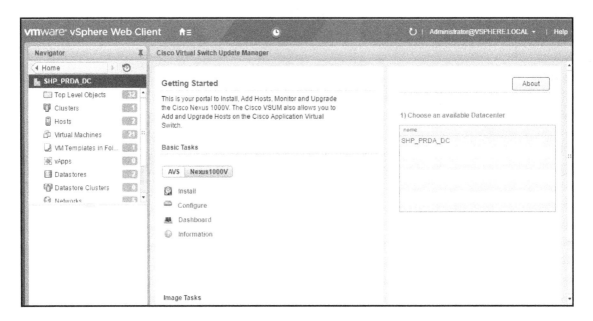

15. In the Nexus 1000V installer page, go to install a new control plane VSM, and select the proper options for **Nexus1000V Switch Deployment Type**, **VSM Version**, and **Choose a Port Group**. Select the host, VSM **Domain ID**, **Switch Name**, **IP Address**, **Username**, and **Password**. Then, click on **Finish**. A window will appear to show the progress:

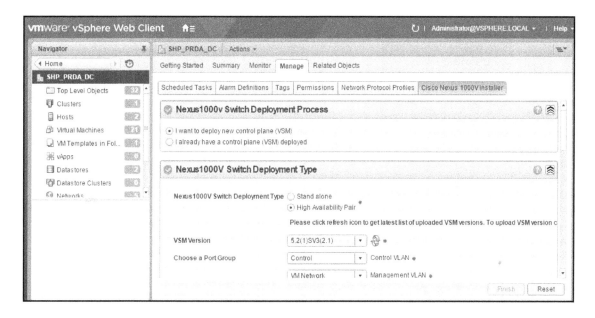

16. Once deployed, select the **Nexus 1000V** VM and click on **Power On** in the **Summary** screen.
17. Go to VSUM GUI, and click on **Dashboard** under **Nexus 1000V Basic Tasks**. Verify that the **VC Connection Status** is green for your installed **VSM:**

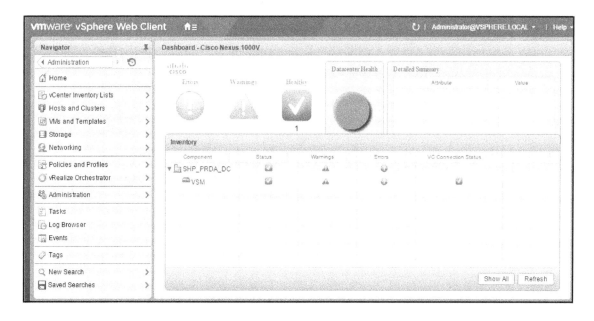

18. You need to create a port profile of Ethernet type for the uplink management. For this, log in to the Nexus 1000V switch using SSH, and type the following commands:

```
port-profile type ethernet system-uplink
  vmware port-group
  switchport mode trunk
  switchport trunk allowed vlan 1-1000
  mtu 9000
  no shutdown
  system vlan 1-1000
  state enabled
```

19. Move over to vCenter and add your ESXi host to the Nexus environment.
20. Open vCenter, click on **Inventory**, and select **Networking**.
21. Expand **Datacenter** and select **Nexus Switch**. Right-click on it and select **Add Host**.
22. Select one of the unused VMNICs on the host, then select the uplink port group created earlier (the one carrying the system VLAN data), and click on **Next**.
23. On the **Network Connectivity** page, click on **Next**.
24. On the **Virtual Machine Networking** page, click on **Next**. Please do not select the checkbox to migrate virtual machine networking.
25. On the **Ready to complete** page, click on **Finish**.
26. Finally, run the `vemcmd show card` command to confirm whether the opaque data is now being received by the VEM.
27. Log in to your Nexus 1000V switch and type in `show module` to check whether your host has been added or not.
28. Log in to your ESXi server and type `VEM Status`. As you can see, VEM is now loaded on VMNIC.

# Communication between VSM and VEM

There are two options for enabling communication between a VSM and a VEM: layer 2 and layer 3 (L2/L3). This is known as the **software virtual switch (SVS)** mode.

# Using layer 2 connectivity

If the VSM and VEM are in the same layer 2 domain, the best way to connect them is to use the layer 2 connectivity mode, which can be done through the following command line:

```
Nexus1000v(config-svs-domain)# svs mode L2
```

# Using layer 3 connectivity

If the VSM and the VEM are in different layer 2 domains, the layer 3 connectivity mode should be used. This can be achieved through the following command line:

```
Nexus1000v(config-svs-domain)# svs mode L3
```

The following diagram explains the layer 3 connectivity in detail:

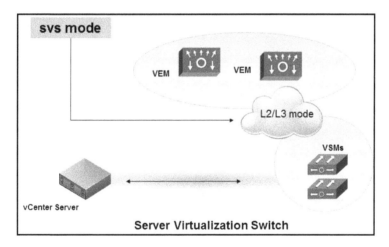

# Using the Domain ID

The control information on a physical switch is normally transparent to the network module. This internal network is isolated by design. However, the N1KV control packets need to traverse the physical network between the VSM and the VEM.

Cisco N1KV uses the Domain ID to identify a VSM and a VEM for ease of relating to one another, so that the VEM only receives the control packets intended for it and from the correct VSM. An SA defines this ID at the time of the VSM installation, and becomes a part of the opaque data that is transmitted to vCenter.

This concept is depicted in the following diagram:

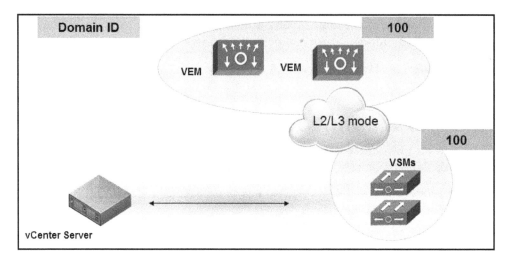

# L2 mode

If you look at the following diagram, you will see that two virtual interfaces are used to communicate between the VSM and the VEM:

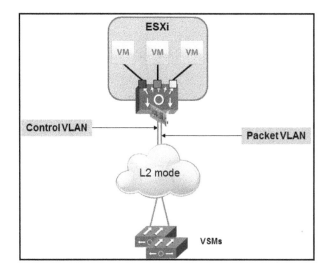

# L3 mode

A VEM will use the VMkernel interface to tunnel the control and packet traffic to the VSM using **User Datagram Protocol** (**UDP**). You can create a VMkernel interface per VEM and attach an L3 control port profile to it.

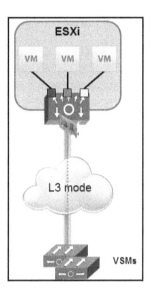

# System VLANs and opaque data

You can add system VLANs as an optional parameter in a port profile. When you use the system VLAN parameter in a port profile, it helps the port profile to act as a special system port profile that is included in the N1KV opaque data. Interfaces that use this type of port profile, along with the members of one of the system VLANs, by default get enabled and forwarded. As a ripple effect, if the VEM does not have communication with the VSM, it still communicates when the ESXi host starts. This enables the use of critical host functions if the ESXi host starts, but it is unable to communicate with the VSM.

As a Cisco best practice, both the control and packet VLANs must be defined as system VLANs. Without this, they will not be included in the opaque data and therefore, the VEM will be unable to communicate with the VSM.

# VSM to vCenter communication

Another important element of Cisco N1KV is VSM to vCenter communication.

The VSM connects via the management interface using a self-signed SSL certificate. It uses the vCenter API. Through this API, it can create port groups and pull data from the vCenter. The VSM can also store the DVS data in the vCenter database through this API.

It can also create dvPort groups, distributed virtual switch port groups, in the vCenter and store the VDS data to be passed to ESXi hosts, which become members of the Nexus switch. It also gets useful information from the vCenter about its current structure.

# Summary

In this chapter, we introduced the Cisco N1KV virtual switch and outlined its implementation and features.

We identified functions of the N1KV components, installed those components, and identified their features too.

In the next chapter, we will talk about the backup, restore, and HA of the Cisco UCS environment.

# 11
# Configuring Backup, Restore, and High Availability

In this chapter, we'll learn how to back up and restore the UCS configuration. There are multiple UCS backup options which can be used either in disaster recovery scenarios to fully restore the Fabric Interconnects configuration and state to export the UCS configuration data to be imported to the same, or a different system. UCS configuration backups are in XML format and hence can be easily modified if required. We'll show different backup options and walk through creating and importing backup jobs from both the GUI and the command line.

In the second half of the chapter, we will learn about the Fabric Interconnect high availability feature. This feature is for control plane functions only. From the data plane perspective, every component is redundant providing multiple data paths. Fabric Interconnects actively participate in data flow and fabric failover can be configured at the vNICs level. For the control plane, one Fabric Interconnect is configured as primary and the other as secondary in a cluster. Most of the high availability configuration is possible from the GUI but there are some configurations and details which are only available through CLI. We will take a look into both GUI and CLI, for backup and high availability.

The following topics will be covered in this chapter:

- Backing up the Cisco UCS configuration
- Creating UCS backup jobs
- Restoring backups using GUI
- Configuring high availability clustering
- Fabric Interconnect elections
- Managing high availability

# Backing up the Cisco UCS configuration

The following are the different options available for UCS data backup:

- **Full state backup**: Full state backup is the backup of an entire system in the binary format. It contains the system configuration, logical configuration, and the state of the system, such as assignment of pools, MAC addresses, FSM, faults, and so on. This type of backup can be used in a disaster recovery scenario to recover the whole configuration of a failed Fabric Interconnect. This type of backup cannot be imported to a different system. Full state backup is a snapshot of the system at a specific time. Any changes to the system render it obsolete. Any changes after the full state backup are lost if a system is restored from the backup.
- **System configuration backup**: System configuration backup consists of administrative settings such as username, RBAC, and locales in XML format. This backup does not contain the system state and hence cannot be used to restore a system. This backup can be used to import system configuration settings to the original or a different Fabric Interconnect.
- **Logical configuration backup**: Logical configuration backup consists of administrative settings such as pools, policies, service profiles, and VLANs in XML format. This backup does not contain the system state and hence cannot be used to restore a system. This backup can be used to import system configuration settings to the original or a different Fabric Interconnect.
- **All configuration backup**: All configuration backup consists of system and logical configuration backups in XML format. This backup does not contain the system state and hence cannot be used to restore a system. This backup can be used to import all configuration settings to the original or a different Fabric Interconnect.

UCS backup is non-disruptive and can be performed while the system is in production without any impact on the operating system running on the blade servers. A backup operation can be used to take a one-time backup or it can be scheduled to take a full state or all configuration backup using the backup and export policy. Backups can be exported to multiple types of destinations including the local filesystem (the filesystem of the computer where UCS Manager is running), FTP, TFTP, SCP, and SFTP.

UCS Manager backup is not intended for taking server operating system level backup, which is running on the blade servers.

# Creating UCS backup jobs

UCS backup job creation is done in the administrative configuration area of the UCS Manager GUI, or it could be accomplished using the admin scope in the CLI mode. We will first walk through the graphical interface configuration and explain the various options and then we will walk through the command-line configuration.

# Creating a manually run backup job using GUI

UCS backup jobs can be either run manually or can be programmed to run at specific schedules. We will first look at how to create a manual job. In order to create a manually run job, follow these steps:

1. Log in to UCS Manager.
2. Click on the **Admin** tab in the navigation pane.
3. Click on the **All** tab in the navigation pane and click on **Backup Configuration** in the work pane in the **General** tab:

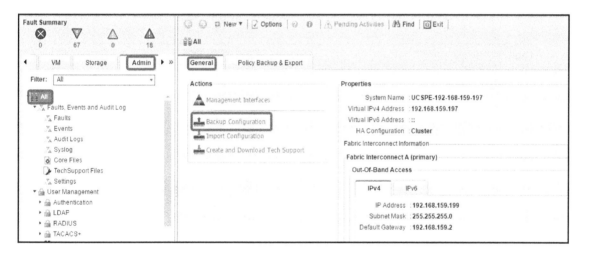

4. Click on **Create Backup Operation**:

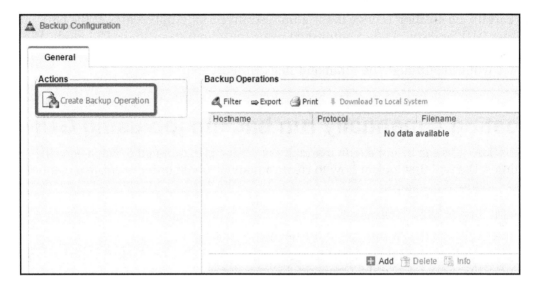

5. On the next pop-up screen, provide details for the backup job:

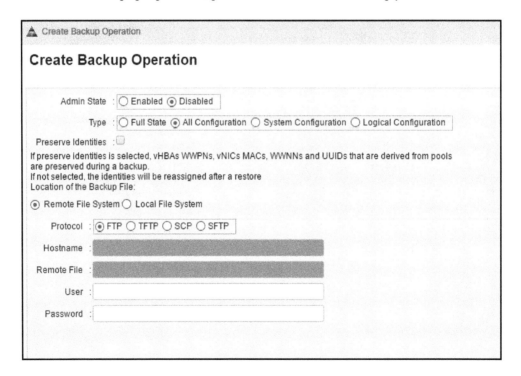

6. The following table provides a description of the configuration options available in the previous screenshot:

| Configuration | Description |
|---|---|
| Admin State | **Enabled**: The backup job runs immediately after the configuration is complete.<br>**Disabled**: The backup configuration is completed but the job is not run immediately which could be manually run at a later time. |
| Type | Select the type of backup which could be **Full State**, **All Configuration**, **System Configuration**, or **Logical Configuration**. |
| Preserve Identities | A checkbox to preserve all identities derived from pools, including the UUIDs, MAC addresses, and WWNN and WWPN. |
| Location of the Backup File | **Local File System**: Backup is saved locally on the computer where UCS Manager is running. The screen changes to display the **Browse** button for storing the file.<br>**Remote File System**: Backup is saved to a remote server using one of the protocols mentioned. |
| Protocol | For remote location, protocol selection could be **FTP**, **TFTP**, **SCP**, or **SFTP**. |
| Hostname | Remote server hostname or IP where the backup is stored. |
| Remote File | Remote filename with full path. |
| User | User having write permissions on the specified remote server.<br>The **User** field will disappear for the **TFTP** selection. |
| Password | User password.<br>The **Password** field will disappear for TFTP selection. |

We will configure a local **All Configuration** backup as an example:

1. Select **Admin State** as **Disabled**.
2. Select **Type** as **All Configuration**.
3. Select the **Preserve Identities** checkbox.
4. Select **Location of the Backup File** as **Local File System**.

5. Enter **Filename** with the `<filename>.xml` extension to store on the local system:

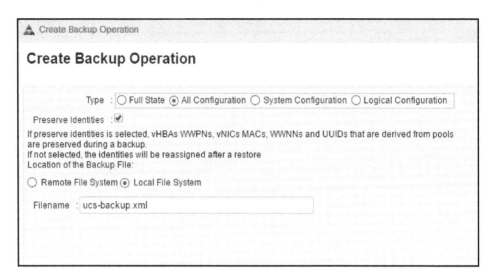

6. Click on **OK**.
7. In order to run the job at a later time, select the job and click on **Download to Local System**.
8. If it is required to delete a backup job, right-click on the job and select **Delete** as shown in the following screenshot:

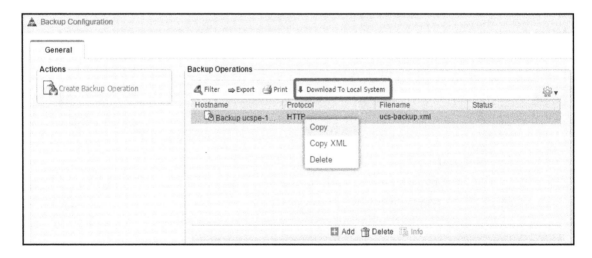

9. The same screen provides the status of the backup task in the form of **finite state machine** (**FSM**). Scroll down and expand **FSM Details**:

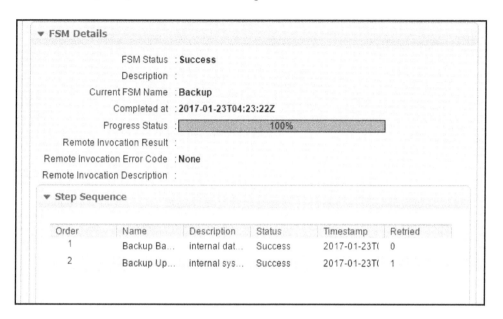

# Creating a scheduled backup job using GUI

In order to schedule a backup job, it is required to configure the backup and export policy. Using this policy setting, it is possible to schedule a full state backup or full configuration backup export job on a daily, weekly, or biweekly basis. Follow these steps for configuration:

1. Log in to UCS Manager.
2. Click on the **Admin** tab in the navigation pane.
3. Click on the **All** tab in the navigation pane and click on **Policy Backup & Export** in the work pane.

4. Information to be entered here is identical to backup job creation under the **General** tab except for **Schedule** which can be set as **Daily**, **Weekly**, or **Bi Weekly**:

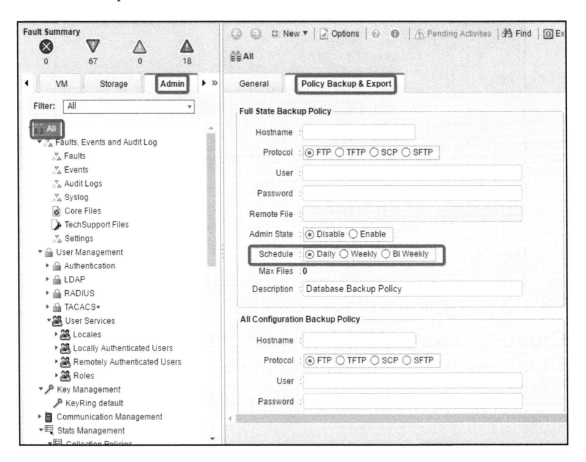

# Creating a backup job using CLI

In order to perform the backup using CLI commands, follow these steps to create a weekly scheduled backup job to export a file using the SCP protocol to a remote server. Connect with FI CLI using SSH and run these scope commands:

1. Select the organization scope:

```
FI-A# scope org /
```

2. Select a backup policy:

```
FI-A /org # scope backup-policy default
```

3. Select a remote hostname:

```
FI-A /org/backup-policy # set hostname server
```

4. Select a protocol for the backup job:

```
FI-A /org/backup-policy* # set protocol scp
```

5. Set the remote server username:

```
FI-A /org/backup-policy* # set user username
```

6. Set a password:

```
FI-A /backup-policy* # set password
Password:
```

7. Select a remote server filename:

```
FI-A /backup-policy* # set remote-file /backups/full-state1.bak
```

8. Select the admin state of the job to be enabled:

```
FI-A /backup-policy* # set adminstate enable
```

9. Select a schedule:

```
FI-A /backup-policy* # set schedule weekly
```

10. Optionally add a description:

```
FI-A /backup-policy* # set descr "This is a full state
weekly backup."
```

11. Execute and save changes to the configuration:

```
FI-A /backup-policy* # commit-buffer
```

# Restoring backups using GUI

UCS restore job creation is also done in the administrative configuration area of the UCS Manager GUI or it could be accomplished using admin scope in the CLI mode. We will walk through the configuration of the graphical interface and explain various options:

1. Log in to UCS Manager.
2. Click on the **Admin** tab in the navigation pane.
3. Click on the **All** tab in the navigation pane and click on **Import Configuration** in the work pane in the **General** tab as shown in the following screenshot:

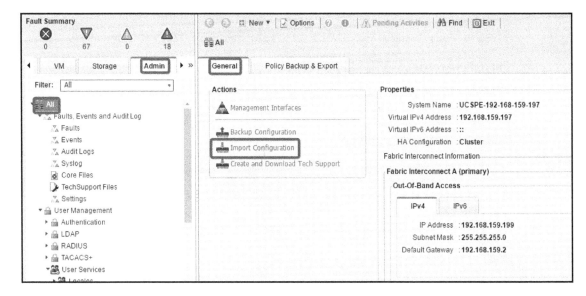

4. Click on **Create Import Operation**:

5. On the next screen, provide details for the backup job as follows:

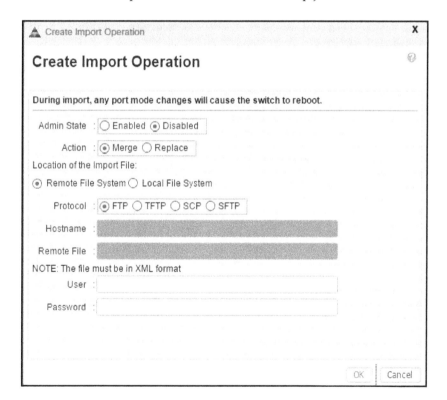

6. The following table provides a description of the configuration options available in the preceding screenshot:

| Configuration | Description |
|---|---|
| **Admin State** | **Enabled**: Import job runs immediately after the configuration is complete.<br>**Disabled**: Import configuration is completed but the job is not run immediately, which could be manually run at a later time. |
| **Action** | **Merge**: Merge into the existing configuration.<br>**Replace**: Replace the existing configuration. |
| **Location of the Import File** | **Local File System**: Import is fetched locally from the computer where UCS Manager is running. The screen changes to display the **Browse** button for storing files.<br>**Remote File System**: Import is fetched from a remote server using one of the protocols mentioned. |
| **Protocol** | For remote location, protocol selection could be **FTP**, **TFTP**, **SCP**, or **SFTP**. |
| **Hostname** | Remote server hostname or IP from where backup is restored. |
| **Remote File** | Remote filename with full path. |
| **User** | User having write permissions on the specified remote server. The **User** field will disappear for the **TFTP** selection. |
| **Password** | User password.<br>The **Password** field will disappear for the **TFTP** selection. |

We will restore from a local backup file as an example:

1. Select **Admin State** as **Disabled** (if it is to be run at a later time).
2. Select **Action** as **Merge** or **Replace**.
3. Select **Location of the Import File** as **Local File System**.
4. Click on **Browse** and browse to the path of the local folder on the system where UCS Manager is running.
5. Select the backup and click on **OK**.
6. In order to run the job at a later time, select the job and click on **Import From Local System**.
7. If it is required to delete a backup job, right-click on the job and select **Delete**:

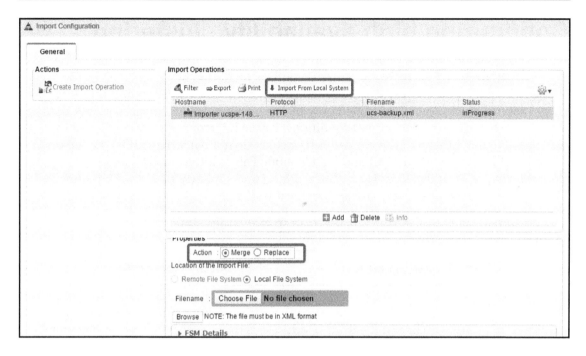

8. The same screen provides the status of the import task in the form of FSM. To see the details, scroll down and expand **FSM Details**:

# Configuring high availability clustering

A UCS Fabric Interconnects pair can be configured in a high availability cluster. In the cluster configuration, FIs create a primary secondary affiliation to control data traffic flow whereas the data plane forwards simultaneously on both Fabric Interconnects. This means cluster control traffic flow is controlled only by the primary node whereas network data can flow through both FIs under normal conditions. Fabric Interconnects are connected through dedicated Gigabit Ethernet UTP copper ports, which do not participate in the data plane. These interfaces are marked as **L1** and **L2**. **L1** of one Fabric Interconnect should be connected to the **L1** of the other Fabric Interconnect and similarly **L2** should be connected to **L2** of the peer. These links carry cluster heartbeat traffic.

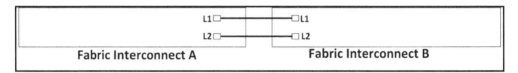

High availability configuration requires three IP addresses. Both Fabric Interconnects require an IP address each, and the third IP address is the cluster IP for the management that floats between the peers A and B depending on which peer is primary.

Under normal conditions, both Fabric Interconnect peers must have the same hardware platform and software version. For example, a UCS 6332 cannot be peered with 6332-16UP. However, this requirement may temporarily be allowed during an FI upgrade. Peers are upgraded one by one, which means that for a brief period, they can have different software and hardware.

Once cluster physical cabling is complete, both FIs go through the initial setup process. During the initial setup of the first Fabric Interconnect, it must be enabled for cluster configuration and it is configured as primary and assigned a cluster management IP. When the second FI is configured, it automatically detects the cluster peer and is configured as secondary.

# Configuring the first Fabric Interconnect

After establishing the cabling discussed earlier, Cisco UCS Fabric Interconnect needs to be initially configured with a management IP address. This will allow the system to manage it remotely through GUI or CLI. Connect to the first Fabric Interconnect console using a serial connection. Configure the first Fabric Interconnect using the following steps:

1. Select the installation method:

   ```
   Enter the installation method (console/gui)? Console
   ```

2. Select the initial setup:

   ```
   Enter the setup mode (restore from backup or initial setup)
   [restore/setup]? Setup
   ```

3. Type in y to continue:

   ```
   You have chosen to setup a new switch. Continue? (y/n): y
   ```

4. Choose a complex password:

   ```
   Enter the password for "admin": password
   ```

5. Retype the password:

   ```
   Confirm the password for "admin": password
   ```

6. Choose the creation of a new cluster by selecting yes:

   ```
   Do you want to create a new cluster on this switch
   (select 'no' for standalone setup or if you want this switch
   to be added to an existing cluster)? (yes/no) [n]: yes
   ```

7. A or B will be suffixed to the name defined in the next step:

   ```
   Enter the switch fabric (A/B): A
   ```

8. Enter the name of the Fabric Interconnect:

   ```
   Enter the system name: FI
   ```

9. Enter the management IP address:

   ```
   Mgmt0 IPv4 address: 172.16.1.10
   ```

10. Enter the subnet mask:

    ```
    Mgmt0 IPv4 netmask: 255.255.255.0
    ```

11. Enter the address of the default gateway of the management network:

    ```
    IPv4 address of the default gateway: 172.16.1.1
    ```

12. Enter the shared IP of the cluster:

    ```
    Virtual IPv4 address : 172.16.1.12
    ```

13. Type in yes to configure the DNS:

    ```
    Configure the DNS Server IPv4 address? (yes/no) [n]: yes
    ```

14. Enter the DNS server IP address which is providing name services:

    ```
    DNS IPv4 address: 8.8.8.8
    ```

15. Type in yes to configure the domain name:

    ```
    Configure the default domain name? (yes/no) [n]: yes
    ```

16. Enter the domain name of the company:

    ```
    Default domain name: yourcompany.com
    ```

17. After pressing *Enter*, the cluster configuration will be confirmed with a summary of configurations. The following configurations will be applied:
    - Switch Fabric = A
    - System Name = FI
    - Management IP Address = 172.16.1.10
    - Management IP Netmask = 255.255.255.0
    - Default Gateway = 172.16.1.1
    - Cluster Enabled = yes
    - Virtual IP Address = 172.16.1.10
    - DNS Server = 8.8.8.8
    - Domain Name = yourcompany.com

18. Type in yes to save the changes:

    ```
    Apply and save the configuration (select 'no' if you
    want to re-enter)? (yes/no): yes
    ```

# Configuring the second Fabric Interconnect

Once the first Fabric Interconnect is configured, the secondary Fabric Interconnect requires very minimum configuration. It will detect the primary Fabric Interconnect through the L1/L2 connections and pull the remaining configuration from it. To configure the second Fabric Interconnect, connect its console using a serial connection. Configure the Fabric Interconnect using the following steps:

1. Choose the installation method:

   ```
   Enter the installation method (console/gui)? Console
   ```

2. If the physical cabling is done accurately, the secondary Fabric Interconnect will automatically be detected. Type y to configure it as secondary:

   ```
   Installer has detected the presence of a peer switch.
   This switch will be added to the cluster. Continue?[y/n] y
   ```

3. Use the same password as configured for the primary Fabric Interconnect:

   ```
   Enter the admin password of the peer switch: password
   ```

4. Enter the management IP address:

   ```
   Mgmt0 IPv4 address: 172.16.1.11
   ```

5. Enter the subnet mask:

   ```
   Mgmt0 IPv4 netmask: 255.255.255.0
   ```

6. Save the configuration:

   ```
   Apply and save the configuration (select 'no' if you
   want to re-enter)? (yes/no): yes
   ```

 Note that the number of configuration steps for the secondary Fabric Interconnect is far less than that for the primary Fabric Interconnect. The secondary Fabric Interconnect automatically acquires all the configuration information from the primary Fabric Interconnect.

If the Fabric Interconnect was initially configured as standalone (a POC deployment), it can be converted to be a cluster-aware configuration using the following steps.

Connect to the Fabric Interconnect using the serial console or SSH connection. Once connected, apply the following commands:

1.  Connect to the CLI local management interface:

    ```
    FI-A# connect local-mgmt
    ```

2.  Type in `enable cluster` with the shared cluster IP:

    ```
    FI-A(local-mgmt)# enable cluster 172.16.1.12
    ```

3.  Type in `yes` to configure clustering. Note that once a standalone Fabric Interconnect is converted to a cluster, it cannot be converted back to the standalone state:

    ```
    This command will enable cluster mode on this setup.
    You cannot change it back to stand-alone. Are you sure you
    want to continue? (yes/no) : yes
    ```

4.  Once the standalone Fabric Interconnect is converted to the primary cluster peer, configure the second Fabric Interconnect following the same steps but for the secondary Fabric Interconnect.

# Fabric Interconnect elections

**Fabric Interconnect elections** are infrequent and may only occur under an equipment failure or user-forced conditions. A user-forced condition may occur during the firmware upgrade of the Fabric Interconnects. Firmware is upgraded on the subordinate Fabric Interconnect first and after the reboot of the FI, it is converted to primary and then the firmware of the current primary is upgraded. In order to force an election, connection to the local-management interface using CLI is required:

1.  UCS-A `#connect local-mgmt`: This connects to the local management interface of the cluster.
2.  UCS-A `(local-mgmt) #cluster{force primary|lead{a|b}}`: The `cluster lead` command and `cluster force primary` command are two separate commands that can be used to start an election. The `cluster force primary` command can be used on the secondary Fabric Interconnect to make it primary. It can be used in critical situations where the primary Fabric Interconnect has failed. The `cluster lead a|b` command can be used on Fabric Interconnects to change the current cluster lead to peer A or peer B.

# Managing high availability

The Fabric Interconnect cluster can be monitored from the UCS Manager GUI. The GUI provides information of the primary and secondary peers and management IP. Perform the following steps to do this:

1. Log in to UCS Manager.
2. Click on the **Equipment** tab in the navigation pane.
3. Click on the **Fabric Interconnects** tab on the navigation pane and the work pane shows the high availability status on the right-hand side pane:

4. The preceding screenshot shows that this is the active primary Fabric Interconnect because the **Leadership** status is indicated as **Primary**.

The Fabric Interconnect IP or the **shared cluster IP** (also known as **VIP**) can also be changed from the GUI. Follow these steps to configure the IPs:

1. Log in to UCS Manager.
2. Click on the **Admin** tab on the navigation pane.
3. Click on the **All** tab on the navigation pane and the **General** tab on the work pane.

4. Click on **Management Interfaces** on the work pane.
5. A new pop-up window will show all the IP settings:

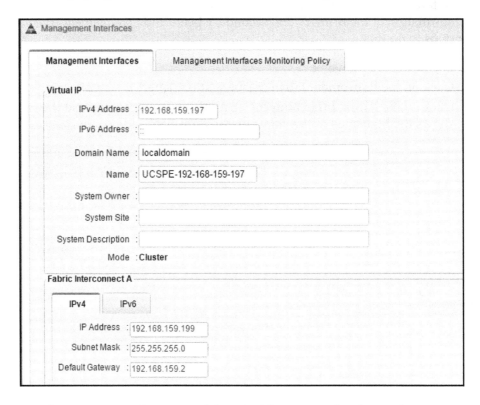

6. In the pop-up window, any of the IP addresses can be changed.
7. Cluster and Fabric Interconnect IP addresses can also be changed from the CLI.
8. The cluster status can also be confirmed from CLI commands:

```
FI-A# show cluster state
```

This command provides the status summary of the cluster as follows:

```
A: UP, PRIMARY
B: UP, SUBORDINATE
HA READY
FI-A# show cluster extended-state
Cluster Id: 0x4690d6b6eafa11e1-0x8ed3547fee9ebb84

Start time: Mon Nov 12 12:00:16 2012
Last election time: Mon Nov 12 12:00:17 2012
```

```
A: UP, PRIMARY
B: UP, SUBORDINATE

A: memb state UP, lead state PRIMARY, mgmt services state: UP
B: memb state UP, lead state SUBORDINATE, mgmt services state: UP
heartbeat state PRIMARY_OK

INTERNAL NETWORK INTERFACES:
eth1, UP
eth2, UP

HA READY
Detailed state of the device selected for HA storage:
Chassis 1, serial: FOX1622G490, state: active
Chassis 2, serial: FOX1616GSPV, state: active
```

Certain failure scenarios may impact the Fabric Interconnect high availability configuration. A number of techniques are used to avoid issues. These scenarios occur due to the network failure between the L1, L2 dedicated network.

# The split brain scenario

Under normal running conditions, one Fabric Interconnect (primary) serves as an *active* member and the other Fabric Interconnect serves as a *standby*. A **split brain** occurs when there is L1, L2 network failure between the primary and secondary Fabric Interconnects. Cisco developed the chassis midplane in such a way that there is EEPROM divided into sections, one for each Fabric Interconnect.

Fabric Interconnect A has the read/write access to one section of EEPROM through the chassis management controller and the read-only access to the other EEPROM.

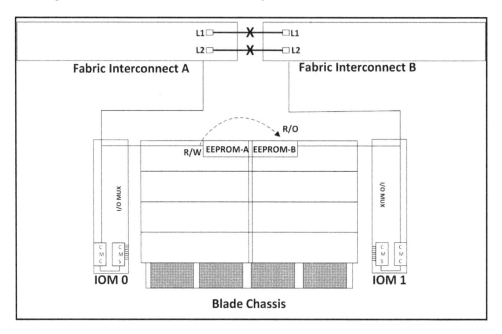

# Partition in space

When the L1, L2 network between the two Fabric Interconnects is disconnected or fails, the primary FI continues to serve as the primary; however, the secondary FI concludes that the primary FI is dead and tries to become the primary. This is split brain partition in space because each Fabric Interconnect considers itself to be in control of the cluster.

When a partition in space is detected, both FIs immediately demote themselves, start the election process, and start claiming chassis resources (known as **quorum**). The FI that claims more resources wins the election and stays in the cluster whereas the other FI aborts. When the link is restored, the second node can rejoin the cluster as a subordinate.

# Partition in time

This condition may occur when one of the nodes stays down for a significant time period, in which configuration changes are made to the active node. Obviously, these changes are not available to the failed node. Now, if the primary node shuts down for some reason and the previously downed node is brought up alone in the cluster with an old database revision, there is a likely chance of configuration corruption. This condition is known as **partition in time**.

To resolve this split brain condition, each Fabric Interconnect writes a database version number to its section of EEPROM. Now when a Fabric Interconnect is brought alone in the cluster, it can still read the EEPROM database version and compare it to its own information. If the version number is the same or higher, the FI can become the active member and if the version number is lower, the FI does not become the active member. This mechanism thus protects against applying an older version of the UCS configuration.

# Summary

In this chapter, we learned about the different UCS backup and restore options available. Different types of backups are possible and the administrator may configure any combination of backup strategies according to the requirement. It is possible to back up both to the local computer and remote server using various protocols. Backups can also be scheduled. Restore also has different options in terms of local or remote location and the same selection of protocols as available for the backup jobs. We then learned about the Fabric Interconnect high availability. We learned how high availability is configured and managed. We looked at high availability election and some high availability failure conditions which result in the split brain condition and how various split brain conditions are resolved.

In the next chapter, we will be discussing the common failure scenarios which will be very helpful in troubleshooting problems with UCS components.

# 12
# Cisco UCS Failure Scenarios Testing

In this chapter, we will walk through the different types of failure scenarios that can occur in Cisco UCS. UCS solution components have excellent redundancy for critical equipment such as chassis and Fabric Interconnects. However, in an unexpected situation such as a physical component's failure, we should be able to identify the failed component and possibly conduct some troubleshooting before contacting Cisco TAC. The most common equipment that fails for the UCS are chassis/Fabric Interconnect power supplies, fan units, IOMs and SFPs for both IOMs, and Fabric Interconnect ports. If proper failover is configured for the network adapters (vNICs) and proper connectivity is configured for the storage adapters (vHBAs), the majority of single component failures do not result in data or management traffic disruption.

UCS failures may also be related to configuration issues, firmware mismatches, temperature issues due to air flow obstruction, and physical cabling issues. In this chapter, we will look into how we can identify these issues from the UCS Manager GUI and also look into LEDs on UCS components.

The following are the topics that will be covered in this chapter:

- Port channel uplink failure and recovery on Fabric Interconnect
- Server link to Fabric Interconnect failure and recovery
- FEX IO modules—failure and recovery
- Fabric Interconnect device failure and recovery
- UCS chassis failure, reporting, and recovery

- Single Fibre Channel failure and recovery on Fabric Interconnects
- Indicating a status with Beacon LEDs
- Creating a tech-support file

In order to dive deep into various troubleshooting scenarios, we will first look at the network and storage connectivity from the mezzanine adapter to the northbound LAN or switch. Different types of ports are involved in this connectivity. They are as follows:

- **IOM backplane ports**: IOM backplane ports connect to the southbound server mezzanine card through midplane traces. Second and third-generation 2200/2300 series IOM FEXs can provide a maximum of 32 backplane ports.
- **IOM Fabric ports**: IOM Fabric ports connect to Fabric Interconnect for northbound connectivity. Second-generation 2200 series IOM FEX have four/eight ports 10G each for 2204 and 2208 respectively, whereas third-generation 2300 series IOM FEX have four ports 40G each for 2304.
- **Fabric Interconnect server ports**: UCS Fabric Interconnect 6332-16UP has a first 16 unified ports. The unified ports and remaining non-unified ports can be configured as server ports to provide southbound connectivity to the UCS chassis IOM module fabric ports.
- **Fabric Interconnect uplink ports**: UCS ports configured as uplink ports provide northbound connectivity to upstream network switches.
- **Fabric Interconnect FC**: UCS Fabric Interconnect 6332-16UP includes first 16 unified ports, that can be configured as Fibre Channel ports to provide SAN connectivity. Port reconfiguration between Ethernet and FC requires a reboot of the FI or expansion module.
- **Fabric Interconnect FCoE ports**: UCS unified Ethernet ports can also be configured as **Fibre Channel over Ethernet** (**FCoE**) ports for SAN connectivity using the FCoE protocol.
- **Fabric Interconnect Appliance ports**: UCS unified Ethernet ports can also be configured as **Appliance** ports for directly connecting storage appliance to Fabric Interconnect.

The following diagram shows the different ports for both IOM modules and Fabric Interconnects:

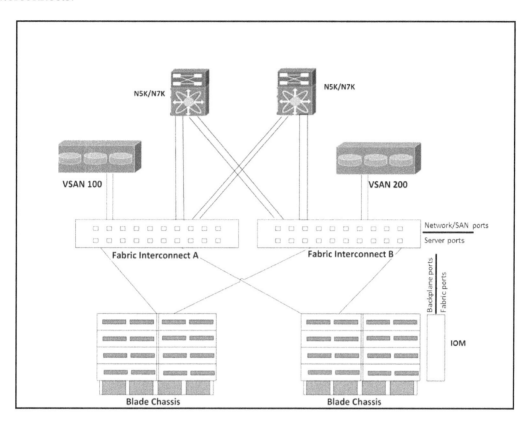

# Port channel uplink failure and recovery on Fabric Interconnects

Fabric Interconnects can connect to northbound Nexus switches either directly or using a port channel/vPC. Port channel configuration, which not only load-balances bandwidth utilization but also avoids unnecessary reconvergence in the case of partial link failures, is recommended as multiple uplink ports can be aggregated.

Use the following procedure to verify northbound port channel configuration and the operational state:

1. Log in to UCS Manager.
2. Click on the **LAN** tab in the navigation pane.
3. In the **LAN Cloud** tab, expand **Fabric A** and **Port Channels**.
4. In the work pane, the **Status** of **Port Channels** is shown in the **General** tab as follows:

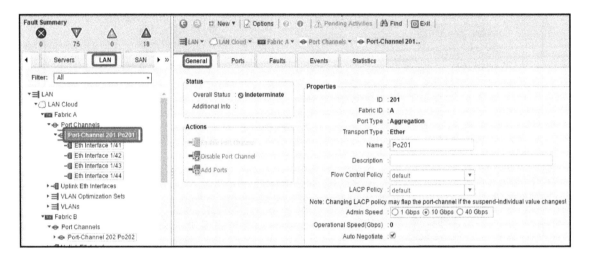

5. The **Ports** tab shows member ports and the **Faults** tab shows any faults as shown in the following screenshot:

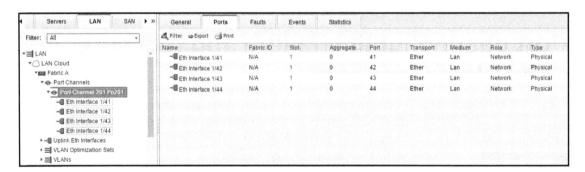

The following screenshot shows the error message that is displayed when a port channel cannot be brought up due to a mismatch in speed between the Fabric Interconnects and uplink Nexus ports:

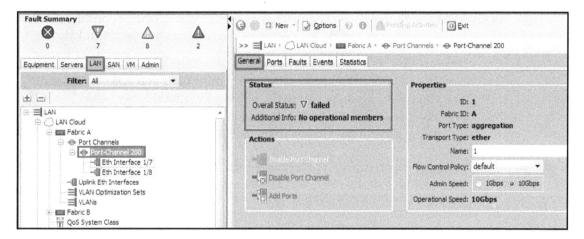

Some other common upstream port channel issues and recommended solutions are as follows:

| Issue | Recommended solution |
|---|---|
| Port channel does not come up. | Verify cable connectivity and look for any physical SFP failure. Verify that there is no protocol or speed mismatch between the connected ports. Verify individual connectivity by removing the port channel configuration. |
| Port channel member failure. The error message in GUI is **membership-down**. | Verify cable connectivity and look for any physical SFP failure. Verify any speed mismatch and correct the issue. |

# Server link to Fabric Interconnect failure and recovery

For blade server and Fabric Interconnect connectivity, there are two connections involved between the server mezzanine card, IOM backplane ports, IOM fabric ports, and Fabric Interconnect server ports. These connections are as follows:

- The connection between the blade server mezzanine card and IOM backplane port that connects the blade server to the IOM in the chassis
- The connection between the IOM fabric port and Fabric Interconnect server port that connects the IOM in the chassis to the Fabric Interconnect

Connectivity failure can happen due to a mezzanine card, IOM ports, or Fabric Interconnect server ports. We will now look at different port failure scenarios.

## Identifying a mezzanine adapter failure

The first requirement is to identify and isolate the source of the issue, which can be the server mezzanine card, IOM card ports, or Fabric Interconnect server ports. To determine that the issue is with the server mezzanine card and not with the IOM or Fabric Interconnect ports, physically have a look at the server motherboard LED's status at the front of the server as follows:

- If the network link LED at the front of the blade server is off, the adapter will not be able to establish the network link
- The network link LED will be green if one or more links are active

The network link LED for the UCS blade B22 M3 is shown in the following illustration:

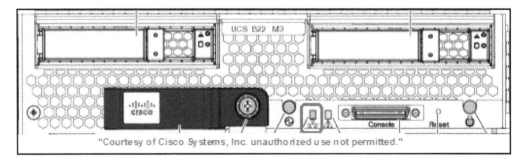

Once the physical connectivity is verified by the LED indicator status, you can also look into the UCS Manager for any issues related to the server adapter.

Use the following procedure to determine the type of server mezzanine adapter errors being experienced:

1. Log in to UCS Manager.
2. Click on the **Equipment** tab in the navigation pane.
3. In the **Equipment** tab, expand the desired server in the desired chassis.
4. Expand the desired adapter, and the **Overall Status** of that adapter will be shown in the work pane.
5. This is a quick view for looking at any adapter errors on that server. In order to see the details of the errors, click on the **Faults** tab in the work pane that will provide all the error messages related to the adapter as shown in the following screenshot:

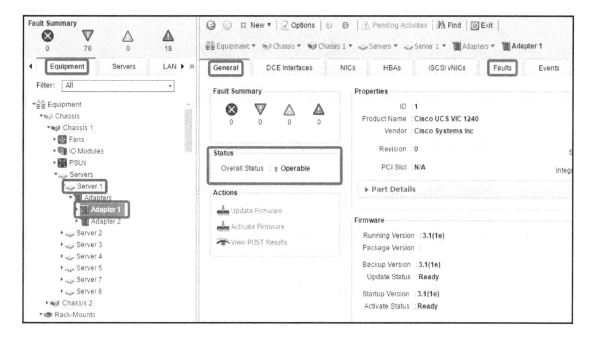

## Common mezzanine adapter error messages

The following is a list of some common adapter issues and recommended solutions to troubleshoot and fix adapter issues. This information is an excerpt from the *Cisco UCS Faults and Error Messages Reference* guide available on the Cisco website at `http://www.cisco.com/en/US/docs/unified_computing/ucs/ts/faults/reference/UCS_S EMs.html`.

Some other common mezzanine adapter error messages and recommended solutions are as follows. For a detailed list of UCS error messages, follow the preceding link:

| Issue | Recommended solution |
|---|---|
| The adapter is reported as *inoperable* in Cisco UCS Manager | For a new installation, verify that the adapter is compatible with the blade server. In case of a UCS Manager firmware upgrade, verify that the adapter has the required firmware version to work with the version of Cisco UCS Manager. Verify that the adapter is seated properly in the slot on the motherboard. Reseat to ensure good contact, reinsert the server, and rerun the POST. Verify that the adapter is the problem by trying it in a server that is known to be functioning correctly and that uses the same adapter type. |
| The adapter is reported as degraded in UCS Manager | Reseat the blade server in the chassis. |
| The adapter is reported as overheating | Verify that the adapter is seated properly in the slot. Reseat it to assure good contact and rerun the POST. Verify if there are any server/chassis airflow issues and correct these issues. |

# FEX IO modules – failure and recovery

IOM provides southbound connectivity to servers using backplane ports and northbound connectivity to Fabric Interconnects using fabric ports. When a service profile is successfully associated with the server, the backplane port's status shows as **Up**.

Perform the following procedure to look into the status of IOM backplane and fabric ports:

1. Log in to UCS Manager.
2. Click on the **Equipment** tab in the navigation pane.

3. In the **Equipment** tab, expand the desired server in the desired chassis.

4. Expand the desired IO module by expanding **IO Modules**, and the status of **Backplane Ports** and **Fabric Ports** will be shown in the work pane.

5. The following screenshot shows the **Backplane Ports** statuses that are connected to the server's mezzanine card:

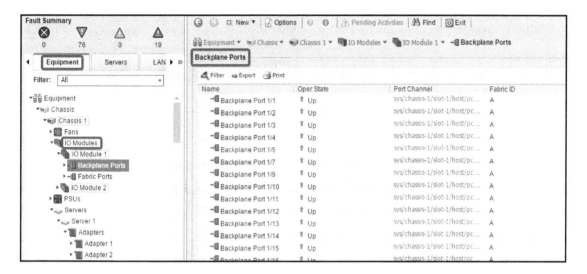

6. The following screenshot shows the **Fabric Ports** statuses that are connected with Fabric Interconnect server ports:

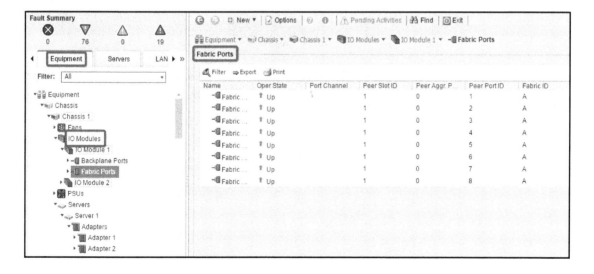

It is also possible to configure a port channel for the IOM fabric ports connected to Fabric Interconnect. This configuration is different as compared to the north switch port channel, and this port channel is configured using the **Chassis/FEX Discovery Policy** section as shown in the following screenshot:

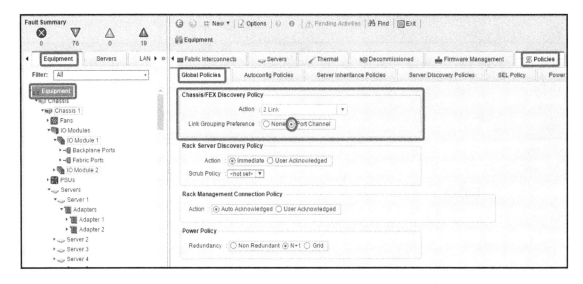

# Common IOM error messages

This information is an excerpt from the *Cisco UCS Faults and Error Messages Reference* guide available on the Cisco website at
http://www.cisco.com/en/US/docs/unified_computing/ucs/ts/faults/reference/UCS_S
EMs.html.

A list of some of the common IOM FEX issues and recommended solutions to troubleshoot and fix these issues is as follows. For a detailed list of UCS error messages, follow the preceding link.

| Issue | Recommended solution |
|---|---|
| The IOM port fails | • For this fault, generate a tech-support file for Cisco UCS Manager and the chassis or FEX module<br>• Contact Cisco TAC |
| The IOM shows *insufficient-resources* | • Verify the VIF namespace size and its usage<br>• Delete all vNICs on the adapter over the maximum number<br>• Add additional fabric uplinks from the IOM to the Fabric Interconnect and re-acknowledge the chassis<br>• If the preceding actions did not resolve the issue, generate a tech-support file and contact Cisco TAC |
| The IOM shows *satellite-connection-absent* | • Verify that the Fabric Interconnect server port is configured and enabled<br>• Verify that the links are plugged in properly, and re-acknowledge the chassis<br>• If the preceding actions did not resolve the issue, generate a tech-support file and contact Cisco TAC |
| The IOM displays *satellite-mis-connected* | • Make sure that each I/O module is connected to only one Fabric Interconnect<br>• Verify that the links are plugged in properly, and re-acknowledge the chassis<br>• If the preceding actions did not resolve the issue, generate a tech-support file and contact Cisco TAC |
| The IOM displays *equipment-removed* | • Reinsert the IOM module and wait a few minutes to see if the fault clears<br>• If the preceding action did not resolve the issue, generate a tech-support file and contact Cisco TAC |
| The IOM shows *unsupported-connectivity* | • Verify that the number of links in the chassis discovery policy are correct<br>• Re-acknowledge the chassis<br>• If the preceding actions did not resolve the issue, generate a tech-support file and contact Cisco TAC |

# Fabric Interconnect server port failure

For troubleshooting connectivity issues, it is also necessary to look into the status of the Fabric Interconnect ports where the IOM fabric ports are connected. These Fabric Interconnect ports are configured as **Server** ports.

Perform the following procedure to have a look at IOM backplane and fabric ports:

1. Log in to UCS Manager.
2. Click on the **Equipment** tab in the navigation pane.
3. In the **Equipment** tab, expand the desired Fabric Interconnects.
4. Change the **General** tab to the **Ethernet Ports** module, and **Overall Status** of the backplane and fabric ports will be shown in the work pane.
5. In the **Filter** bar, uncheck **All** and check the **Server** checkbox to display server ports only. The port's status and any adapter errors on that server port will be displayed on the screen as shown in the following screenshot:

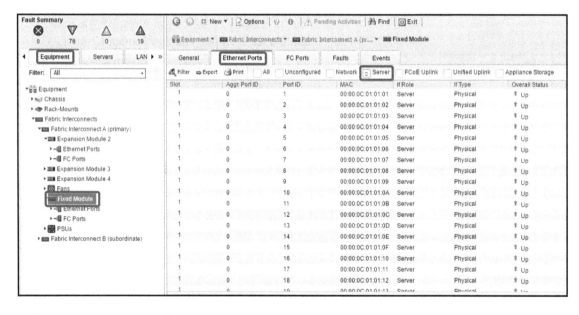

If there are some errors, the **Overall Status** tab in the work pane will indicate the issue: for example, **link-down** in case of a physical SFP failure.

# Rectifying the global Chassis/FEX Discovery Policy configuration error

In Chapter 4, *Configuring Cisco UCS Using UCS Manager*, we discussed and configured the global **Chassis/FEX Discovery Policy**, which dictates the number of physical connections from the UCS chassis expected by the UCS Manager software to acknowledge the chassis. UCS Manager generates an error if IOM connectivity with the Fabric Interconnect is not compliant with the global **Chassis/FEX Discovery Policy**.

The following screenshot shows a **fabric-unsupported-conn** error due to a misconfigured chassis discovery policy. In order to rectify this issue, configure the global **Chassis/FEX Discovery Policy** according to the number of physical links (one, two, four, or eight) connected from the IOM to the Fabric Interconnect using the steps provided in Chapter 4, *Configuring Cisco UCS Using UCS Manager*, and re-acknowledge the chassis.

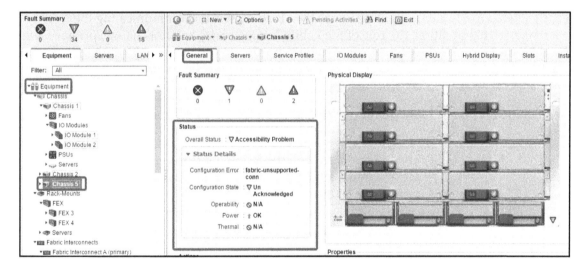

# Fabric Interconnect device failure and recovery

UCS Fabric Interconnects are deployed in a cluster configuration from the control plane perspective. A Fabric Interconnect pair is in active/standby configuration. The active Fabric Interconnect is called **primary** and the standby Fabric Interconnect is called **subordinate**.

All control plane communication is handled by the primary Fabric Interconnect that manages the main configuration database. The main configuration database is stored on the primary and replicated on the subordinate Fabric Interconnect. The primary sends updates to the subordinate when configuration changes occur through dedicated Ethernet links called **L1/L2**.

In a situation where the Fabric Interconnect running the primary instance fails, the subordinate Fabric Interconnect takes the role of primary instantaneously. Access to UCS Manager stops, and you need to log out and log back in. In a split brain situation, where both Fabric Interconnects try to come online as the primary, the Fabric Interconnect database version gets checked, and the Fabric Interconnect with the higher database revision number becomes the primary. We discussed a split brain situation in Chapter 11, *Configuring Backup, Restore, and High Availability*, and learned that the UCS chassis midplane has been designed such that it is helpful in resolving split brain scenarios.

If the dedicated communication links L1/L2 between two Fabric Interconnects fail, the Fabric Interconnects have special access to the blade chassis for communicating the heartbeat. In this situation, the role of the Fabric Interconnects will not change; primary will remain primary, and subordinate will remain subordinate. However, any configuration changes made on the primary will not be reflected on the secondary database until the dedicated Ethernet links are restored.

The following procedure should be performed to replace a failed Fabric Interconnect:

1. Upgrade the firmware of the replacement Fabric Interconnect to the same level as the running Fabric Interconnect with the following steps:
    1. Connect the new Fabric Interconnect to the management network (do not connect the L1 and L2 cables).
    2. Convert the new Fabric Interconnect into an SSH, and run through the setup wizard by configuring the Fabric Interconnect as a standalone.
    3. Update both UCS Manager and the Fabric Interconnect firmware code to the code running on the existing cluster member.
    4. Once the upgrades are complete, verify that the running and startup versions match those of the existing cluster member.
2. Once the firmware is updated, use the following commands to erase the configuration on the standalone Fabric Interconnect:

```
UCS # connect local-mgmt
UCS # erase configuration
UCS # yes (to reboot)
```

3. Connect the L1 and L2 cables between the Fabric Interconnect.

4. Erase the configuration; this will cause the setup wizard to run again on the new Fabric Interconnect and detect the presence of a peer Fabric Interconnect. When prompted for the detection of a peer Fabric Interconnect, type y to add the new Fabric Interconnect to the existing cluster. Save the configuration and reboot.

5. Log in to the UCS Manager, or use the following command line to verify the cluster state:

```
UCS # connect local-mgmt
UCS # show cluster state
Cluster Id: 0x633acf7e9b7611e1-0x9587147fbb1fc579
A: UP, PRIMARY
B: UP, SUBORDINATE
HA READY
```

Sometimes, it may also become necessary to change the current primary Fabric Interconnect in the cluster. One such situation is during a Fabric Interconnect's firmware upgrade, where it is necessary to switch the cluster lead while upgrading code on the primary cluster.

Use the following commands to change the cluster lead:

```
UCS # cluster lead a
UCS # cluster force primary
```

Either of these two commands can be used to make **Fabric A** the primary Fabric Interconnect:

```
UCS # show cluster state
```

(if done quickly, you'll see the status of SWITCHOVER IN PROGRESS)

 Fabric Interconnects have redundant power supply and fan units so they can avoid a complete failure. With this built-in redundancy, it is very rare that Fabric Interconnects will go down completely. The redundant parts of Fabric Interconnects are hot swappable and can be changed without any disruption.

# Common error messages with Fabric Interconnects

This information is an excerpt from the *Cisco UCS Faults and Error Messages Reference* guide available on the Cisco website at
`http://www.cisco.com/en/US/docs/unified_computing/ucs/ts/faults/reference/UCS_S`
`EMs.html`.

Some other common error messages with Fabric Interconnects and recommended solutions are as follows. For a detailed list of UCS error messages, follow the preceding link:

| Issue | Recommended solution |
|---|---|
| Management entity degraded Management entity down | • Verify that both L1 and L2 links have proper connectivity between the Fabric Interconnects<br>• If the preceding action did not resolve the issue, generate a tech-support file and contact Cisco TAC |
| Management entity election failure | • Verify that the initial setup configuration is correct on both the Fabric Interconnects and the L1/L2 links are properly connected<br>• Convert SSH to CLI and run the `cluster force primary` command in the `local-mgmt` command on one Fabric Interconnect<br>• Reboot the Fabric Interconnects<br>• If the preceding actions did not resolve the issue, generate a tech-support file and contact Cisco TAC |
| HA not ready | • Verify that the initial setup configuration is correct on both the Fabric Interconnects and the L1/L2 links are properly connected<br>• Verify IOM connectivity<br>• If the preceding actions did not resolve the issue, generate a tech-support file and contact Cisco TAC |
| Version incompatible | • Upgrade the Cisco UCS Manager software on the subordinate Fabric Interconnect to the same release as the primary Fabric Interconnect<br>• If the preceding action did not resolve the issue, generate a tech-support file and contact Cisco TAC |
| Equipment inoperable | • Reseat the failed equipment, such as fans, power-supply, or SFP |

# UCS chassis failure, reporting, and recovery

The UCS 5100 series chassis is a critical component of the UCS solution and is fully redundant. The redundant components of the UCS chassis are as follows:

- Eight fans for proper airflow
- Four power supplies for power redundancy
- Two redundant IOM module slots for northbound connectivity
- Redundant midplane traces for data and management traces

It is very rare that the UCS chassis will fail completely. The most common failure suspects for the UCS chassis are components such as fan modules, power supplies, IOM modules, or blade servers inserted into the chassis. All UCS chassis components are hot pluggable, so in the case of a failure, the failed component can be replaced without disruption.

## Common failure messages for the UCS chassis

This information is an excerpt from the *Cisco UCS Faults and Error Messages Reference* guide available on the Cisco website at `http://www.cisco.com/en/US/docs/unified_computing/ucs/ts/faults/reference/UCS_S EMs.html`. For a detailed list of UCS error messages, follow the preceding link.

Some common failure messages for the UCS chassis and their recommended solutions are as follows:

| Issue | Recommended solution |
|-------|----------------------|
| Server identification problem | • Remove and reinsert the server card<br>• Re-acknowledge the server<br>• If the preceding actions did not resolve the issue, generate a tech-support file and contact Cisco TAC |
| Port failed | • Re-insert the IOM module<br>• If this did not resolve the issue, contact Cisco TAC |

| Issue | Recommended solution |
|---|---|
| Equipment inoperable | • Re-acknowledge the chassis that raised the fault<br>• Physically unplug and replug the power cord to the chassis<br>• Verify that the I/O modules are functional<br>• If the preceding actions did not resolve the issue, execute the `show tech-support` command and contact Cisco technical support<br>• This error message may also appear for the fan and power supply units |
| Unsupported connectivity | • Verify that the number of links in the chassis discovery policy is correct<br>• Re-acknowledge the chassis<br>• If the preceding action did not resolve the issue, generate a tech-support file and contact Cisco TAC |
| Equipment unacknowledged | • Verify the connectivity state of the I/O module links<br>• Re-acknowledge the chassis<br>• If the preceding actions did not resolve the issue, execute the `show tech-support` command and contact Cisco technical support |

# Single Fibre Channel failure and recovery on Fabric Interconnects

In virtualized environments, SAN connectivity is very crucial for hypervisors as a shared SAN is a critical component for advanced virtualization features, such as migrating and then running virtual machines between different hosts. A problem with the connectivity of the SAN array can also cause issues with the SAN boot.

SAN could be connected to Fabric Interconnects directly or through a northbound Nexus, MDS, or third-party switch. Proper connectivity between Fabric Interconnects and SAN storage processors or Fabric Interconnects and SAN fabric switches is necessary. SAN connectivity is also configured as redundant. However, unlike Ethernet, where a northbound vPC that is using a cross-switch connection can protect against a complete switch failure, the connectivity between SAN switches and Fabric Interconnects can only be a straight connection. It is, however, possible to create a Fibre Channel port channel for protection against a single port failure if SAN supports it.

Perform the following procedure to look into SAN connectivity (the screenshot is showing direct attached FCoE storage):

1. Log in to UCS Manager.
2. Click on the **SAN** tab in the navigation pane.
3. In the **SAN** tab, expand the Fabric Interconnects in the **Storage Cloud** expand list.
4. Expand **Storage FCoE Interfaces**, and the status of the SAN connectivity will be shown in the work pane as follows:

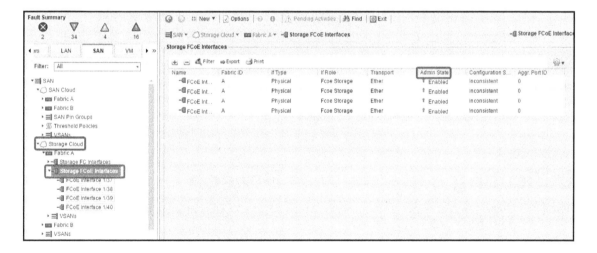

5. The following screenshot shows a port connectivity issue in the form of **membership-down**; this means that the physical connectivity between the Fabric Interconnect and its storage is down:

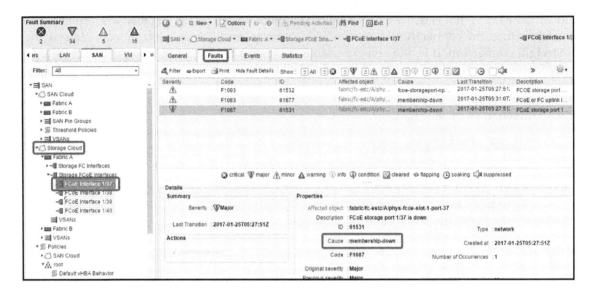

In order to mitigate the risk of Fibre Channel single link failures, Fibre Channel port channels or trunking can be established to ensure uninterrupted connectivity. Refer to Chapter 6, *Configuring SAN Connectivity*, which discusses the procedure for the creation of a Fibre Channel port channel for storage connectivity.

# Indicating a status with Beacon LEDs

The UCS chassis and components have different colored LEDs and flashing patterns. Looking at the LED's status can also help identify various issues. All UCS components, including the chassis, IOMs, power supplies, fan units, blade servers, and Fabric Interconnects have different LED indicators that can provide information about the component's location, faults, or operational status. Locator LEDs are blue in color, operational status LEDs are usually green or a blinking green color, and faults are identified with solid, amber-colored LEDs. The UCS chassis and blade servers have some buttons as well; these can be pushed to turn the locator LED on/off.

The following table describes how to interpret the LED indicators on various UCS components:

| LED status | Interpretation |
|---|---|
| Off | Not connected. No power. |
| Green | Normal operation. |
| Blinking green | Normal traffic activity. |
| Amber | Booting up, then running diagnostics or a minor temperature alarm. |
| Blinking amber | Failed component or major temperature alarm. |
| Locator LED (blinking blue) | Locator feature enabled. |

# Creating a tech-support file

In the event of an equipment failure, perform the following procedure to create a tech-support file for Cisco TAC:

1. Log in to UCS Manager.
2. Click on the **Admin** tab in the navigation pane.
3. In the **Admin** tab, click on the **All expandable** list.

4. In the work pane, click on **Create and Download Tech Support** as shown in the following screenshot:

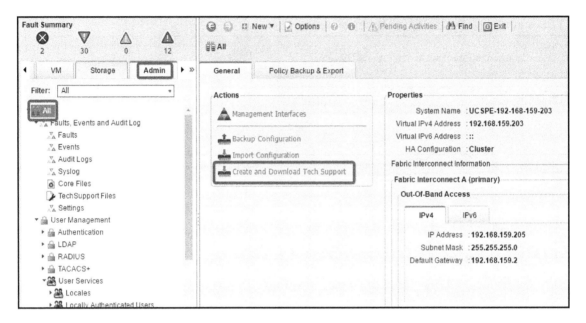

5. In the pop-up window that opens, select the desired option to create the tech-support file and browse to a local location on the PC to save the file as shown in the following screenshot:

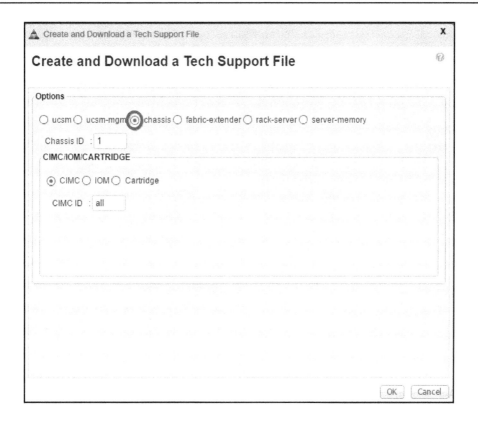

# Summary

In this chapter, we walked through some failure scenarios that are mostly related to connectivity issues or physical components, such as power supplies, fans, or SFP failures. We looked at how to acquire information for troubleshooting and identify failed components or misconfiguration that results in a connectivity failure. We looked into the issues related to network connectivity with northbound port channels. We also looked into complete connectivity, from mezzanine adapters to IOM backplane ports, to IOM fabric ports, to northbound Fabric Interconnect server ports. We also looked into Fibre Channel connectivity issues.

We then looked into a complete Fabric Interconnect or blade server chassis failure. We discovered that as there are redundant parts in both Fabric Interconnects and the chassis, it is very rare that complete equipment will fail. We looked into the most common failures, such as SFPs, power supplies, and fan units. We also looked into IOM connectivity and some possible failure scenarios. We learned about various LEDs on the UCS and how we can use these LED indicators to identify a possible issue with a UCS component.

In the next chapter, we will be looking at the integration of some third-party applications, such as VMware vCenter extension and EMC Unified Infrastructure Manager, and Cisco tools, such as UCS power tools and goUCS.

# 13
# Third-Party Application Integration

Cisco UCS has all the capability to get integrated with third-party applications. In this chapter, we will show you three application integrations. The aspects of those integrations are as follows:

- Integration with EMC Unified Infrastructure Manager for provisioning
- Integration with VMware vCenter Server
- Integration with Cisco UCS PowerTool

## Understanding the challenges in infrastructure

As you support your growing business, what challenges do you face when asked to create an infrastructure that is ready to support a virtual application or test beds for a new line of business request?

- When there are too many highly technical people involved, in a provisioning process, it wastes time
- These guys can take weeks or months to deliver the infrastructure for a new service, which will certainly delay the rollout and impact the bottom line business

- The normal human tendency is to make mistakes in manually-intensive processes, which becomes costly and also takes time to determine the issue
- You may be unaware of the changes that may take the infrastructure configuration out of compliance, and this significantly leads to hardware issues in the future

If you have ever faced these problem, EMC **Unified Infrastructure Manager** (**UIM**) is the solution for you. In the next section, we will go through UIM and its benefits.

# Going deep with UIM

UIM is a purpose-built service for Vblock Infrastructure Platforms that has centralized interaction with element managers to define available resource *pools* and then view their capacity through a single dashboard. It creates policy-based, automated, converged infrastructure provisioning templates that can be used on any Vblock platform.

A UIM service offering is a template that you can create in anticipation of the applications that will be deployed on your Vblock platform. Once created, the templates are placed into the UIM/P catalog, ready for provisioning and activation when needed. Service offerings contain all except components needed to have a complete foundational infrastructure, such as storage, compute, network, and operating system.

UIM/Provisioning provides administrators with a tool to provision the VCE Vblock system from one location. Compute, storage, and SAN components are discovered in UIM. The discovered resources can then be provisioned with UIM, making it a simplified approach to end-to-end provisioning.

A base configuration is required for provisioning to occur. As an example, the UCS must be configured with a number of policies, Fabric Interconnect connectivity, and so on. Storage must have the RAID groups and/or pools. The following diagram shows the overall architecture of UIM and its component connectivity diagram:

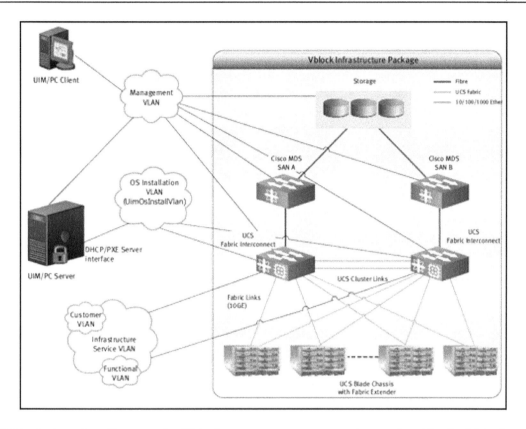

UIM is designed to discover the Vblock components, attempting to simplify the Vblock system into a single entity, create infrastructure services for automated provisioning of the Vblock system, and integrate the provisioned ESXi clusters with vCenter.

# Understanding the discovery mechanism of UIM

The **discovery mechanism** is designed to pull and import the device data from all Vblock components into a single database. UIM utilizes HTTP(S) to communicate via the XML API to the UCS.

A list of items is required for the discovery of a Vblock system. Each Vblock system must have a unique name. The **Description** field is optional but is displayed on the **Vblock** tab, so if there is a good business use to distinguish Vblock systems, it is a useful entry.

The high-level results of the discovery will be displayed within the **Results** screen. Details about the blades, storage, and network can be viewed on their respective tabs in the **Administration** view. For example, storage details can be seen in the **Storage Pool** tab.

When discovery finishes, you will see a **Blade Pool** that identifies all UCS blades with the chassis, slot, model, CPU, and memory. Also, it discovers network profiles that identify attributes from UCS to associate vNICs with VLANs, QoS, and adapter policies.

The following screenshot is an example of the discovery screen for a Vblock 300. The only optional items on this screen are **Description** and the **Use SSL** checkboxes. By default, all VCE builds use SSL for UCS communication.

Once all of the details have been entered, clicking on **Add and Discover** will automatically start the discovery. Clicking on **Add** will only add the Vblock system to the list, but will not begin the discovery:

The following screenshot is an example of the discovery results in the **Details** view. As you can see, **UCS**, **Network**, **Storage**, and **SAN** information are shown.

This is just the high level. The details can be seen in the **Blade Pool**, **Storage Pool**, and **Network Profiles** tabs:

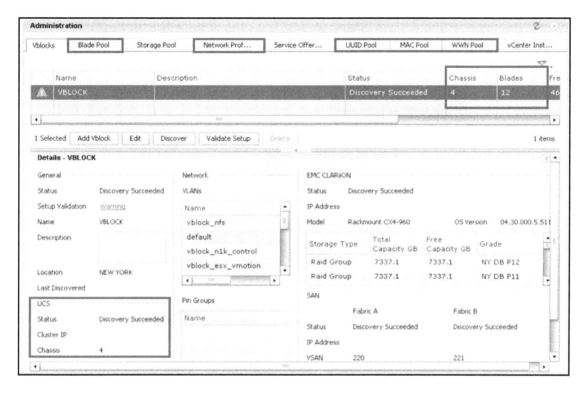

The following is a list of the details that are pulled from the UCS in the Vblock system:

- UCSM version
- Number of chassis
- Number of blades
- Blade location
- Blade model
- Blade CPU
- Blade memory
- All S/N info
- VLANs created
- QoS
- Adapter policies
- PIN groups

# Learning about the UIM service life cycle

An **infrastructure service** is a cluster of servers packaged together with the network and storage resources required to enable the cluster. The Unified Infrastructure Manager/Provisioning Center provides **Infrastructure as a Service (IaaS)** for Vblock systems:

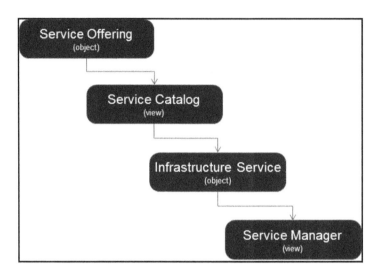

This life cycle shows the overview of the service life cycle as it pertains to an infrastructure service. It starts off as a generic template. The catalog displays a list of all templates (offerings). Based on the current need, selecting the proper template (offering) will allow the administrator to create the desired infrastructure service for provisioning.

As mentioned before, **Service Offerings** is a template. Within the template, there are minimum and maximum allocations that can be used. For example, you can have a template that allows a minimum of two and a maximum of eight blades.

**Service Offerings** also identifies whether an OS will be installed with the infrastructure service, and if yes, then which OS. It might be a good idea to have duplicates of each service offering, one with and one without an OS, in case the option is needed.

Anyone creating an infrastructure service will be bound to the resource restrictions defined in the service offering.

The following is an example of what a completed service offering may look like. Notice the minimum and maximum in the **Servers** section. There is also a default number that can be used to minimize infrastructure service creation. This example shows a range of 1-12 servers, with a default of 1. When the infrastructure service is created, there will be one server, and any more servers needed will require a click of the **Add** button. If four is the normal number of servers, 4 should be the default value:

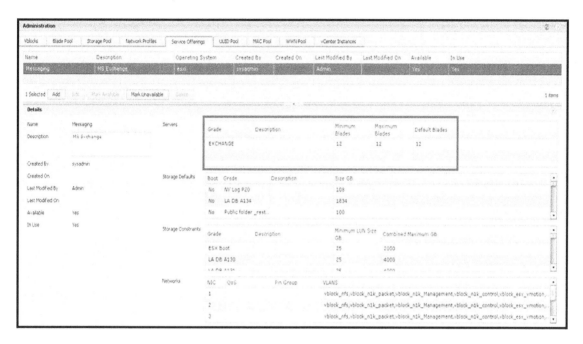

Service offerings cannot be created until the **Blade Pool** and **Storage Pool** objects are graded. The grade can be considered similar to a **class of service**. The way the pools are graded completely depends on the business requirements for the Vblock system.

The methods of grading are as follows:

- **Performance factor**: CPU speed or amount of available memory (blades)
- **Resource configuration**: Half-width versus full-width (blades)
- **BU/Customer allocation**: Finance group purchased the resource
- **Cluster-specific**: Granular selection of components for each vCenter cluster

Since this is a virtualized environment, these well-known identifiers need to be configured on each component as the provisioning occurs. The pool should be a unique pool, not overlapping with any other system.

Each pool will be completely consumed before moving on to the next pool. For instance, if you create a pool of 100 addresses for the first UUID pool, that pool will be completely used before moving to the second pool that you create.

For the WWPN and MAC pools, you can create separate pools for A and B sides, allowing easy identification of where the address resides.

All pools are created as global or Vblock-specific pools. This comes into play more when there are multiple Vblock systems managed by one UIM instance.

To recap the service offering, it is just a template. The details of each server and data store can be edited before provisioning. For example, the hostname, IP address, data store name, and so on.

Now let us move to the integration of UCS Manager with VMware vCenter Server.

# Integrating VMware vCenter Server with UCSM

Do you use Cisco UCS servers in your VMware virtualized environment and use different management tools to manage the blades and your virtual environment?

Then you should start using the Cisco UCS Manager plugin for VMware vCenter that can manage all your virtual and physical servers in a single management pane in your vCenter.

The Cisco UCS vCenter integration plugin brings the capabilities of UCS Manager into vCenter and you can use your vCenter to manage all your Cisco blades. The result is a single pane of glass for vCenter users to get both physical and virtual infrastructure information for a given hypervisor.

Before you start the integration of UCSM with VMware vCenter, you first need to check the following prerequisites for this setup:

- vSphere Enterprise Plus License
- Support for **pass-through switching** (**PTS**)
- Minimum Cisco UCSM release of 1.2 (1d)
- VLANs configured in UCSM for exposing it to your VMs
- Data center object created in vCenter Server to contain the PTS DVS

You can either use the automated wizard to integrate vCenter Server in UCSM or you can also choose the manual integration method.

If you use the wizard, you will perform the following steps:

1. Install a plugin on vCenter Server.
2. Define DVS.
3. Define a port profile and a port profile client.
4. Apply a port profile to VMs.

# Configuring vCenter with UCSM

Let us start looking at the configuration steps for UCS integration in vCenter Server.

1. Log in to the UCS Manager.
2. From the main page, click on the **VM** tab:

3. Click on **Export vCenter Extension**.
4. Choose a location to save and click on **OK**:

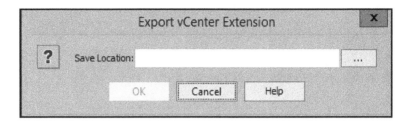

5. After exporting the XML file, copy this to VMware vCenter Server.
6. Log in to the vCenter Server.
7. From the **Plug-Ins** menu, choose **Plug-In Manager**.
8. Right-click on the **Plug-In Manager** window and select **New Plug-In**.
9. In the **Register Plug-In** window, click on the **Browse** button and select the XML file you copied to the server.
10. After installing the extension XML file, click on the **Register Plug-In** button in the **Register Plug-In** window.
11. Once the plugin registration process is done, return to the UCS Manager window.
12. Click on **Configure VMware Integration**.

13. Click on **Next.**

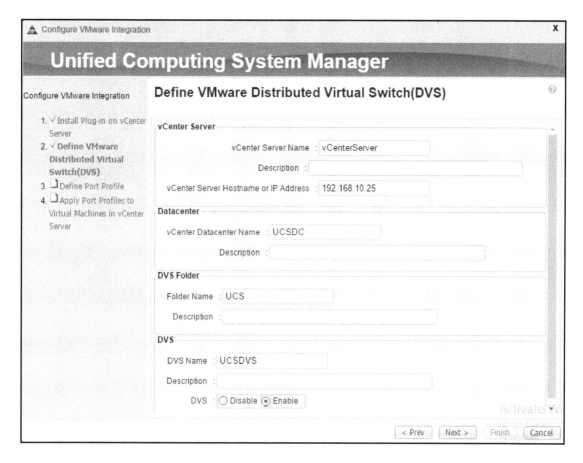

14. In the **vCenter Server** area, complete the fields to define the connection to VMware vCenter.

15. In the **Datacenter** area, complete the fields to create the data center in VMware vCenter.

16. In the **DVS Folder** area, complete the fields to create a folder to contain the distributed virtual switch in VMware vCenter.

17. In the **DVS** area, complete the fields to create the distributed virtual switch in VMware vCenter.

18. Click on **Next**.

19. In the **Port Profile** area, complete the fields to define the port profile.

20. In the **VLANs** area, do the following to assign one or more VLANs to the port profile:

    1. In the **Select** column, check the checkbox in the appropriate row for each VLAN that you want to use in the port profile.

    2. In the **Native VLAN** column, click on the radio button in the appropriate row for the VLAN that you want to designate as the native VLAN:

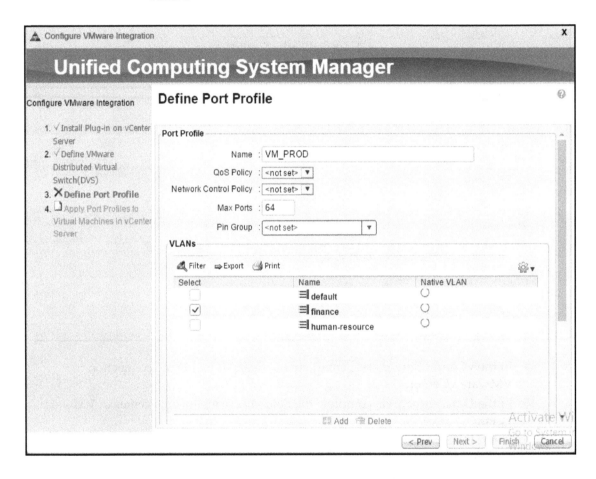

21. In the **Client Profile** area, specify the information on those fields to create a profile client for the port profile:

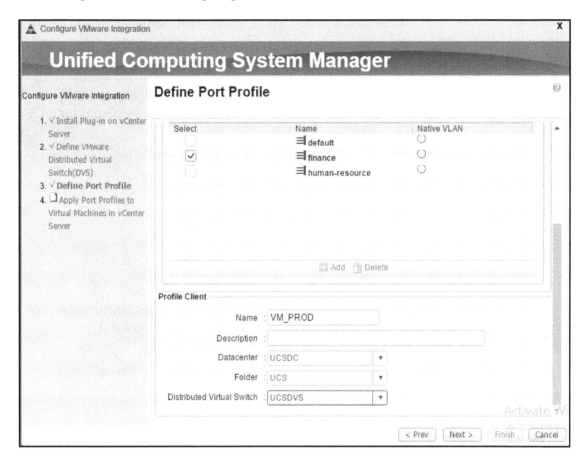

22. Click on **Next**.
23. Review the text on the page in the **Configure VMware Integration** wizard.
24. Click on **Finish.**

Cisco UCS Manager connects to the vCenter Server, creates the specified DVS, and applies the port profiles.

# Integration with Cisco UCS PowerTool Suite

Have you ever faced a challenge in managing multiple UCS systems? Have you encountered problems in maintaining an overarching system that maintains resource pools, users, and policies, and so on?

If yes, you need automation in place, and Cisco UCS PowerTool Suite is a good choice.

You can use UCS PowerTool Suite to monitor event streams and to export entire UCS configuration. Using UCS PowerTool Suite, you can manage the following objects for UCS Manager, UCS Central, and UCS IMC:

- Service profiles
- Global service profiles
- Power actions
- Servers
- Chassis
- Fabric Interconnects
- Configuration operations

Cisco UCS PowerTool Suite is a Windows PowerShell tool that provides functionalities for managing your Cisco UCS, UCS Central, and UCS IMC. It has more than 2,000 commandlets to let you better manage your UCS platform as a module.

> The latest version that you get is 2.1.1. You can download it from `https ://software.cisco.com/download/release.html?mdfid=286305108&fl owid=79283&softwareid=284574017&release=2.1.1&relind=AVAILABLE &rellifecycle=&reltype=latest`.

Installing PowerTool is pretty much similar to the way you install any Windows-based application with the following pre-requisites:

- Windows PowerShell 3.0 or higher version
- PowerShell 4.0 or higher version for UCS **Desired State Configuration** (**DSC**)
- .NET Framework version 4.5 or higher

# Connecting your UCS Manager using PowerTool Suite

The first thing you have to do is to connect to UCS Manager. To do that, double-click on the PowerTool Suite icon to open up the PowerShell window and run the following command:

```
Connect-Ucs <IP Address of UCSM>
```

It will immediately ask you for the username and password of UCSM, as shown in the following screenshot:

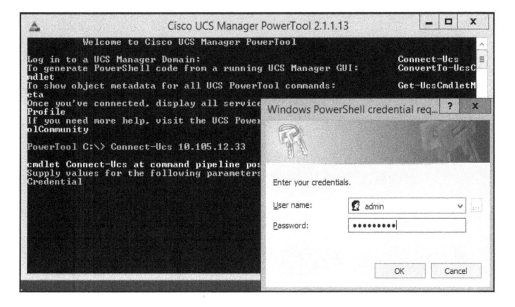

Once it authenticates, it will show the details of the UCS system, as shown in the following screenshot:

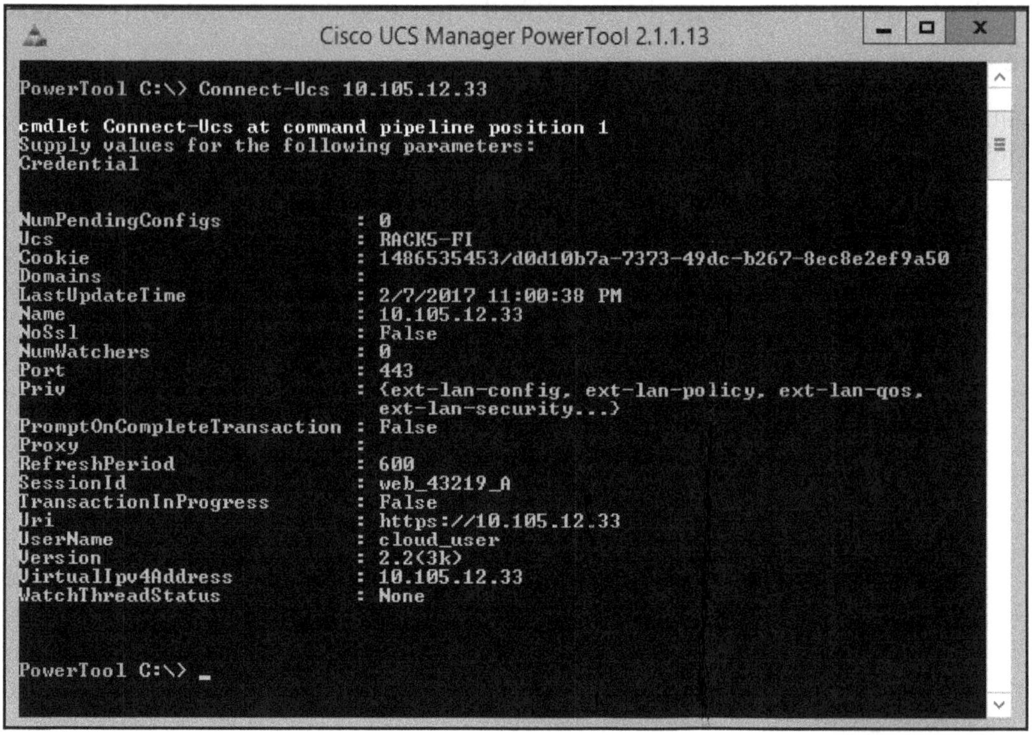

```
Cisco UCS Manager PowerTool 2.1.1.13

PowerTool C:\> Connect-Ucs 10.105.12.33

cmdlet Connect-Ucs at command pipeline position 1
Supply values for the following parameters:
Credential

NumPendingConfigs            : 0
Ucs                          : RACK5-FI
Cookie                       : 1486535453/d0d10b7a-7373-49dc-b267-8ec8e2ef9a50
Domains                      :
LastUpdateTime               : 2/7/2017 11:00:38 PM
Name                         : 10.105.12.33
NoSsl                        : False
NumWatchers                  : 0
Port                         : 443
Priv                         : {ext-lan-config, ext-lan-policy, ext-lan-qos,
                               ext-lan-security...}
PromptOnCompleteTransaction  : False
Proxy                        :
RefreshPeriod                : 600
SessionId                    : web_43219_A
TransactionInProgress        : False
Uri                          : https://10.105.12.33
UserName                     : cloud_user
Version                      : 2.2(3k)
VirtualIpv4Address           : 10.105.12.33
WatchThreadStatus            : None


PowerTool C:\> _
```

One of the main tasks using this PowerTool is to see how to use the commandlets and how to get more help for this. Cisco really did a good job in bringing all of the commandlets help within the PowerTool. Let me show you an example of it. If you want to get help on the get-UcsBlade, run the following command:

```
Get-Help get-UcsBlade
```

You will see a full blown output of what you can do with the specified commandlet, as shown in the following screenshot:

If you want to get some examples of the commandlet you want to use, you should add –
examples at the end of the get-help command. The following is an example output of the
command:

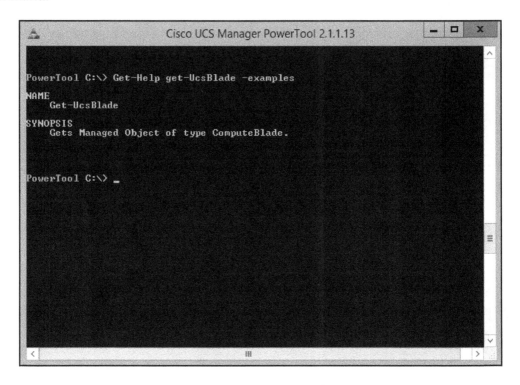

If you want to get the status of the UCS chassis, run the following command:

```
Get-UcsChassis
```

The following screenshot is an example output of the command:

Similarly, if you want to get the statistics of the UCS chassis, such as `InputPower`, `OutputPower`, and so on, run the following command:

```
Get-UcsChassisStats
```

A sample output should look like the following screenshot:

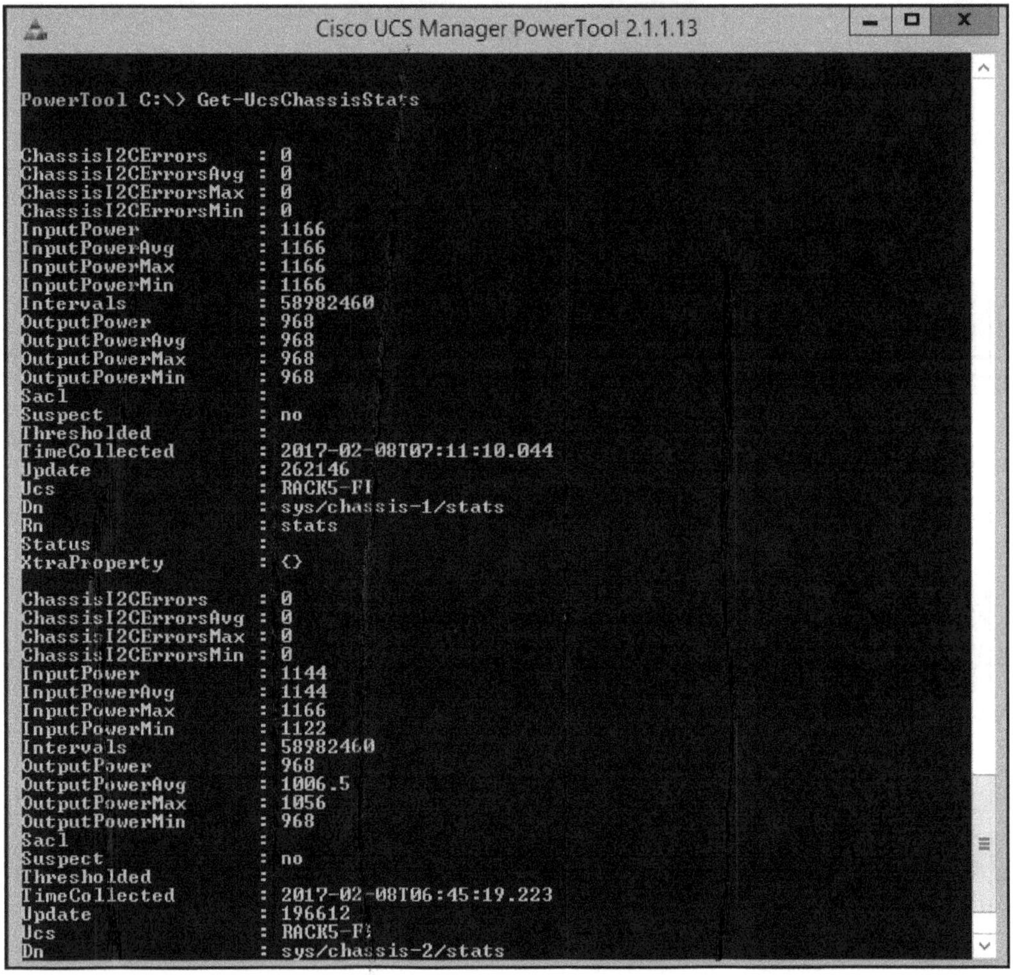

So, you can see how easily you can manage your UCSM through PowerTool. But this is not the end; there is something which will give you tremendous help in building your script for your future task automation.

If you want to automate what you do through GUI without the knowledge of all of the commandlets, wouldn't that be great? Yes, of course! Cisco has thought about this and provided a wizard to help us understand what the backend command looks like if you perform any frontend operation through GUI.

To do that, run the following command from the PowerTool prompt:

```
ConvertTo-UcsCmdlet
```

At this point, open up the GUI and perform any task. This tool will capture those frontend operations and will generate the backend commands on your screen.

# Summary

In this chapter, the aspects of EMC UIM/Provisioning and VMware vCenter integration with UCS Manager were discussed. The chapter described how efficiently UCS Manager can integrate third-party applications and provide a better way to manage, compute, and network in the real world.

UCS PowerTool Suite can be a handy tool whenever you require changes at scale and you can expect quick results with all queries related to infrastructure. It provides complete programming compatibility to manage and monitor all the infrastructure components without spending any additional capital.

The next chapter explains how efficiently multiple UCS domains can be managed in the data center and looks at proactive monitoring of the performance and health of UCS and integrated components. It shows how to automate and orchestrate the data center components with advanced workflows to provision services from weeks to minutes.

# 14
# Automation and Orchestration of Cisco UCS

Scalability and unified management across multiple Cisco UCS domains can be challenging for system admins and IT architects. Cisco UCS Central manages multiple UCS domains deployed at single or multiple locations and supports management of inventory and resources such as global resource pools, service profiles, policies, and templates. Similarly, UCS Performance Manager provides health monitoring and visibility into multiple UCS domains, whereas UCS Director can help in achieving the deployment of infrastructure components from multiple weeks to a few minutes with automation and orchestration.

In this chapter, we will introduce you to the following components to manage, monitor, and automate your data center:

- Multiple UCS domain management
- Performance monitoring and capacity planning
- Powering infrastructure with a cloud solution

## Multiple UCS domain management

Growing business and application requirements in the data center can demand more infrastructure, which can lead to more than one UCS domain in the data center. This will bring more complexity and administration overhead to manage multiple UCS Managers. To overcome the compliance and risks associated with multiple UCS domains, Cisco has developed a single pane of management for multiple UCS Managers, called **UCS Central** software (Manager of UCS Managers).

UCS Central software delivers centralized unified management and scalability of multiple Cisco UCS domains for up to 10,000 servers, whether they are located in a single data center or spread across multiple data centers. It provides a single control point for the core aspects of UCS management, such as policies, service profiles, pools, inventory, and faults, to simplify the operations and administer across multiple domains at a global scale where UCS Manager provides policy-driven management for a single UCS domain. UCS Central serves as an image repository for all firmware bundles and provides consistent firmware management across all the domains with minimum intervention. It provides centralized visibility into a complete inventory and reports on information across all the domains.

# UCS Central architecture

UCS Central uses the same model-based architecture framework as UCS Manager by extending APIs for global automation among multiple UCS domains. It simplifies UCS management by standardization, aggregation, global policy enforcement, and global ID consistency. Each UCS domain will get registered with UCS Central to provide centralized policy-driven automation. These UCS domains can be configured as a UCS domain group in UCS Central and multiple UCS domain groups can be created in it:

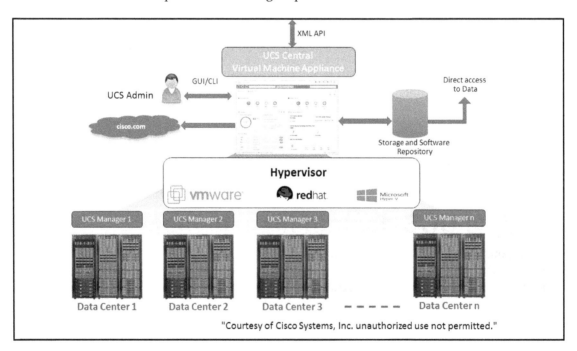

It offers two modes for deployment: **standalone** and **clustered** modes. The cluster mode is required where you don't have high availability provided by the hypervisor. You can deploy two virtual machines in the cluster mode with a shared disk. The standalone mode can be deployed with high availability offered by the hypervisors.

It is software that can be installed as a virtual machine appliance either through an OVA file or ISO image. It supports all the major hypervisors such as VMware ESXi, RedHat KVM, and Microsoft Hyper-V.

The following is the list of supported hypervisors on which UCS Central 1.5 software can be installed. It can be downloaded from `https://software.cisco.com/`:

- VMWare ESXi 5/6
- KVM hypervisor on RedHat Enterprise Linux 6.5 and 7.2
- Microsoft Hyper-V server 2012 R2/2016

Scalability of UCS Central doesn't depends upon the number of UCS domain registrations; instead, it depends upon the total number of blade servers that are getting managed through it. The underlying hardware requirements for UCS Central should be a minimum of four vCPUs, 16 GB memory, and 80 GB space. For medium to large UCS domain deployments, it is recommended to monitor the performance of UCS Central VM and increase the resources such as vCPU and memory according to your requirements. It is always recommended that UCS Central should be installed on a high-speed data store for better performance.

# Why UCS Central?

Centralized management of UCS infrastructure can provide the following benefits to the customers:

- Better visibility into local or remote UCS domain infrastructures
- Reduced administrative overheads by centralized monitoring, troubleshooting, inventory, and reporting
- Direct logging into KVM sessions from single interface for all the servers
- Automatic backup of UCS domains to a centralized location, making it easy to restore them
- Faster setup of new domains with global standardization of resources and reduced configuration issues

- Quick provisioning and de-provisioning of workloads across multiple domains
- Automatic and consistent UCS firmware management
- Hardware compatibility reports providing interoperability information for UCS components

# UCS domain registration with UCS Central

The latest UCS Central 1.5 can manage the UCS domain registration directly from UCS Central and doesn't need to configure each UCS domain to register with it individually. UCS Central interacts with admin users and doesn't need to enter the shared-secret password, as this will push the configuration to the UCS domain. It is recommended that the hostname should be used for UCS domain registration instead of using an IP address.

UCS Central establishes a secure connection with UCS Manager Central and uses entered admin credentials to accomplish a successful registration with the domain as shown in the following screenshot. Registration can also be done from the Central CLI:

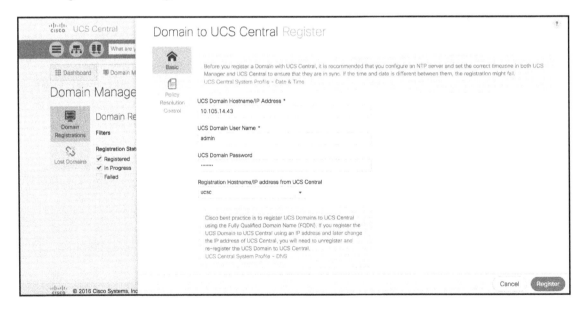

The **Policy Resolution Control** tab in the **Domain to UCS Central Register** window provides control to select either a **Local** or **Global** policy for UCS domain management. Users can select the choice according to what functions they need to leverage through UCS Central:

Once the UCS domain has been registered with Central, the **Registration Status** comes up as **Registered** in the domain under the **Admin** tab as shown in the following screenshot:

Once the UCS domain is registered on Central, you can manage all the pools, policies, templates, service profiles, and service profile templates globally. UCS Central will push this configuration to the selected UCS domain and the domain will store it locally. Central will keep monitoring the usage of these identities across all the domains as shown in the following screenshot:

The **UCS Central** dashboard can provide complete visibility of all the UCS domains, as shown in the following screenshot:

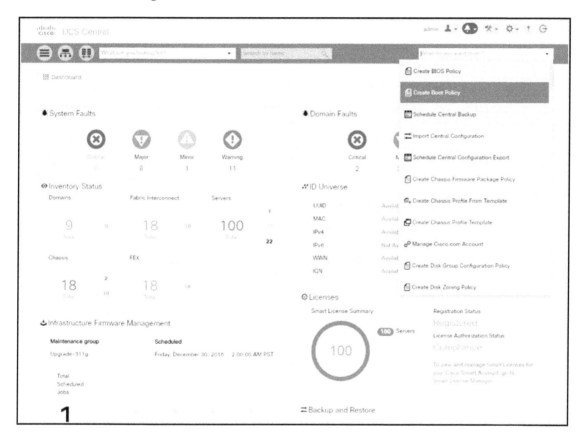

# Performance monitoring and capacity planning

Proactive monitoring of data center resources can reduce the risks involved in running business critical applications and prevent any unpredictable disasters. UCS Manager provides capabilities such as faults, logs, errors, and events to the administrator, but it lacks in providing granular visibility into performance and real-time statistics of all the components. **UCS Performance Manager** (**UCSPM**) is a purpose-built data center operation management solution, which doesn't only provide performance monitoring of Cisco UCS, an integrated infrastructure network, storage, and virtualization components ,but it also helps in capacity planning of resources in the data center. It is an agentless architecture that supports Cisco UCS Central, UCS domains, network devices, storage devices, the Control Center, hypervisor servers, Linux, and Microsoft Windows servers. It allows you to optimize resources and deliver better SLAs for your applications.

## UCS Performance Manager architecture

Based on Zenoss technology, UCS Performance Manager is a subset system of it and delivers granular device monitoring and real-time performance matrices for all the components. It uses the Cisco UCS API and other native APIs to collect the data from Cisco UCS Manager and other integrated infrastructure endpoints, to display comprehensive useful information to easily detect issues and problems in all the components. It is a graphical based web interface to monitor and visualize the UCS infrastructure and it helps in reducing risk associated with the failure of devices and components. It triggers the alerts to administrators for any current problems and future problems in advance for both physical and virtual components, including compute, network, storage and virtual components:

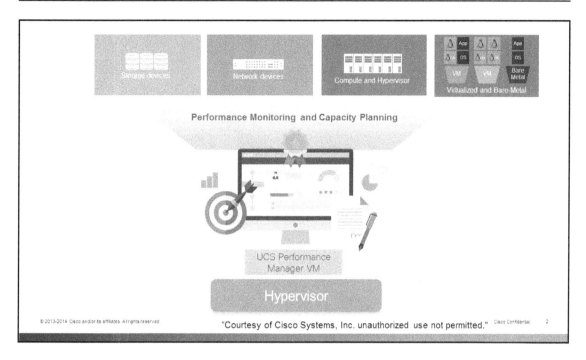

"Courtesy of Cisco Systems, Inc. unauthorized use not permitted."

UCSPM can be deployed as a single host or multi-host deployment. Single-host deployment can support up to 500 servers, where multi-host deployment can scale up to 2,500 servers. UCSPM v2 can be downloaded as an OVA or ISO image from the Cisco portal and requires 64 GB memory for providing better performance.

After installing the UCSPM virtual machine, it requires virtual hostname configuration in the Control Center. It doesn't listen directly on TCP ports and it would need DNS configuration to reach a virtual hostname. The Control Center provides the configuration to carry out the required modifications. It provides an intuitive HTML5 web interface for monitoring the UCS infrastructure and its components.

UCSPM provides the following capabilities to actively monitor the infrastructure:

- Single console for device health and performance monitoring of physical and virtual components
- Dependency mapping for all the components
- Forecast utilization of resource capacity
- A comparison of current and historical performance issues impacting on any application workloads

- Identification of congestion sources for IOM server ports, Ethernet uplinks, and FC uplinks, providing fixes
- Fabric utilization trends, graphs, and reports
- Scalable and module architecture for expansion

UCSPM is packaged as a Docker container to provide horizontal scalability to multiple virtual machines as an underlying service in the Control Center. The Control Center is based on a service-oriented architecture, which enables applications to run as a set of distributed services across multiple virtual machines. It manages the pools of VM resources (compute, storage, and network) for UCSPM and provides a high-performance Hadoop database with Apache HBase. The following screenshot displays the consolidated dashboard of UCSPM. It provides an additional dashboard and portlet to customize the dashboard with the desired graphs and stats monitoring:

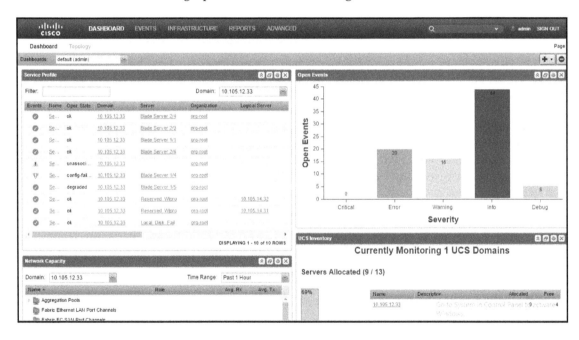

The following screenshot shows the physical topology of UCS and the integrated components:

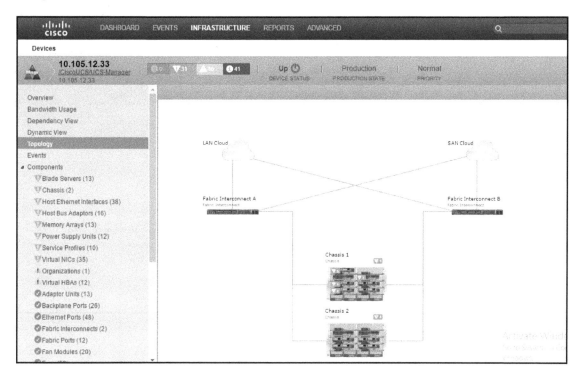

The following screenshot shows the visibility of virtual infrastructure components integrated with UCS:

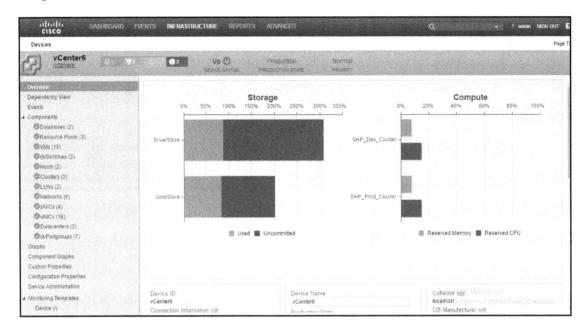

# Powering infrastructure with a cloud solution

Consolidating the physical and virtual infrastructures into a single domain to rapidly provision resources through all the components can be challenging in data centers. The solutions available in the market can provide some level of functionality and capabilities across some components but mostly fail to abstract the underlying infrastructure to automate them. They can interface with supported vendors but are limited with other management components. **Cisco UCS Director** (formerly **Cisco Cloupia**) can be a misleading name for Cisco UCS servers only, but it is a unique tool that can automate and orchestrate all the components such as network, storage, compute, and virtualization.

It is a robust and validated converged infrastructure solution that provides unified management, simplicity, and a comprehensive ability to automate all the components in the data center. Northbound and southbound API integration with device managers and third-party ecosystems makes it a more agile and powerful tool for data center automation and operations. It provides an HTML5-based web interface to end users, providing on-demand services through a self-service catalog, and can charge them based on a consumption model by leveraging existing compute, network, storage, and virtualization stacks under complete administrator control.

# UCS Director overview

**UCS Director** is multi-tenant and multi-vendor cloud platform solution that can deliver on-demand IT services through a self-service catalog to end users. It provides end-to-end provisioning, monitoring, and management of the infrastructure in a secure multi-tenant fashion. It is a centralized unified management and orchestrator solution for Cisco data center products that can connect with physical and virtual infrastructure domain managers and rapidly provision resources available through the service catalog. It can discover, control, and exchange resource information with other compute, network storage, and virtual elements in the data center. It can collect inventory of all the components and provides various reporting across them.

UCS Director plays a central role in interfacing with admin, tenants, end users, physical and virtual domain managers, third-party management tools, public clouds, and system integrators. Admin can log in to the admin portal to add all the infrastructure components, develop workflows, create policies, publish service catalogs, generate various reports, and so on, where end users can submit the request for provisioning applications, servers, and resources available through the self-service catalog.

UCS Director can authenticate through local, LDAP, and **single sign-on** (**SSO**) and provides RBAC for authorization of services.

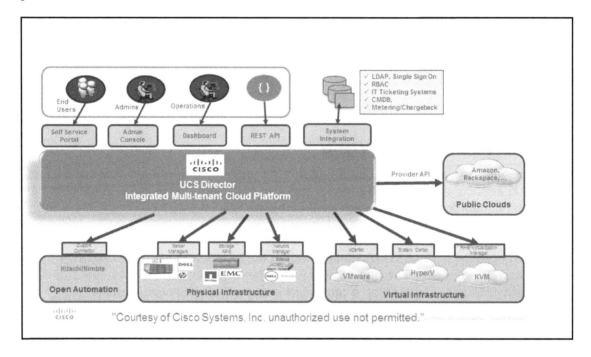

UCS Director is a virtual appliance model that can be downloaded from Cisco CCO portal. It is available in OVA and ISO image format and supports all major hypervisors, such as VMware ESXi, Microsoft Hyper-V, RedHat KVM, and the OpenStack cloud platform.

# UCS Director solutions

UCS Director solutions include two components for deployment:

- UCS Director
- UCS Director Baremetal Agent

# UCS Director

UCS Director is based on Cent OS based virtual appliance and hosts most of the services including MySQL database for storing all the configuration details; however, you can still use an external database. It includes the following services:

- Apache Tomcat
- Secure domain controller
- Identity and access manager
- Infra manager
- Event manager
- MySQL database

Users can interact with UCS Director through a web-based interface, shell admin (CLI), and REST API. It includes the **software development kit** (**SDK**) that provides the REST-based API library for integration with other components. It provides both northbound APIs for interacting with UCS Director and southbound for development of other infrastructure components and complex scripting workflows.

# UCS Director Baremetal Agent

**UCS Director Baremetal Agent** is another appliance that provides the physical Baremetal provisioning for all major operating systems; it is also called **BMA**. It includes the following services to automate the provisioning process for servers through the **Preboot Execution Environment (PXE)**:

- **Dynamic Host Control Protocol (DHCP)**
- **Hypertext Transfer Protocol (HTTP)**
- **Trivial File Transfer Protocol (TFTP)**

The UCSD BMA appliance needs to be integrated with the UCS Director appliance for server provisioning. There are two NICs available on BMA: one communicates on a management network with UCS Director and the second NIC is used for server provisioning.

UCS Director Scalability can be scaled from single node to multi-node mode. Multi-node mode is deployed for workload sharing the services across multiple services nodes but it doesn't provide high availability as this relies on the hypervisor high availability feature. Multi-node can be deployed where virtual machines are more than 5,000.

The UCS Director **Dashboard** tab can provide a single console to monitor all the trends, graphs, and bars for all the physical and virtual infrastructure components, as shown in the following screenshot:

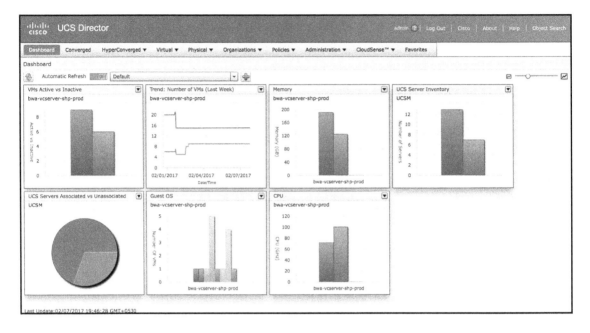

It is a model-based orchestrator that allows the IT admin to customize and automate components with an easy-to-use workflow UI designer. It provides a comprehensive task library, with more than 2,000 tasks for compute, network, storage, and virtualization domain elements to create the workflow for automating the IT process. It provides a drag and drop mechanism to simply call the existing tasks, as shown in the following screenshot:

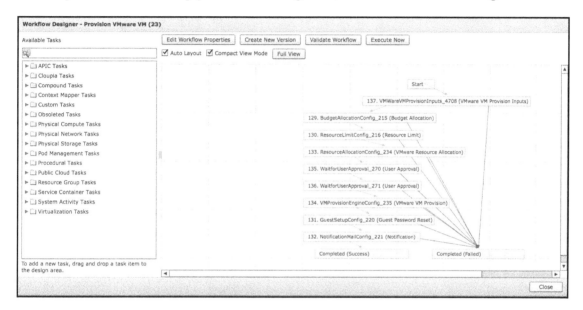

End users can check the status of the requested services, where admin can check status and detailed log information for any errors in the workflows, as shown in the following screenshot. It provides a real-time log mechanism to easily troubleshoot any kind of errors and a rollback mechanism to simply go back to a previous state:

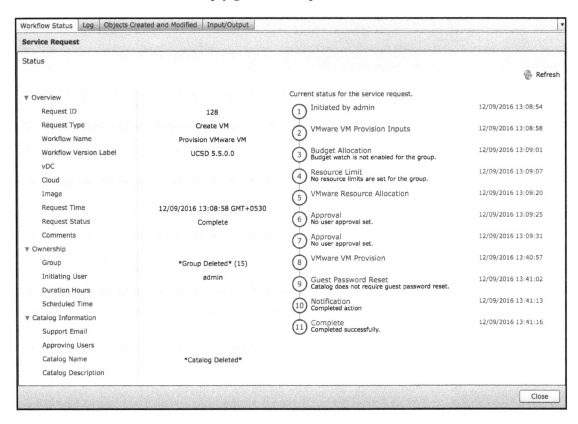

UCS Director CloudSense Analytics provides visibility into the utilization of resources and performance metrics in real time. It provides a wide variety of reports and assessments for physical and virtual infrastructures. The reports can be generated in PDF or HTML format. The following example shows the inventory report of UCS servers in a data center:

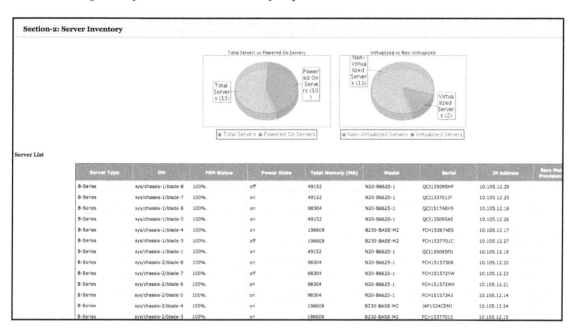

**Section-2: Server Inventory**

Server List

| Server Type | DN | FSM Status | Power State | Total Memory (MB) | Model | Serial | IP Address | Bare Metal Provision |
|---|---|---|---|---|---|---|---|---|
| B-Series | sys/chassis-1/blade-8 | 100%. | off | 49152 | N20-B6620-1 | QCI135095HP | 10.105.12.20 | |
| B-Series | sys/chassis-1/blade-7 | 100%. | on | 49152 | N20-B6620-1 | QCI1333701JF | 10.105.12.25 | |
| B-Series | sys/chassis-1/blade-6 | 100%. | on | 98304 | N20-B6625-1 | QCI1517A6V9 | 10.105.12.16 | |
| B-Series | sys/chassis-1/blade-5 | 100%. | on | 49152 | N20-B6620-1 | QCI135095AE | 10.105.12.26 | |
| B-Series | sys/chassis-1/blade-4 | 100%. | on | 196608 | B230-BASE-M2 | FCH153674ES | 10.105.12.17 | |
| B-Series | sys/chassis-1/blade-3 | 100%. | off | 196608 | B230-BASE-M2 | FCH1537701C | 10.105.12.27 | |
| B-Series | sys/chassis-1/blade-1 | 100%. | on | 49152 | N20-B6620-1 | QCI135095FD | 10.105.12.19 | |
| B-Series | sys/chassis-2/blade-8 | 100%. | on | 98304 | N20-B6625-1 | FCH1515730R | 10.105.12.22 | |
| B-Series | sys/chassis-2/blade-7 | 100%. | off | 98304 | N20-B6625-1 | FCH151572YW | 10.105.12.23 | |
| B-Series | sys/chassis-2/blade-6 | 100%. | on | 98304 | N20-B6625-1 | FCH151572WK | 10.105.12.21 | |
| B-Series | sys/chassis-2/blade-5 | 100%. | on | 98304 | N20-B6625-1 | FCH15157343 | 10.105.12.14 | |
| B-Series | sys/chassis-2/blade-4 | 100%. | on | 196608 | B230-BASE-M2 | JAF1524CEMJ | 10.105.12.24 | |
| B-Series | sys/chassis-2/blade-3 | 100%. | on | 196608 | B230-BASE-M2 | FCH15377015 | 10.105.12.15 | |

# Summary

In this chapter, we have discussed Cisco UCS Central, UCS Performance Manager, and UCS Director. These tools will enhance the administration and operations of all the data center components and help in optimizing and automating the infrastructure with centralized and unified management.

You will have seen throughout this book that Cisco UCS provides unique features for contemporary data centers. Cisco UCS is a unified solution that consolidates computing, network, and storage connectivity components along with centralized management.

# Index

www.ingramcontent.com/pod-product-compliance
Lightning Source LLC
Chambersburg PA
CBHW081455050326
40690CB00015B/2812